CANADA'S TRIAL COURTS:
TWO TIERS OR ONE?

EDITED BY
PETER H. RUSSELL

# Canada's Trial Courts:
# Two Tiers or One?

UNIVERSITY OF TORONTO PRESS
Toronto   Buffalo   London

ISBN 978-0-8020-9323-3

Printed on acid-free paper

---

**Library and Archives Canada Cataloguing in Publication**

Canada's trial courts: two tiers or one? / edited by Peter H. Russell.

ISBN 978-0-8020-9323-3

1. Courts – Canada – Provinces.  2. Court administration – Canada – Provinces.
I. Russell, Peter H.  II. Title.

KE8200.C33 2007          347.71'01          C2007-901147-0
KF8700.C33 2007

---

This book has been published with the assistance of grants from the Canadian
Association of Court Administrators and the Canadian Association of Provincial Court Judges.

University of Toronto Press acknowledges the financial assistance to its publishing program of the Canada Council for the Arts and the Ontario Arts
Council.

University of Toronto Press acknowledges the financial support for its publishing activities of the Government of Canada through the Book Publishing
Industry Development Program (BPIDP).

*In memory of the Honourable Ian Scott,*
*who was deeply committed to the cause of a single-tier trial court*

# Contents

viii   Contents

# Acknowledgments

Nearly all Canadians at some time will find themselves involved in the proceedings of the country's trial courts. Many thousands of lawyers, judges, and justice officials work in these courts, but only a very tiny group of Canadians is deeply engaged in dealing with the structure of the trial court system. This group is made up of lawyers, judges, court administrators, academics, and occasionally one or two politicians. This book owes its genesis to some members of this group who came together in 2001 and proposed a conference on the future of Canada's trial courts. This group included Richard Mosely, who was then a senior official with the federal Department of Justice, Professor John Whyte, who at that time held a similar position with the Saskatchewan Department of Justice, Stephen Bindman, an experienced journalist now working with the federal Department of Justice, George Thompson, director of the National Judicial Institute, and Professors Carl Baar, Tony Doob, Martin Friedland, and Kent Roach. All of the above, and many others, made important contributions to the conference and this book.

The driving force from the beginning and all the way through to the Conference on the Future of the Trial Courts at Saskatoon in 2002 and to the publication of its proceedings were two people – Barbara Hookenson and Gerry Seniuk. Barbara headed up court administration in Saskatchewan's Department of Justice. She subsequently moved to a similar position in Alberta. Gerry is the chief justice of Saskatchewan's Provincial Court. Without the talent and commitment of Barbara and Gerry the conference and the book to which it has given rise would never have happened.

I would also like to thank the Canadian Association of Court Administrators and the Canadian Association of Provincial Court Judges for their financial support for the editing and publication of this book. Two other institutions that were very helpful at different stages of this project were the Faculty of Law at the University of Toronto and the College of Law at the University of Saskatchewan.

Finally, as editor of this volume, I am much indebted to B.J. Wray, who assisted me at every stage of the editing. With a PhD in English literature, professional editorial experience, and, as a first-year law student at the University of Toronto, a burgeoning interest in the law, B.J. was a marvellous assistant. Her editorial judgment, polite perseverance with tardy writers, and technical know-how were invaluable in steering this volume to completion.

Peter H. Russell
August 2006

CANADA'S TRIAL COURTS:
TWO TIERS OR ONE?

# Introduction: How We Got Here

PETER H. RUSSELL

The title of this book poses a question that is not likely to leap to mind when Canadians think about the country's trial courts. The limited public discussion that goes on about such courts is most often concerned with whether justice was done in specific cases or whether the punishment meted out was too lenient. There is very little interest in or knowledge of the courts themselves: They are simply accepted as part of the institutional fabric of our society.

And yet backstage, behind the scenes, so to speak, a vigorous debate has been going on about the structure of our trial court system. The central issue in this debate is whether the courts in the provinces that try criminal and civil cases should continue to be organized in two tiers – a higher level of Superior Courts staffed by federally appointed judges for the most serious cases, and a lower level of Provincial Courts staffed by provincially appointed judges for the less serious cases. The alternative to this system would be the unification of some or all trial court jurisdiction in the Superior Court or the Provincial Court. Up to now, the main participants in these discussions have been the judges themselves, a small section of the legal profession, senior court administrators, and a handful of academics. Politicians occasionally get involved in this debate but most who do tend not to engage in it for very long. In the media, even among that tiny coterie of journalists who do stories on the courts, eyes are apt to glaze over when issues of court structure are discussed.

If the question of whether Canada should continue with a two-tier system of trial courts or move to a one-tier system has not become a major issue of public debate, one might ask why a book should be devoted to it. The answer is that those of us who are engaged in the question – on both sides of it – believe that working out the right answer to this question matters a great deal to the quality of justice that Canadians experience in their courts and to the good governance of their country. Moreover, the political struggle that has gone on over this issue, precisely because to a large extent it goes on within the judiciary, reveals an important and mostly unseen facet of judicial politics in Canada. The issue also invites us to think about one of the most exceptional, but least noticed, features of Canada's federal structure.

Canada is by no means unique in being engaged, at least at the elite level, in questions of trial court unification or amalgamation. For over a century the simplification and consolidation of courts has been a feature of court restructuring projects throughout the common law world. The essays in the final section of this volume provide accounts of such projects and issues in the United States and England. However, the judicial system bequeathed to Canada by its constitutional founders and the evolution of that system over nearly a century and a half give a distinctive Canadian hue to the question of trial court unification. To understand how and why this has become an important question among those who work in and study Canadian courts, we must turn to the constitutional underpinnings of our court system and the forces that have shaped its evolution.

## Constitutional Foundations

The Fathers of Confederation expended little effort in designing the judicial system of Canada. Essentially they took the system that they already had as British colonists and adapted it to a federal system of governance. As with their treatment of parliamentary government, the Constitution they framed has little to say about the judicial institutions of the federation they were founding.

The only section of Canada's founding Constitution, the *British North America Act*, that makes any reference to specific courts is section 96 which states that 'The Governor General,' that is the federal government, 'shall appoint the judges of the Superior, District and County Courts in each province.'[1] These were the courts that were already functioning in the 'common law provinces' – New Brunswick, Nova Scotia, and Ontario. A Superior Court based in the provincial capital with its judges going on circuit to hear the most serious cases was supplemented by locally based District or County Courts. Quebec was a little bit different: instead of District or County Courts, it had a decentralized Superior Court.

The founding fathers clearly envisaged the Superior Courts as Canada's most important judicial institutions, part of Canada's English constitutional inheritance. As I.R. Scott explains in his contribution to this volume, the English Superior Courts consist of the judges: the judges are the court. The judges of England's Superior Courts did not get their jurisdiction from Parliament. Their original authority to hear cases came from the Crown but no legislation defined the cases they could try. Over the centuries Superior Court judges simply asserted an inherent jurisdiction to hear and decide criminal and civil cases of all kinds, including, in the course of time, claims against the Crown itself. Although the jurisdiction of superior court judges in Canada as in England is inherent and was not created by Parliament, it can be and has been reduced by legislation. This has been done in both countries so that cases deemed to be less serious may be assigned to 'inferior courts,' which are virtually any courts of first instance that are not Superior Courts. An important constitutional issue in Canada, and one that is carefully explored in Patrick Healy's chapter, is whether there is any constitutional limit on Parliament's power to reduce the jurisdiction of provincial Superior Courts with respect to the trial of criminal offences.

County and District Courts, the other courts specifically mentioned in the Constitution, are examples of 'inferior courts.' These courts were an Upper Canadian colonial invention, established by Governor Simcoe in 1794 primarily to provide a judicial service to merchants in frontier towns who found it inconvenient to wait for the infrequent visit of a Superior Court judge from the capital to settle legal disputes involving modest amounts of money. County Courts were not established in England until 1846. After Confederation, these inferior courts continued to operate in the common law provinces, their name depending on whether a province's regional administration was set up on a county or district basis.

While the variation in the names of these courts – County or District – is easy to understand, the variety of names bestowed by the Canadian provinces on their superior courts can be bewildering. Quebec is the only Canadian province that has used the generic name and from the beginning called its general jurisdiction trial court the Superior Court. The three Prairie provinces and New Brunswick call their superior court the Court of Queen's Bench (or King's Bench). The superior courts of three Atlantic provinces are called Trial Divisions of the Supreme Court (to distinguish them from their courts of appeal). British Columbia has always called its superior trial court simply the

Supreme Court of British Columbia (even though it isn't supreme). The superior courts of the Northwest Territories and Yukon are also called Supreme Courts. The Nunavut Court of Justice, the focus of Nora Sanders's chapter, is Canada's newest Superior Court. It is also Canada's first one-tier trial court carrying out the functions of a Superior Court as well as all of the functions that in other jurisdictions are assigned to so-called inferior courts.

The Superior Courts of the provinces were meant to be the keystone institutions of the new country's judicial structure. The judiciary of both the Country and District Courts and the Superior Courts of the provinces would be appointed by the federal government and their salaries would be fixed and provided by the federal Parliament. But it is only the Superior Court judiciary whose tenure is constitutionally secured. Section 99 of the Constitution states that 'Judges of the Superior Courts shall hold office during good behavior, but shall be removable by the Governor General on Address of the Senate and House of Commons.'[2] This language is modelled on the *Act of Settlement of 1701*, the charter of judicial independence in the United Kingdom.

It would be a mistake to consider the courts recognized in section 96 – the Superior Courts[3] as well as the County and District Courts – as either federal or provincial institutions. They are both; they are hybrid institutions, partly federal and partly provincial. Their judges are appointed, paid, and removed by the federal government while the courts themselves are organized, managed, and supported by provincial governments. Section 92 (14) of the Constitution gives the provincial legislature exclusive jurisdiction over 'the Administration of Justice in the Province, including the Constitution, Maintenance, and Organization of Provincial Courts, both of Civil and Criminal Jurisdiction ...' The combination of section 92(14) and 96 of the Constitution meant that federal appointees would staff the two top levels of provincial courts.

The judicature sections of Canada's founding constitution pointed towards its having a court structure more akin to that of a unitary state than a federal state. By way of contrast, the judicial structure of the American federation has developed along the lines of a dual court system. In the United States each state has its own system of courts presided over by its own state-appointed judiciary. Alongside these state courts, the federal government has developed an extensive system of trial and appeal courts to hear a broad range of federal law matters as well as diversity suits – that is, suits between citizens from different states. Canada's system of provincial courts with federally appointed judges removed grounds for fearing parochial justice for citizens who find themselves going to court outside their home province. Hence, there was no pressure to set up a parallel system of federal courts for 'diversity suits.' For a federation with more than its share of regional cleavages, the integrated nature of its foundational courts should be considered a blessing.

It would be nice to report that this advantage of the judicature provisions in the Canadian Constitution is the product of the Founding Fathers' visionary statecraft. But there is no evidence of any deep thinking about Canada's judicial system in the deliberations that produced the 1867 Constitution. Gerry Seniuk and John Borrows, in their chapter of this book, expound a vision that draws on the full potential of the country's founding structure. But the explanation of section 96 comes down basically to the assumption on the part of leaders of the Confederation project that the leading judges of the new nation would be centrally appointed as they were in Great Britain. This assumption was fortified by an interest in keeping plum appointments to judicial office in their own hands that would soon be on the levers of power in Ottawa.[4] Some justified this arrangement by expressing fear of the parochial politics that might influence judicial appointments if left in the hands of provincial politicians.[5] The assumption that federal politicians would rise above party politics in discharging their responsibility of appointing judges has, to put it kindly, an ironic ring today.

Though the section 96 courts were the only courts specifically mentioned in Canada's founding Constitution, other sections contained the seeds of other courts. Unlike the courts recognized in section 96, these other courts would be either purely provincial or purely federal in nature. The constitutional seed with the greatest potential was section 92(14) which we have already mentioned with its carte blanche mandate to provincial governments to constitute, maintain and organize provincial courts of civil and criminal jurisdiction. Besides giving the provinces legislative jurisdiction and administrative responsibility over the Superior, County, and District courts, this section gave the provinces power to create other provincial courts, and for these additional provincial courts, provincial governments would have the responsibility of providing the judiciary. At the time of Confederation these entirely provincial courts dealt with minor criminal and civil matters, and instead of having a professional, legally trained judiciary, drew on the English tradition of lay justices of the peace. This rudimentary form of local lay justice would over time evolve into an extensive system of provincial courts that, in a quantitative sense, became the major trial court system in the country.

The other judicial seed, which proves to be much less fertile, is section 101 of the Constitution. Section 101 empowers the federal Parliament to establish, if and when it wishes, 'a General Court of Appeal for Canada,' and then adds, almost as an afterthought, that Parliament can also establish 'any Additional Courts for the Better Administration of the Laws of Canada.' The first part of section 101 provides the constitutional authority for the creation of the Supreme Court of Canada. It was not until 1875, eight years after Confederation, that Parliament exercised its power to create the Supreme Court as a general court of appeal for Canada – but not Canada's highest court of appeal. That function would continue to be served, right up until 1949, by the highest court in the British Empire, the Judicial Committee of the Privy Council. At the time of Confederation and for a long time thereafter, appeal rights were severely limited and there were no courts specializing in appeals under the Supreme Court of Canada. Appeals below the Supreme Court were handled by judges of the provincial Superior Court hearing appeals from judges of their own court or reviewing decisions of 'inferior courts.'[6] The second part of section 101 – the bit about 'Additional Courts for the Better Administration of the Laws of Canada' – had the potential to set up a dual system of federal and provincial courts like the American system. However, for over a century that section was scarcely used.[7] The Federal Court of Canada, with jurisdiction over a very limited number of federal law matters, was not established until 1971. So, while a dual court system developed in Canada, it was not a system of federal and provincial courts, but a two-tiered system of provincial trial courts, one with a federally appointed and remunerated judiciary, the other with a provincially appointed and remunerated judiciary.

## Evolution of the Trial Court System

Since Confederation, the trial court system has evolved in a manner unforeseen by the founding fathers. The ever-increasing demands for court services generated by the urbanization and industrialization of the country were met mostly at the lowest level of the provincial court system where responsibility for appointing and paying the judiciary rested entirely with the provinces. So it was the Provincial Courts that became the growth engine of the country's trial court system.

In the field of criminal justice most of the expanding caseloads were taken over by salaried magistrates who replaced the benches of local gentry serving as justices of the peace. For a long time the provinces delegated the management and support of these Magistrates Courts to municipalities. Martin Friedland's chapter describes these courts as he found them in the late 1960s when provincial governments were beginning to centralize their administration. The picture he paints is not pretty: a poorly qualified, mostly lay judiciary, operating inefficiently in shoddy surroundings and often closely associated with the police, had become the workhorse of the criminal justice system, the portal through which every case that entered the system was processed. The picture was a little different in Quebec where the province had converted its Court of Sessions of the Peace into a professional single-judge court that tried the criminal cases which in common law Canada were heard in County or District Courts. But Quebec also had Magistrates and Municipal Courts for less serious criminal cases. In the civil area it was also the purely provincial courts that provided the new kinds of judicial service required for handling family and consumer disputes. With the advance of the welfare state, the provinces established family and youth court services in a variety of institutional forms and expanded the small claims jurisdiction of the provincially appointed judiciary.

Beginning in the mid-1960s, in what Carl Baar in his chapter calls the first wave of reform of provincial court systems, the Magistrates Courts were judicialized. By the end of the 1970s in all the provinces Provincial Courts replaced Magistrates Courts. The Provincial Courts were staffed by a legally trained judiciary whose professional qualifications soon came to equal those of the federally appointed section 96 judiciary. The Provincial Court judiciary also came to enjoy security of tenure and judicial independence on a par with the federally appointed provincial judiciary. This upgrading of the professional qualifications and terms of office of Provincial Court judges was accompanied by a significant expansion of their jurisdiction. In the criminal justice area the federal Parliament kept increasing the serious indictable offences for which trial before a Provincial Court judge was an option and increasingly this was the option chosen by defendants. Anthony Doob's and Cheryl Webster's quantitative study, presented in the third chapter of this volume, shows that by the end of the twentieth century 98 per cent of the adult criminal court case load in Canada was being resolved in the Provincial Courts. Provincial Courts were also taking over virtually all aspects of family court adjudication short of the divorce and related property matters that remain attached to the Superior Courts. Similarly, for civil suits, the monetary limit of the Provincial Courts so-called small claims jurisdiction continued to creep upwards, eventually reaching $70,000 in Quebec.

While Provincial Courts were emerging as a major system of trial courts, the second level of trial courts provided for in the Constitution – the County and District Courts – were fading away. The second wave of reform discussed in Baar's chapter was the merger of this lower level of section 96 courts into the provinces' Superior Courts. Maintaining a locally based County or District Court judiciary with a jurisdiction just slightly less than that of a capital-based, itinerant Superior Court judiciary no longer made any sense. Still, it took nearly twenty years, from 1973 to 1992, for merger to be completed and it was only accomplished without a good deal of political skirmishing along the way.

A crucial consequence of the integrated nature of Canada's section 96 courts is that changes in them require joint action by federal and provincial authorities. While it is provincial governments and legislatures that must introduce and implement any legislation restructuring these courts, for these changes to come into effect, the federal government and Parliament must make the appropriate changes in the number of judges and provide for their remuneration. In 1969, when the first request for terminating the County and District Courts and 'elevating' the judges of these courts to the Superior Courts came from British Columbia, the federal government refused to cooperate. No public reason was offered for turning down this request, although it seems unlikely that federal reluctance stemmed from the modest increase in judicial salaries it would have to pay. A more plausible explanation is that Superior Court judges who were opposed to the merger had the ear of federal ministers. Certainly, the heart of opposition to merger came from the Superior Court judiciary. The crux of their concern was that such an enlargement of their numbers as the merger entailed would undermine the collegiality essential to maintaining the high quality of their work.[8] In the end, the practical arguments of provincial attorneys general about the inefficiencies of maintaining what in effect had become a three-tiered system of trial courts prevailed, and by 1992 the County and District Courts had disappeared from the Canadian judicial scene.

The Canadian judicial system had evolved in ways unforeseen by the Fathers of Confederation. Most of Canada's adjudicative services were now provided by a two-tier system. But the two tiers were not the two levels of courts recognized in the founding constitution. The Superior Courts of the provinces with their federally appointed judiciary remained as the highest general jurisdiction courts but under them there was now a much more extensive system of Provincial Courts staffed by a provincially appointed judiciary. In law these Provincial Courts were considered to be 'inferior courts,' even though the qualifications of their judges had become comparable to those of the Superior Court judiciary, and their adjudicative responsibilities had expanded to cover the bulk of criminal justice as well as civil matters of great social concern. This same dualism was now established in Yukon and the Northwest Territories where residential Territorial Courts mirrored the Provincial Courts[9] and visiting justices from the provinces' Superior Courts provided higher court services.

To complete the picture of the court system that had evolved, two other developments should be noted. By the end of the 1980s all of the provinces, even tiny Prince Edward Island, had established Courts of Appeal to hear appeals from the trial courts. These Courts of Appeal were emanations of the Superior Courts of the provinces. They were, in effect, section 96 courts, their judges appointed and paid by Ottawa. This meant that the Superior Court judiciary now had two layers – a top layer specializing in appeals and the lower level functioning as a general jurisdiction trial court, although Superior Court judges at the trial level, as is pointed out in the Ontario Superior Court judges'contribution to this book, continue to have responsibilities for reviewing decisions of subordinate judicial officials.

The other development is the rather sudden appearance of those 'additional courts' that the federal Parliament, under section 101 of the Constitution, can establish. In 1971, as noted above, the tiny Exchequer Court of Canada was folded into the new Federal Court of Canada with a trial and appeal division. The Federal Court specializes in several fields of federal public law – notably immigration, maritime law, patents and challenges to federal administrative bodies. In giving the Federal Court (which is not a Superior Court) exclusive jurisdiction to deal with challenges to federal administration the federal Parliament stripped this jurisdiction away from the provincial Superior Courts. In the light of claims that the Superior Courts have an irreducible core of jurisdiction (a claim that Patrick Healy examines in his chapter) this was an interesting development that raised jurisprudential eyebrows at the time.[10] After the establishment of the Federal Court there were two further exercises of the federal power to establish courts: the creation of the Tax Court of Canada in 1983 and the establishment of the Court Martial Appeal Court. Though the emergence of these small specialist federal courts does not substantially alter the picture of a Canada-wide two-tier trial court system, as purely federal courts they do mark a further departure from the system mandated in the original Constitution of integrated federal-provincial courts as the core institutions of Canada's judicial system.

*Emergence of the Court Unification Issue*

Once the provincially appointed judiciary had acquired professional qualifications and adjudicative responsibilities commensurate with those of the federally appointed provincial judiciary, it became difficult to defend the distinction between the two groups of provincial judges. It did not seem to make any sense, for instance, to authorize a judge of the Provincial Court to conduct a judge-alone trial that could send a person to prison for life but to insist that only a federally appointed Superior Court judge could conduct a jury trial. Martin Friedland was one of the first to challenge the logic of maintaining the two-tier system in the 1968 report he wrote for the Ouimet Commission on Corrections, a report he revisits in the first chapter of this book. In 1973 Darrell Roberts, in a report written for the Law Commission of Canada, came to the same conclusion as Friedland. 'Our whole criminal process,' wrote Roberts, 'is debased by the system of various grades of courts when its most important court is looked upon as inferior and subordinate.'[11] Two years later, the Law Reform Commission published a country-wide study of family law litigation that highlighted the pernicious effects of divided jurisdiction between Superior Courts and ('inferior') Family Courts for the handling of family-related disputes.[12] For example, while only Superior Courts could issue divorce decrees and the settlement of family property, disputes arising from the enforcement of settlements would come before a Family Court judge who had no power to adjust the settlement ordered by the higher court. Maintaining and coordinating two separate tiers of trial courts was adding considerably to the cost of administering justice within the province and was increasingly seen as an impediment to modernizing judicial administration.[13]

It is not surprising then that provincial governments soon joined the academics and law reformers in questioning the two-tier system.

Besides the extra cost and inconvenience of the two-tier system, federal control over appointment of the senior provincial judiciary did not sit well with provincial governments in an era when province-building had become a major force in the politics of the federation. Nowhere was this more evident than in Quebec where the justice minister (in a federalist government), Jerome Choquette, issued a ringing denunciation of section 96 of the Constitution.[14] In the constitutional negotiations of 1978–9 the provinces pressed to have section 96 amended so that all aspects of family law could be dealt with by provincially appointed judges,[15] and in 1980 they raised the ante, with nine of the ten provinces calling for the termination of section 96 so that the provinces would have the power to appoint the judges of all provincial courts.[16]

The provinces' constitutional assault on section 96 came to nought as Pierre Trudeau was able to resist the provinces' agenda for constitutional reform and push through his own nation-building agenda. Not only were the provinces being rebuffed at the political level, but in the judicial arena Supreme Court of Canada decisions were throwing up additional roadblocks to their court reform projects. In a series of cases in the early 1980s, the Court used an expansive interpretation of the federal power to appoint Superior Court judges in section 96 to restrict provincial legislative power over the administration of justice in the province. A residential tenancy commission could not decide landlord and tenant disputes;[17] a professions tribunal could not hear appeals from professional discipline committees;[18] a provincial Family Court could deal with custody of children but not occupancy of the family home.[19] A core of inherent jurisdiction must be preserved for federally appointed Superior Court judges, otherwise reasoned Justice Brian Dickson, 'what was conceived as a strong constitutional base of national unity, through a unitary judicial system, would be gravely undermined.'[20]

The climax came in 1983 when New Brunswick, one of several provinces seeking to unify criminal jurisdiction in a single court, persuaded the federal government to join it in asking the Supreme Court whether the federal Criminal Code could be amended so that a court staffed by provincially appointed judges could hear all criminal cases. The question was answered in the negative through an unsigned 'opinion of the Court' which held that section 96 limited not only provincial jurisdiction over the administration of justice but federal legislative power as well. Here it was the protection of independence afforded by section 99 uniquely to Superior Court judges that was the key rationale of the decision. The reappraisal of the Supreme Court's decision in *McEvoy* that Patrick Healy offers in this book is partly based on the Supreme Court's subsequent recognition of the constitutional protection of the independence of provincially appointed judges. Healy's reappraisal of *McEvoy* is extremely important as it reopens the possibility of filling the few missing pieces in the criminal trial jurisdiction of the Provincial Courts.

As the chapters by Friedland and Baar relate, after *McEvoy* provincial attorneys general continued to work for a unified criminal court. By 1990 all of the provinces supported the principle of a unified provincial criminal court. But now these efforts assumed that the only way to do this constitutionally was to have provincially appointed judges 'elevated' to the Superior Court. A province that took this path to unification would have to hand over its judicial appointment responsibilities to Ottawa. Such a transfer of appointing power would be unattractive at any time, but it was doubly problematic in a context that found the provinces reforming their system of appointing Provincial Court judges much more thoroughly than the federal government was reforming its system of appointing Superior Court judges. While the provinces and territories were establishing true merit systems through the use of independent nominating committees or councils, the federal process of appointing section 96 judges remained mired in political patronage.[21] To provide some check on the federal government's control of the appointing process, proposals were put forward to have provincial governments represented on the committees that advise the federal government on judicial appointments. Borrows and Seniuk return to these proposals in their chapter, adding the need to have representatives of Aboriginal governments on these committees.

While progress towards unifying criminal trial jurisdiction stalled in the 1990s, some progress was made in unifying family court jurisdiction. Carl Baar describes the process of Family Court unification, beginning with Prince Edward Island and a few cities in the 1970s and then spreading to other provinces until there was some Family Court unification in every province except British Columbia and Quebec. These Family Court unification projects were achieved by the federal government making appointments to a special family law division of the provincial Superior Court. As Baar explains, this model of unification caused tensions and political friction. It stalled in Ontario because of the Superior Court's resistance to the rigid specialization it introduces into the Superior Court which has a long tradition of being a court of general jurisdiction. Provinces that had well-developed, highly professional provincial Family Courts working in close collaboration with a network of social agencies were not about to scrap these institutions. This certainly has had much to do with the reluctance of British Columbia and Quebec to become involved in family court unification at the Superior Court level. Indeed, Huguette St-Louis's chapter makes it clear that with the consolidation of provincial courts and tribunals into the Court of Quebec any further unification of that province's courts will be done through the Court of Quebec structure. The piecemeal family court unification that has occurred in some provinces has caused many stresses and strains. Marian Tyson describes the uncertainty and administrative headaches that have resulted from such a patchwork approach in her own province, Nova Scotia. Tyson, an experienced court administrator, also shows the practical need for centralizing the administration of a province's court services and facilities, regardless of which government appointed the judges who adjudicate in these courts.

By the end of the century, efforts to sort out the proper roles for the federally appointed and provincially appointed judiciaries had reached an unsatisfactory point. Provincial Court judiciaries with qualifications at least commensurate with those of the Superior Court jurisdiction and adjudicative responsibilities of a very serious kind (particularly in the field of criminal justice) had outgrown their original status as inferior court judges. In a seminal article published in 2000, Noel Lyon and Gerald Seniuk posed the question: 'If the Provincial Court is neither functionally an *inferior* nor constitutionally a *superior* court, then in which of these two categories should it belong?' Lyon and Seniuk proposed that the time had come to address this question through a dialogue among 'the various groups responsible for maintaining confidence in the administration of justice.'[22] It is this proposal that led to organizing the 2002 Conference on the Trial Courts of the Future, the conference that gave rise to this book.

### The Trial Courts of the Future Conference

The organizers of the conference had the misfortune of scheduling it for 12–13 September 2001. The terrifying and tragic events of 9/11 meant that the conference had to be postponed for a few months. On 16 May 2002, Lorne Calvert, the premier of Saskatchewan, welcomed three hundred participants from all parts of Canada and all parts of the justice system to Saskatoon to take part in the Trial Courts of the Future Conference, the first ever conference 'on the evolving role of trial courts and how they serve the needs of Canadians, and to consider options and constraints for structural reform.'[23] The attendees included lawyers and citizens who use the courts, justice department officials from both levels of government, court administrators, provincial justice ministers, legal and social science academics, journalists, persons experienced in mediation and other forms of alternative dispute resolution, and judges, lots of them, from both the Provincial and Superior Courts. It was, without a doubt, a gathering whose composition met the organizers' objective of bringing together a comprehensive assembly of persons to discuss the future of the country's trial courts – in other words, the institutions in which Canadians are most likely to experience the administration of justice.

The agenda of the two-day conference flowed along the two streams referred to by Premier Calvert in his welcome: the evolving needs of those who use the courts and issues of structure arising from the evolving roles of the courts.[24] The latter issues covered many of the points dealt with in this introduction and in the chapters that follow. There was much interest in the possibility of overcoming jurisdictional fragmentation and moving towards a system in which the responsibilities of the Provincial and Superior Courts are based on functional considerations rather than on an out-dated hierarchy of status. To reformers of this persuasion, the contributions of two law professors, Patrick Healy and Alan Manson, on constitutional and legal constraints to restructuring were encouraging. Healy carefully analysed the logic of the Supreme Court decision in *McEvoy*, pointing out why it may no longer bar the federal Parliament from granting full criminal trial jurisdiction to provincially appointed judges. Manson's paper looked at the judicial review functions carried out through the centuries-old prerogative writ remedies that are part of the inherent jurisdiction of Superior Court judges, and concluded that if Provincial Court judges were to be given a full criminal trial jurisdiction, these traditional common law paths to judicial review could be replaced by statutory rights of appeal.[25] The presentations of Clark Kelso from the United States and Ian Scott from the United Kingdom brought Canadians up to date on trial court reform in their respective countries. A common theme of both was the importance of unifying the administration of trial court services and facilities even if there are different strata or divisions of the judiciary.

The presentations that dealt with evolving needs covered many subjects. That the public who use the courts are far from satisfied with the courts was evident in the public opinion data brought to the conference's attention by Richard Mosley, at the time an assistant deputy minister in the federal Department of Justice and now a Federal Court judge. In contrast to data collected by commercial polling companies showing a high degree of respect for the courts, a more in-depth and extensive survey by the Canadian Centre for Judicial Statistics found considerable public dissatisfaction. For instance, on what is surely the most fundamental expectation of citizens – do the courts ensure a fair trial? – only 40 per cent of those surveyed gave a positive answer. Only 15 per cent believed the criminal courts were helping the victim, and only 13 per cent thought the criminal courts were providing justice quickly. Stephen Bindman, an experienced journalist and special advisor to the federal Department of Justice, also emphasized the fundamental importance of public trust for the effective functioning of any court structure. The deplorable physical conditions experienced all too often in court houses across the country, he observed, do not inspire public confidence in the quality of justice served up in such shabby and congested surroundings. The inadequacy of court facilities was a major point in the presentation of Dr Deborah Parker-Loewen, president of the Canadian Council of Provincial Child and Youth Advocates. She pointed to the many ways in which Canada's trial courts fail to respect the rights of children. Children, she argued, need to be able to participate, either directly or through a representative, not only in youth justice but in proceedings dealing with custody, access, and child welfare.

The capacity of the court system to administer justice for Aboriginal peoples was a focus of several presentations. Bevann Fox, a community development worker with the File Hills Qu'Appelle Tribal Council, vividly described the alienation and disrespect experienced by Aboriginal people when a member of their community is taken for trial to a distant court whose formal, adversarial proceedings show not a glimmer of understanding of their own traditions. Grand Chief Gary Merasty of the Prince Albert Grand Council, an experienced Aboriginal educator, explained how essential it was for judges administering justice in Cree communities to have 'solid knowledge of tribal customs, languages and practices.' Judge Gerald Morin, a Provincial Court judge in Saskatchewan, told the conference how he had developed a modus operandi that enabled his court to function as a Cree court. Persons who appear in the Cree court have the option of speaking and being spoken to in their own language. Judge Morin's account demonstrated the importance of this linguistic facility in giving reality to the provisions of the Criminal Code and the Supreme Court's *Gladue* decision[26] that require sensitivity to aboriginal heritage in the Canadian criminal justice process. Professor John Borrows, an Aboriginal law professor of Ojibwa background, explored how Aboriginal tradition could be effectively incorporated into the House of Justice model of a unified court put forward in the paper by himself and Gerry Seniuk, Chief Justice of Saskatchewan's Provincial Court.

An overarching question of the Trial Courts of the Future Conference was whether the capacity of the trial courts to meet public expectations and changing needs would be significantly enhanced by structural reform. While the conference did not attempt to give a definitive answer to that question, many of the presentations and discussants in break-out groups aspired to a more holistic approach to the administration of justice than is possible when jurisdiction is split up along lines that make no functional sense. Some of those concerned with strengthening court services did not think that progress should depend on structural reforms that may be constitutionally and politically difficult to achieve. Others were more strongly convinced that justice fragmented is justice denied and were keen to see progress towards achieving a court system that efficiently harnesses the justice resources of Canadian communities and transcends irrelevant differences of status between federally and provincially appointed judiciaries.

## Organization of the Book

Originally the organizers of the Trial Courts of the Future Conference intended to publish the entire conference proceedings. However, when as editor I began to work on turning the proceedings into a book, I found that they were too voluminous and their content too disparate to be put together in a manageable and coherent book. After consultation with the conference sponsors and my editorial assistant, B.J. Wray, I decided to organize the book around the issue of structural reform. Issues of improving court services, ranging from alternative dispute resolution, to proper treatment of victims and children, to the use of minority languages, to administering justice for Aboriginal peoples, to reducing delay and increasing efficiency, cover too vast a field to be dealt with adequately in any single volume. The structural issue of whether the trial courts of Canada should continue to be structured on

a two-tier basis seemed much more amenable to serving as the organizing theme for a volume of essays.

The book is divided into four parts. The background of the structural issue and various approaches to it are the common theme of the
four chapters that form Part One. Martin Friedland's chapter focuses
on the criminal courts and the challenge posed to the superior court/
inferior court dichotomy by reform of the Provincial Courts. In the
chapter that follows, Carl Baar provides an overview of trial court
reorganization in the fields of criminal, civil, and family law and considers various models for further merger of the courts. The chapter by
Cheryl Marie Webster and Anthony Doob presents an empirical analysis of the criminal caseloads of the Superior and Provincial Courts,
which shows that the latter have become the primary criminal trial
court in Canada for both summary and indictable offences. Patrick
Healy's chapter critically examines the jurisprudence of the Supreme
Court of Canada that has created a constitutional barrier to further unification of criminal trial jurisdiction at the level of the Provincial Court.
These four papers were included in a special issue of the *Criminal Law
Quarterly* published in 2003. I am grateful to Professor Kent Roach, the
editor of that issue, for permitting publication of these articles in this
volume. I should note that to meet the space limitations of this book, it
was necessary to do some editing of the articles, particularly those by
Webster and Doob, and Healy.

In Part Two we move from academic analyses to presentations given
by four persons who have been actively engaged in the administration
of justice. Huguette St-Louis, at the time chief judge of the Court of
Quebec, leads off with an account of the past, present, and future of the
court she headed, the most extensive and comprehensive Provincial
Court in Canada. Following this, Marion Tyson, president of the Association of Court Administrators, looks at court reform from the perspective of a court administrator. Then Nora Saunders who served as
deputy minister of justice in the Territory of Nunavut describes the
rationale and reality of Canada's fully unified trial court, the Nunavut
Court of Justice. This part concludes with the presentation of David
Hancock, then minister of justice and attorney general of Alberta, who
at the conference committed himself to working for the unification of
trial courts in his province. These four chapters are based on presentations given at the conference with a little updating and editing.

Part Three presents two contrasting visions of the future of Canada's trial courts. The first by John Borrows and Gerry Seniuk puts

forward the ideal of the trial court serving Canadians in each community as an all-purpose 'house of justice' staffed by a judiciary selected by federal-provincial nominating commissions. This paper is based on an article included in the same special issue of the *Criminal Law Quarterly* that published the papers in Part One. The second chapter in Part Three is based on a report written by a group of Ontario Superior Court judges and subsequently endorsed by the whole court. It was written in response to the suggestion of Ontario's then attorney general, James Flaherty, that a unified criminal court might provide the best platform for improving the administration of criminal justice in the province. The report sets out the advantages of continuing with the existing division of responsibilities between the Superior Court and the Provincial Court.

The final section of the book provides some comparative perspectives on court reform in Canada. Its two chapters, one on trial court unification in California, by Clark Kelso, and the other on trial court integration in England, by Ian Scott, give readers thorough and up-to-date accounts of trial court reform in two other common law jurisdictions. Kelso and Scott are leading scholars of both the law and the politics of court reform in their respective countries. Both chapters are based on presentations given at the Trial Courts of the Future Conference.

I introduce each of the chapters with a short editorial note on its background, context, its relation with other chapters, and its contribution to the overall theme of the book. In a short conclusion I draw together points that emerge from the twelve chapters which will have an important bearing on the future of court reform in Canada and which may also be relevant to court reform elsewhere.

NOTES

1 In 1982 the original Constitution was renamed *The Constitution Act, 1867*.
2 In 1960 section 99 was amended to provide for the mandatory retirement of Superior Court judges at age 75.
3 Despite the different names given to superior courts, throughout this book Superior Courts will be capitalized.
4 See, for instance, the speech of John Rose, *Parliamentary Debates on the Subject of the Confederation of the British North American Provinces*, 3rd. Sess., 8th Provincial Parliament of Canada (Quebec: Hinter Rose, 1865) 387.

5 This is a key point in the speech of Hector Langevin, who gave the only sustained defence of federal control over the appointment of provincial judges. See ibid., 387–8.

6 For an account of the development of provincial courts of appeal, see Peter H. Russell, *The Judiciary in Canada: The Third Branch of Government* (Toronto: McGraw-Hill Ryerson, 1987), ch. 12.

7 The only federal court established under this power was the Exchequer Court of Canada that dealt mostly with cases involving federal revenue and intellectual property. In 1971, when it was incorporated into the Federal Court, it had only eight judges.

8 For a discussion of the debate over merger of the section 96 courts, see Russell, *The Judiciary in Canada*, 268–73.

9 Except that the Territorial Courts had to be established by federal legislation because the federal Parliament has a plenary legislative authority over the territories.

10 See, for instance, G.V.V. Nicholls, 'Federal Proposals for Review of Tribunal Decisions' (1970) *Chitty's Law Review* 257.

11 Darrell Roberts, 'The Structure and Jurisdiction of the Courts and Classification of Offences' (paper prepared for the Law Commission of Canada, 1973), 23.

12 Law Reform Commission of Canada, *Working Paper No.1, The Family Court* (Ottawa: Ministry of Supply and Services, 1975).

13 See Perry S. Millar and Carl Baar, *Judicial Administration in Canada* (Montreal and Kingston: McGill-Queen's University Press, 1981), ch. 3.

14 Jerôme Choquette, *Justice Today* (Quebec: Gouvernment de Québec, 1975).

15 Roy Romanow, John Whyte, and Howard Leeson, *Canada Not Withstanding: The Making of the Constitution, 1976–1982* (Toronto: Carswell/Methuen, 1984), 39.

16 Russell, *The Judiciary in Canada*, 55.

17 *Re Residential Tenancies Act*, [1981] 1 S.C.R. 714.

18 *Crevier v. A.G. Quebec*, [1981] 2 S.C.R. 230.

19 *B.C. Family Relations Act Reference*, [1982] 1 S.C.R. 62.

20 *Re Residential Tenancies Act* at 723.

21 See Peter H.Russell and Jacob S. Zeigel, 'Federal Judicial Appointments: An Appraisal of the First Mulroney Government's Appointments' (1991) 41 *University of Toronto Law Journal* 4.

22 Gerald T.G. Seniuk and Noel Lyon, 'The Supreme Court of Canada and the Provincial Court of Canada' (2000) *Canadian Bar Review* 79 at 80.

23 Lorne Calvert, 'A Message from the Premier of Saskatchewan,' Trial Court of the Future Proceedings, Saskatoon, 2002.

24 An electronic and hard-copy transcript of the conference proceedings is available at the University of Toronto Faculty of Law Library.
25 Professor Manson's paper, 'The Constitutional Dimensions of Prerogative Writs and the Implications for Criminal Court Re-Structuring' could not be included in this volume.
26 *R. v. Gladue*, [1999] 1 S.C.R. 688.

# PART ONE

---

## Emergence of the Issue

# 1 The Provincial Court and the Criminal Law

MARTIN L. FRIEDLAND

*The article Martin Friedland published on Magistrates Courts in 1968 in the* Criminal Law Quarterly *marks the beginning of public discussion in Canada of unifying criminal trial courts. In his forthright manner, Friedland reported on the depressing conditions he found in the Magistrates Courts in various parts of the country. He referred to these lower criminal courts as 'the forgotten child of our system of criminal justice.' Their physical conditions were appalling, their process inefficient and slow, and their personnel ill-qualified and lacking terms of office appropriate for judges. Yet, except in Quebec, Magistrates Courts were responsible for trying the majority of criminal cases, including offences that could result in life imprisonment. Friedland's solution was to move away from a system of inferior and superior criminal courts to one in which all those trying criminal cases had the same status and pay and enjoyed the same quality of institutional support and respect.*

*In this chapter, Friedland revisits the 1968 article and updates it in the light of changes that have taken place in the criminal court system and various efforts to restructure it over the nearly forty years since he wrote his seminal article. He notes the great improvement in the quality of the lower criminal courts as they have been transformed from Magistrates Courts to Provincial Courts. The improvement is evident in both their physical facilities and the quality and terms of office of their judiciary. So much have they improved and so much have they become the principal locus of criminal justice in Canada that first-rate lawyers whose interests lie in the field of criminal law may well prefer an appointment to the Provincial Court over an appointment to the Superior Court. Despite efforts at the political level in a number of provinces and for a time at the federal level, elimination of the structural distinction between the two courts has still not been removed.*

*Friedland's account of the resistance to a single-tier system focuses on the judiciary itself. At the political level, he observes how strenuous and persistent Superior Court judges have been in resisting merger of their court with lower courts – first with County and District Courts and now with Provincial Courts. His chapter also shows that in cases on court structure that have reached it, the Supreme Court of Canada has not been friendly to a one-tier system. He acknowledges his surprise at the outcome of the* McEvoy *case in 1983 when the Supreme Court ruled that the Constitution is a bar to bestowing full criminal trial jurisdiction on Provincial Court judges even when both levels of government support the change. Yet Friedland concludes on an optimistic note: in time political support for unification will grow, Superior Court judges' resistance will wane, and Canada will have a unified criminal court.*

In 1968 – over a third of a century ago – I traveled across Canada to examine the Magistrates' Courts, as they were then called. The study was commissioned by the Canadian Committee on Correction – the Ouimet Committee, named after its chair, Quebec Superior Court justice Roger Ouimet.[1] The resulting paper, entitled 'Magistrates' Courts: Functioning and Facilities', was published that year in the *Criminal Law Quarterly.*

I painted a depressing picture, stating that the magistrates' court was 'the forgotten child of our system of criminal justice.' 'For the most part,' I wrote,

> the lower courts in the larger urban centres in Canada operate with neither dignity nor efficiency, yet both these qualities are essential to any well-conceived system of justice. A certain degree of dignity is necessary to promote respect for the law and administration of justice and to create an atmosphere which will help ensure that the rights of the individual are not forgotten. Efficiency helps to conserve much-needed resources and tends to prevent the congestion which in turn militates against the maintenance of a dignified system.[2]

There were a number of key problems. One was the often close relationship between the courts and the police. The court was generally referred to as a 'police court.' In most of the principal cities in the West and the Maritimes the police and the Magistrates' Courts occupied the same building, sometimes euphemistically described as a 'public safety building.' The police liked it that way. One chief of police in a large Canadian city stated in his annual report: 'When apprehension, detention and Magistrate's level of prosecution are conjoined, efficiency of operation in these fields is at its peak, and I would solicit your serious consideration of this aspect.'[3]

Another problem was that the Magistrates' Courts had been for the most part a municipal responsibility, and a coordinated provincial policy, with adequate funding, was difficult to develop. At about the time I was conducting my study, the provinces across the country were centralizing the administration of the criminal courts. In Ontario, for example, the McRuer Commission into Civil Rights played an important role in bringing this about.[4]

The physical facilities were for the most part deplorable. In one court in Vancouver, one had to walk through the morgue to get to the courtroom. 'In many courts,' I wrote, 'the only way of providing any ventilation ... is to open the windows, bringing in outside noise and making it difficult to hear what is going on inside the courtroom. This is the choice faced by many courts: whether to hear or to breathe.' I commented on the design of the court building, stating:

> Perhaps the first obvious deficiency in design is the too common difficulty of finding the specific courtroom one is looking for – assuming one has found the proper court building. In many cases there are no visible directions when one enters the building and one is forced to ask a somewhat unobliging clerk where the court is. When there is more than one courtroom in which a case might be tried, it is usually difficult to decipher the posted court list, particularly when there are a great many other persons crowded around the area where the list is posted. [5]

In order to get provincial cooperation for the study, the understanding between the Ouimet Committee and the provinces was that I would not criticize individual jurisdictions. In looking at my old files, I came across a letter from the deputy attorney general of Saskatchewan to the committee, stating, 'Mr Justice Ouimet advised that any report made would not refer in any way to specific cities and provinces, nor any fact given which would enable a reader to know what is referred to.' 'I assume,' he went on to say, 'that this also means that there are not going to be any general statements made that there is such overcrowding or inadequate courtroom facilities in all provinces which would amount to saying that there was overcrowding in Saskatchewan ... I do not consider that there is any overcrowding or inadequate courtroom facilities for our magistrates' courts in the cities of Saskatchewan.'[6]

I guess I did not agree with that assumption because I stated that 'I found a pattern of consistent (although not shocking) delay in almost all of the Magistrates' Courts in the larger centres in Canada.' Viewed from today's perspective, however, the delay found then does not appear too bad. 'In the cases in which both the Crown and defence wished the case to proceed,' I noted, 'there were periods of delay ranging from approximately two weeks to two months.'[7]

In the 1990s, I had an opportunity to revisit the criminal courts across the country in connection with my study on judicial independence and accountability for the Canadian Judicial Council. The physical facilities had clearly improved. In my report, I noted that the 'present funding system, whatever its defects, has over the past few decades been reasonably good to the judiciary.' I then referred to my visits twenty-five years earlier for the Ouimet Committee, stating: 'It was a grim picture. The courts were often housed in basements or as an adjunct to police stations ... For the most part, the lower courts in the larger urban centres in Canada operate with neither dignity nor efficiency.' 'On my visits to courts across the country in connection with the present project', I stated, 'I was impressed with the facilities for the courts in almost every major city I visited.'[8] I have no doubt, however, that others can offer a long list of specific problems. While this was being written I noticed, for example, an article in the *Toronto Star* referring to the problem of mould in one of the Toronto courtrooms.[9] Moreover, the decrease in funding for legal aid and the proposed closing of courts in some provinces would cause problems.

The last part of my study for the Ouimet Committee looked at the problem of the status of the magistracy, which I concluded, was at a low level. 'This is a matter of great concern,' I went on, 'because a judicial officer who does not engender respect cannot hope to have the law which is being applied respected. The provision of adequate court facilities and the elimination of the congestion described in the previous sections would no doubt help in raising the status.' I then turned to the status of the judge, stating: 'Ensuring reasonable pay, requiring that all magistrates be lawyers, and designating them as "judges" – steps which have now been taken by a number of provinces – will significantly improve the image of the magistrate. Increasing magistrates' salaries will help attract better persons. Requiring that they be lawyers will help to ensure that proper justice will be administered.'[10]

Then came the controversial part: 'These changes are very important,' I wrote. 'But they are not enough. A fundamental change in the position of the magistrate in the judicial hierarchy is necessary. He now suffers from an inferiority complex because the Criminal Code puts him in an inferior position by treating him as a third class judge – below the Supreme and County Court judge.' An example of the inferior status of the magistrate, I noted, was the trial de novo procedure set out in the Code (later repealed), which permitted either the accused or the Crown to appeal from a magistrate's decision in a summary conviction case and have a complete rehearing of the case by a county court judge. 'The most desirable solution', I wrote,

> would be to abolish the present court structure and the distinction between the jurisdiction of the magistrate and Supreme and County Courts, and to give all those trying criminal cases concurrent jurisdiction, equal status and equal pay ... Whatever may have been the justification for the grades of trial courts in the past (when the magistrate was, in fact dealing with minor cases, as in England where to a great extent, he still does), it has long since disappeared in Canada where the magistrate deals with many serious offences for which an accused can be sentenced by the magistrate to life imprisonment.

The proposed scheme was very simple. The exclusive jurisdiction of the Superior Courts and the absolute jurisdiction of the Magistrates' Court should therefore be eliminated and all judicial officers should have concurrent jurisdiction to try all offences, with or without a jury, in a court perhaps called simply the criminal court for the particular province.

I would have excluded from the new criminal court, partly for political reasons, capital offences that would continue to be tried by a Supreme Court judge and jury. I would also have excluded the very minor offences which should be tried by another tribunal not necessarily presided over by a legally trained person. The key question was where to draw the line for these minor offences. The division between summary and indictable offences obviously draws it at too high a level because of the potential seriousness of summary conviction offences. Perhaps the soundest solution, I suggested, would simply be that for certain offences (perhaps the present indictable offences) the accused would have to be tried in the criminal court, and for other offences could not be sent to jail or fined over a certain low amount unless tried in the criminal court. Thus the seriousness of the offence, judged by the prosecutor, would determine the court in which the accused would be tried. I added a caveat, however, giving the accused the right to have his or her case tried in the criminal court.

An accused would be tried, according to his or her election, either with or without a jury by the first judicial officer who was available, whether it was a Superior Court judge, a County Court judge, or a provincially appointed judge of the criminal court. There is no practical reason, although it is arguable that there are constitutional difficulties, why the provincially appointed judge could not also take jury cases. 'After all,' I stated, 'if he is not competent to charge a jury he should not be considered competent to charge himself.'

The breaking down of hierarchies was in line with the emerging trends in the late 1960s. University students, for example, were interested in greater equality with faculty members. I wrote the history of the University of Toronto in 2002 and noted the prevalence of these ideas at the University of Toronto and throughout North America at the time.[11] Students, it was felt, should have equal access to library stacks; honours courses which favoured certain students should be abolished; and the teaching quality of professors should be evaluated. Even separate washrooms for faculty and students were to be eliminated. All of these demands were brought into effect at the University of Toronto.

The proposal was also in line with American ideas with respect to the judiciary. The American Bar Association's Model State Judicial Article of 1962, for example, provided for a unified trial court of limited jurisdiction. The American Bar Association Committee commented: 'It is contemplated to set up ... a single, unified judicial system with a single court of original jurisdiction. This follows the recommendation of advocates of judicial reform from Pound to Vanderbilt.'[12] Similarly, the influential report of the President's Commission on Law Enforcement and Administration of Justice concluded in 1967 that 'all criminal cases should be tried by judges of equal status under generally comparable procedures.'[13]

I did not anticipate serious constitutional problems, except perhaps with respect to jury trials. Such a scheme, I speculated, would simply require complementary federal and provincial legislation. The federal government would have to alter radically the court structure set out in the Criminal Code. The provinces would have to enact legislation to make their magistrates as much like federally appointed judges as possible; for example, by designating them as judges, increasing their pay, providing against their removal without just cause, and assuring adequate pensions that did not depend upon the length of service. Quebec, I noted, had gone part way towards unification. There, the position of magistrate and the criminal jurisdiction of the County

Court judge trying cases without a jury were consolidated into the position of District Court judge, and all jury trials were conducted by a Superior Court judge.[14]

The report was well received by some. The *Globe and Mail*, for example, reprinted it in three instalments in the fall of 1968 and liked the proposals. In a lead editorial, it stated:

> Perhaps none of Prof. Friedland's proposals cuts more deeply into judicial reform than the idea he offers, with reservations, to 'abolish the present court structure and the distinction between the jurisdiction of the magistrate and supreme and county courts' ... Prof. Friedland's willingness to turn the whole court system on end should be of immense value to the [Ouimet Committee] which must be concerned with far more than a patchwork transformation of our correctional system.[15]

It did not get as good a response in other quarters. *Justice Weekly*, for example, a sensational tabloid that followed court proceedings and thus escaped prosecution for obscenity, introduced its analysis with the comment: 'A lemon by any other name.' It didn't think much of the idea of requiring lawyers for the court, stating: 'Naturally the professor wants only lawyers as provincial judges ... seeing that he is a professor in a law school. But our experience has been – and it is a longer one than the professor's – that laymen-magistrates on the whole were as good and often much better than lawyer-magistrates.' It concluded its observations by stating: 'As for jurists having 'an inferiority complex,' as the professor suggests, he must be referring to other than the numerous magistrates we have known down through the years – and still know.'[16]

The Ouimet Committee's report was published in 1969. They accepted most of the suggestions in my study for improving the functioning and facilities of the magistrates' courts, but carefully avoided mentioning unification of the courts. I learned then, if I had not known it before, that Superior Court judges are generally not enthusiastic about what they consider a dilution of the status of the Superior Court by expanding its numbers. The same concern was evident a number of years later when recommendations were made by various committees and commissions, such as the Zuber Commission in Ontario in 1987,[17] that the county court be merged with the Supreme Court. This has now been accomplished throughout Canada and is now so well established that I doubt if many persons would want to re-establish the county court system.

The Law Reform Commission of Canada was established in 1971. The unification of the criminal courts was a natural subject of interest for the commission and one of its senior staff members, Darrell Roberts, prepared a study paper on the classification of offences and the structure of the criminal courts. He concluded that a unified criminal court was desirable.[18] The commission, however, did not go on at that time to prepare a working paper or a report on the subject.

New Brunswick had a strong interest in a unified criminal court. Perhaps some one from New Brunswick can explain why it was attractive there. My own analysis is that in New Brunswick Superior Court judges heard relatively few criminal cases and missed that interesting aspect of judging. With a unified criminal court they would be able to hear more criminal cases. Why accused persons were not electing trial by a higher court is not clear. My guess is that the cost structure of the legal aid system might help explain it. If legal aid limits the amount that can be claimed for preliminary hearings, there is less incentive to seek a trial in a higher court. It may also be because of a difference in sentencing practices in the two courts.

When I did my study on judicial independence for the Canadian Judicial Council in the mid-1990s, I saw first-hand why a unified criminal court was desirable in New Brunswick. Whenever I had a spare moment I would drop into the courts, where I tried to get a flavour of what was happening. In Fredericton and Moncton I found the Provincial Court judges busy with interesting criminal cases, while the Superior Court judges seemed to be spending their time on small claims cases. Perhaps the couple of days I was there were not representative of the true picture, but I note that Carl Baar in his 1991 study for the Canadian Judicial Council confirmed that this tended to be the pattern in New Brunswick.[19]

In the early 1980s, the attorney general of New Brunswick wanted to create a provincially appointed unified criminal court. There were, however, questions raised about the constitutionality of the concept and a reference was made by the New Brunswick cabinet to the New Brunswick Court of Appeal. No specific legislation was put forward and it was not known whether the federal government would support a unified criminal court. In a unanimous judgment, the New Brunswick Court of Appeal upheld the establishment of a unified criminal court set up by the province with complementary federal legislation. This was upheld whether the unified criminal court had exclusive or concurrent jurisdiction.[20] The Supreme Court of Canada, however, in a judgment 'by the Court' in the *McEvoy* case in 1983, rejected the scheme. It was held to breach section 96 of the Constitution, even if the federal government passed the enabling legislation and even if the Superior Court retained concurrent jurisdiction to try criminal cases. 'Parliament can no more give away federal constitutional powers than a province can usurp them,' the Court stated. 'The effect of this proposal would be to deprive the Governor-General of his power under s. 96 to appoint the judges who try indictable offences in New Brunswick.'[21]

This came as a surprise to many persons in an age of cooperative federalism. Peter Russell called the decision 'remarkable.'[22] One can understand why a province should not be allowed unilaterally to usurp the federal appointing power, but why not permit such a transfer if the federal government wants to give it to the provinces, particularly if the Superior Courts still have concurrent jurisdiction? The Supreme Court decision unnecessarily elevates the importance of the federal appointing power, which on my reading of the history of the *British North America Act* came about almost by chance. The administration of justice was given in the *Act* to the provinces. It would have been natural also to give them the power to make judicial appointments. In my study *A Place Apart* I ask why the appointing power was not given to the provinces. My answer: 'Perhaps the main reason is that the key players in Confederation who were moving on to the federal stage wanted to keep patronage over appointments in their own hands.'[23] At an early stage of the deliberations leading to Confederation, one delegate, Sir Samuel Tilley, had urged the delegates to consider 'the adoption of some measure which should entirely remove these appointments from the influence of party politics,' but another participant privately observed in a letter to the colonial secretary that the recommendation met with little enthusiasm. 'Considerable reluctance,' he wrote, 'was exhibited by several of the legal members of the conference to forgo prizes now apparently within their grasp.' Other delegates argued, however, that the quality of appointments would be better if they were made by the federal government.

One lingering problem is the validity of the transfers of criminal jurisdiction to the Provincial Court that have been made over the years and continue to be made. The Supreme Court in *McEvoy* stated: 'What is being contemplated here is not one or a few transfers of criminal law power, such as has already been accomplished under the Criminal Code, but a complete obliteration of superior court criminal law jurisdiction.'[24] In fact, the transfers that had taken place in the past were not limited to a few, but included a great number of indictable offences. No one on the seven-member court had a strong background in criminal law. Neither Justices William McIntyre nor Antonio Lamer, both knowledgeable about the criminal law, sat on the case. They would have pointed out that more than a few transfers had already taken place.

A number of individuals have argued that their convictions should be overturned because transfers of indictable offences to the Provincial Court are unconstitutional. Their arguments have been rejected. In *Trimarchi*, for example, the Ontario Court of Appeal stated in 1987 that it is implicit in the *McEvoy* decision

> that the Criminal Code's present scheme of conferral of jurisdiction on s. 96 courts ... and on the Provincial Courts did not run afoul of the requirements of s. 96. If the Supreme Court was of the view that by reason of s. 96 the Parliament of Canada was disabled from conferring jurisdiction on a provincially appointed judge to try any indictable offence it would have said so because this would have been a more direct basis for its opinion.[25]

Still, the question remains slightly open whether there might be a point where the transfer of jurisdiction would be considered too much in a constitutional sense. I doubt if that point will ever be reached, assuming that murder and treason remain in the Superior Courts.

Because of *McEvoy*, the new route to unification was to have the federal government appoint Provincial Court judges as section 96 judges. Of course, this was more attractive to Provincial Court judges, but politically more difficult to achieve. A special committee of Ontario provincial criminal court judges, chaired by Judge David Vanek, brought forward a proposal in 1987 that all trial courts in Ontario be divided into three divisions – the civil, family, and criminal divisions.[26] The committee did not go into detail about how the court should be established, but simply said: 'Initially members of the above courts might be chosen from among Supreme, District or Provincial Court Judges as suitability and preference might dictate.' That meant, in the light of *McEvoy*, that the federal government would make the appointments.

The attorney general of Ontario, Ian Scott, was interested in a unified criminal court and no doubt hoped that the recently established Ontario Courts Inquiry, headed by Court of Appeal Justice Thomas

Zuber, would look with favour on the concept.[27] Justice Zuber
accepted the idea of a merger of the county court with the Superior
Court, but not a merger with the Provincial Court. 'It is not apparent,'
he wrote, 'that this plan [as suggested by the Vanek committee] contains any substantial benefit to the public in terms of accessibility or
efficiency. The unified criminal court would result in a substantial
improvement in the lot of those who preside in the present Provincial
Court (Criminal Division) but this factor cannot be a sufficient reason
to reorganize the court system.'[28] Scott brought about the county court
merger and renamed the courts. The former Supreme Court of Ontario
now combined with the county court would be called the Ontario
Court of Justice (General Division), a name that was disliked by the
federally appointed judges, and the Provincial Court was called the
Ontario Court of Justice (Provincial Division). The former was subsequently renamed the Superior Court of Justice, which pleased the
judges of that court, but stung the Provincial Court judges, who were
now once again implicitly labelled an 'inferior court.' And so the battle
continues. In Ian Scott's memoirs he refers to what he called the
odium with which unification was regarded by many of the federally
appointed judges.

Interest in a unified criminal court continued. Peter Russell in his
influential 1987 book, *The Judiciary in Canada*, supported the concept, as
implicitly did Carl Baar in his 1991 report for the Canadian Judicial
Council,[29] although he was not permitted to make recommendations
on the concept.[30] The Law Reform Commission of Canada, headed by
Justice Allen Linden, now of the Federal Court of Canada, also promoted the concept. In 1989 the commission produced a working paper,
*Toward a Unified Criminal Court*. On the other hand, a Canadian
Bar Association task force on court reform, chaired by a federally
appointed justice, Peter Seaton of British Columbia, and which
included then professor of law Tom Cromwell as research director,
was opposed to the concept. The task force stated: 'We are not persuaded that there is a public perception of lower quality justice being
administered in the provincial courts. Even if it were, we would not
think the unified criminal court would be a necessary or appropriate
reform strategy to address this problem ... Under a new court structure,
inadequate facilities will remain just as inadequate.'[31] The committee
suggested that if governments do 'decide that the unified criminal
court is a reform worth pursuing, very serious consideration should be
given to establishing one or more pilot projects whose operation could

be professionally and systematically assessed.' This approach was the one that had been taken before the widespread adoption of the unified family courts.

New Brunswick did not give up. They took the hint given by the Canadian Bar Association and proposed that 'New Brunswick become a pilot site for a Unified Criminal Court.' A detailed consultation document was issued by the New Brunswick Department of Justice in May 1994. According to Carl Baar, 'those efforts were derailed after federal Justice Minister Allan Rock's unprecedented undertaking that federal authorization (by amending the Judges Act) would require superior court and provincial bar endorsement of the proposal.'[32]

So far, the territory of Nunavut is the only jurisdiction in Canada to have a unified criminal court. No doubt others will have current information on what is taking place in other provinces. The province of Alberta, for example, has recently expressed great interest in the concept.[33]

Other persons can also comment on steps that are being taken in their jurisdiction to integrate the courts administratively, if not fully. In *A Place Apart*, I argued that the courts would function more efficiently and with greater independence if their administration was handled by an independent Court Services Agency in which all courts played a role, along with the provincial government.[34] As far as I am aware, no jurisdiction in Canada has yet taken up that challenge.

Arguments have been put forward that the *Judges' Reference* case, decided by the Supreme Court of Canada in 1997,[35] will lead to the possibility that the Supreme Court will strike down the existing two-tier structure. Judge Gerald Seniuk and Professor Noel Lyon recently wrote in the Canadian Bar Review about the 'ambiguous status of the Provincial Court' in the light of the *Judges' Reference* case.[36] In the *Judges' Reference* case, the Supreme Court of Canada used the preamble to the Constitution to require the same procedures for dealing with financial security for provincially appointed judges as apply to federally appointed judges.

The most recent Supreme Court of Canada case involving the status of the provincial court, *Therrien v. Québec*, decided in June 2001,[37] suggests, however, that the Supreme Court of Canada is not going to upset the judicial apple-cart. In that case, the then Judge Richard Therrien, who had been dismissed as a Quebec Provincial Court judge because he had not disclosed when appointed his conviction in the early 1970s for activities relating to the FLQ, argued that Provincial Court judges could not be dismissed without a resolution of the Legislative Assembly. Under the Constitution, a Superior Court judge cannot be removed without a joint address by the House of Commons and the Senate. In the case of Quebec, it is the Quebec Court of Appeal that makes the determination whether a provincially appointed judge is to be removed. The Supreme Court of Canada upheld the flexible approach that had been set out in the 1985 *Valente* case.[38] Justice Gonthier stated for a unanimous seven-person court that 'the Constitution cannot afford greater protection than what is guaranteed by s. 11(d) of the Canadian Charter.'[39] *Valente* is therefore still the key decision.

The judicial route is clearly not the most promising avenue to bring about a unified criminal court. The *Judges' Reference* case will, however, have an impact on the debate. It has brought and will continue to bring about improvements in the salary and benefits of Provincial Court judges. The gap between Superior Court and Provincial Court judges will continue to narrow. The quality of appointments to the Provincial Court will continue to improve. There is already in each province, for the most part, a good appointment process for Provincial Court judges. An increasing number of first-rate lawyers will prefer an appointment to the Provincial Court or treat the two benches with equal interest.

There is a growing degree of prestige in the Provincial Court. The criminal work of the Superior Courts will continue to decrease, as more and more crimes are tried in the Provincial Court. The recent move to create more hybrid offences is part of that trend. The decrease in legal aid funding will also be a contributing factor. The interesting criminal cases and Charter issues will increasingly be dealt with by the Provincial Court.[40] The public and the politicians will develop a greater appreciation of the important work done by the Provincial Court. In time, the idea of a unified criminal court will seem more attractive to many Superior Court judges. A couple of pilot projects will be tried in a few judicial districts, just as happened in the family law area. They will prove to be successful. In time, there will be a unified criminal court in Canada.

NOTES

This is the text of a paper delivered at the Trial Courts of the Future Conference, Saskatoon, Saskatchewan, 16 May 2002. I am grateful to Colin Grey for his research assistance.

1 *Report of the Canadian Committee on Corrections – Towards Unity: Canadian Justice and Corrections* (Ouimet Commission) (Ottawa: Queen's Printer, 1969).
2 M.L. Friedland 'Magistrates' Courts: Functioning and Facilities' (1968) 11 *Criminal Law Quarterly* at 53.
3 Ibid., at 55–6.
4 *Ontario: Royal Commission Into Civil Rights* (McRuer Commission) (Toronto: Queen's Printer, 1968), Report No. 1, vol. 2, 866 ff.
5 *Supra*, note 2, 60.
6 Roy Meldrum to W.C. McGrath, the secretary of the Ouimet Committee, May 12, 1967.
7 *Supra*, note 2, 64.
8 M.L. Friedland, *A Place Apart: Judicial Independence and Accountability in Canada* (Ottawa: Canadian Judicial Council, 1995), 220.
9 *Toronto Star*, 9 September 2001.
10 *Supra*, note 2, 70 –3.
11 M.L. Friedland, *The University of Toronto: A History* (Toronto: University of Toronto Press, 2002).
12 Set out in the *Report of the Task Force on the Administration of Justice* (Washington, D.C.: American Bar Association, 1967), 92.
13 *The Challenge of Crime in a Free Society: A Report by the President's Commission on Law Enforcement and Administration of Justice* (Washington, D.C.: Government Printing Office, 1967).
14 *Supra*, note 2, 74–5.
15 *Globe and Mail*, 21 November 1968.
16 *Justice Weekly*, 14 December 1968.
17 The Hon. Thomas G. Zuber, *Report of the Ontario Courts Inquiry* (Toronto: Ontario Ministry of the Attorney General, 1987).
18 Darrell Roberts, 'The Structure and Jurisdiction of the Courts and Classification of Offences' (unpublished paper, 1983).
19 Carl Baar *One Trial Court: Possibilities and Limitations* (Ottawa: Canadian Judicial Council, 1991), 75. According to Baar, small claims cases in New Brunswick are now handled by part-time adjudicators: Baar, 'Background Paper on Trial Court Reorganization' (paper prepared for the Trial Courts of the Future Conference, 16 May 2002), 5.
20 *Reference Re Establishment of a Unified Criminal Court of New Brunswick* (1981), 62 C.C.C. (2d) 165, 127 D.L.R. (3d) 214, 36 N.B.R. (2d) 609 (C.A.).
21 *McEvoy v. New Brunswick (Attorney General)*, [1983] 1 S.C.R. 704, 4 C.C.C. (3d) 289, 148 D.L.R. (3d) 25.
22 Russell *The Judiciary in Canada*, 60.
23 Friedland, *A Place Apart*, 234.
24 *McEvoy v. New Brunswick*, 37.

25 *R. v. Trimarchi* (1987), 63 O.R. (2d) 515 at 525, 40 C.C.C. (3d) 433, 49 D.L.R. (4th) 382 (H.C.J.), leave to appeal to S.C.C. refused 49 D.L.R. (4th) viii, 63 O.R. (2d) x, 41 C.C.C. (3d) vi. See also *R. v. McGann* (1986), 70 N.B.R. (2d) 381, 28 C.C.C. (3d) 215 (Q.B.) (Stevenson J.).

26 *Report of the Provincial Criminal Court Judges Special Committee on Criminal Justice in Ontario*, (Chair, Judge David Vanek) (Toronto: The Association of Provincial Court Judges of Ontario, 1987), 78.

27 See Ian Scott, with Neil McCormick *To Make a Difference: A Memoir* (Toronto: Studdart, 2001), 181.

28 Vanek Committee Report, 79.

29 Russell, *The Judiciary in Canada*, 215–18, Baar, *One Trial Court* and 'Judicial Independence and Judicial Administration: The Case of Provincial Court Judges' (1998) *Constitutional Forum* 9.

30 E-mail to the author from Carl Baar, 6 October 2001.

31 Canadian Bar Association *Report of the Canadian Bar Association Task Force on Court Reform in Canada* (Toronto: The Association, 1991), 113.

32 Baar, 'Judicial Independence and Judicial Administration,' 117.

33 David Hancock, Alberta Minister of Justice and Attorney General; see chapter 8 below.

34 Friedland, *A Place Apart*, ch. 9.

35 *Reference re Independence and Impartiality of Judges of the Provincial Court of Prince Edward Island*, [1997] 3 S.C.R. 3, 118 C.C.C. (3d) 193, 150 D.L.R. (4th) 577, sub nom. *Reference re: Provincial Court Act and Public Sector Pay Reduction Act* (P.E.I.), s. 10, supp. reasons [1998] 1 S.C.R. 3, 121 C.C.C. (3d) 474, 155 D.L.R. (4th) 1, motion for directions refused July 9, 1998, motion to extend period of suspension granted [1998] 2 S.C.R. 443.

36 G.T. Seniuk and Noel Lyon, 'The Supreme Court of Canada and the Provincial Court in Canada,' (2000) 77 *Canadian Bar Review* at 79.

37 *Therrien v. Québec (Ministre de la justice)* (2001), 155 C.C.C. (3d) 1, 200 D.L.R. (4th) 1, 43 C.R. (5th) 1 sub nom.

38 *R. v. Valente*, [1985] 2 S.C.R. 673, 23 C.C.C. (3d) 193, 49 C.R. (3d) 97.

39 *Therrien v. Québec* at 27.

40 According to an analysis by a special committee on court restructuring of the Ontario Superior Court Judges' Association, 'there is still a significant quantity of judicial resources of the superior court in Ontario assigned for criminal work, estimated at roughly 37-38% at any given time.' See *Report of the Special Committee on Court Restructuring* (2000), 14.

# 2 Trial Court Reorganization in Canada: Alternative Futures

CARL BAAR

*Carl Baar is Canada's pre-eminent scholar of judicial structure and administration. His knowledge of courts at all levels, in all areas of law, and in all parts of the country is evident in this chapter – as is his strength as a comparativist. While he focuses on courts exercising criminal jurisdiction, his chapter also discusses structural developments in the field of family law and civil justice in all of Canada's provinces. He also helps us assess trial court structure and reform options in the context of experience elsewhere, in particular in the United States and England.*

*In the first part of his chapter Baar shows how trial court systems in all of Canada's provinces have gone through two major waves of reform. The first is the professionalization of the Provincial Courts that Friedland describes and the second is the merger of the District and County Courts into the provincial Superior Courts. He points out that these two waves have produced a system in which two sets of courts – Provincial Courts with their judges appointed and paid by the provinces and Superior Courts with their judges appointed and paid by Ottawa – are distinguished more by their function than by the professional status of their judiciaries. In every province the Provincial Courts have become the primary criminal court and the Superior Court the primary civil court. A third wave of reform, the creation of a unified family court, remains incomplete, having run into federal-provincial political difficulties and Superior Court judicial opposition to specialization.*

*In the second part of his chapter Baar offers three options to the two-tier system of functionally specialized courts toward which Canada is now uneasily drifting. These are full unification of all trial work in a single court, an extension of the Quebec system in which the Provincial Court takes over virtually all criminal jurisdiction, or an integration of trial court work under a unified system of court management. The last is essentially the direction that trial court reform has taken in England and in many states in the United States.*

*Baar makes two points that are most often lost sight of in discussing trial court reform. One is that no matter what system is adopted – the status quo or any of the reform options on offer – the use of subordinate judicial officers is inevitable. In all court systems there is a growing use of judicial officials to deal with matters considered not sufficiently complex or weighty to require the services of high-salaried professional judges. This does not mean that all trial court systems are inescapably two-tier structures. Justices of the peace and other such subordinate judicial functionaries can work under the direction of a single court or of multiple courts.*

*Baar's other point is that civil justice – in particular adjudicating disputes involving relatively small amounts of money – is the orphan of court reform. Arrangements for trying so-called small claims cases have ranged from trial by Superior Court judges in New Brunswick to trial by lawyers with part-time judicial appointments in four provinces today. In the world of corporate law, a few thousand dollars may be small potatoes, but to millions of Canadians these 'small claims' are often of great importance. Baar underlines the need to give the organization of civil justice much more careful consideration than it has received in the past.*

**Retrospective**

*Provincial Court Structure in Canada's First Century*

From 1867 until 1965 the typical Provincial Court system had three levels of trial courts. First, there was a Superior Court that combined trial and appellate jurisdiction. The Superior Court was a central trial court whose judges had their chambers and permanent residence in one (or perhaps two) locations and went on circuit to other Provincial Court centres. This was the Superior Court with general and inherent jurisdiction that was contemplated in section 96 of the *Constitution Act, 1867*. Judges were appointed and paid by the federal government and served during good behaviour. The court and its judges thus inherited the authority and independence long associated with the English Superior Courts.[1]

Second was a set of County and/or District Courts that would try most civil and criminal cases. County Court judges and District Court judges were also appointed and paid by the federal government, but did not have the same constitutionally entrenched tenure of office.

These courts were, in the language of the time, created to 'bring justice to every man's door.' Because they did not have general or inherent jurisdiction, their authority was governed by provincial statute in civil cases and by a combination of provincial statutes and the Criminal Code of Canada in criminal matters. Again, these courts had an English counterpart, although our earliest pre-Confederation County Courts apparently pre-dated their English counterparts. Quebec was the only province without a separate set of County or District Courts, so while most of the province's Superior Court justices were in Montreal and Quebec City, some resided in smaller centres. In many provinces, county and district judges acquired 'consent jurisdiction' in civil cases, so that if both parties agreed, a judge could try a case involving a sum that exceeded the court's statutory jurisdiction. By the 1970s, for example, Ontario's County Court judges heard million-dollar lawsuits despite a statutory limit of $25,000.

Third was a set of Magistrate's Courts staffed largely by lay judicial officers who were appointed by the provincial government and served at pleasure. The magistrates' jurisdiction was primarily criminal (matters such as pre-trial release, preliminary hearings, and summary conviction offences), but also included all juvenile court proceedings and a wide range of family law matters deemed less important because they involved women and children rather than property.[2] Again, the model was the English lay magistrates, who persist to the present day in part because most are part-time and unpaid. In 1877, in Peel County, Ontario, a population of 26,011 was served by one County Court judge and 168 magistrates. Halton County immediately to the west had one County Court judge and 136 magistrates.[3]

Canadian magistrates were often called police magistrates, and a century ago in Alberta, magistrates could at the same time be senior RCMP officers. The position's lower status and the absence of legal qualifications, combined with the court's jurisdiction over youth and family matters, meant that the first women to hold judicial office in Canada were provincial appointees to Police Court and Juvenile Court. Emily Murphy of the Persons case served as a magistrate in Edmonton as did Helen Gregory MacGill in Vancouver.[4]

Justices of the peace often shared responsibility for judicial functions in these courts, and were typically paid on a piece-work basis, a sure incentive to sign search warrants brought to them by local police officers. In British Columbia, even magistrates 'were only paid a fee by the government if the accused was convicted.'[5] By the 1930s, it was common practice for defence counsel to offer to match the fee if an acquittal was entered.

## Waves of Reform

Since 1965 the structure of Canadian Provincial Court systems has undergone changes that belie the image of conservative and unresponsive judicial institutions. Two waves of reform are complete, and a third is firmly established.

First came the professionalization of the magistracy through the creation of Provincial Courts staffed by legally qualified provincially appointed judges. Beginning with Quebec in 1965 and then Ontario in 1968, every province had replaced its Magistrate's Courts with Provincial Courts by 1978. A few lay judges remained by the 1990s, but Newfoundland was the last province to appoint judges without legal training, and has not done so in over twenty years.

Professionalization was accompanied by the expansion of jurisdiction, both by statute and in practice. Accused persons more frequently exercised their option to be tried before a Provincial Court judge for an indictable offence rather than before a judge alone or a judge and jury in a County Court. Family Court jurisdiction expanded to the extent that constitutional limitations allowed,[6] and in half the provinces, small claims went to Provincial Court judges, and the dollar limit edged upward.

Quebec led the way with the highest civil jurisdiction of any Provincial Court, and a unique model for its Court of Sessions of the Peace (which functioned as the criminal division of its Provincial Court). Sessions Court judges not only had jurisdiction over summary offences and over those indictable offences in which an accused elected trial by Provincial Court judge, but also had jurisdiction in 'judge alone' trials conducted by County or District Court in every other province. This has meant that Quebec Superior Court judges try criminal cases only when a jury is either required (for example, for murder) or elected by an accused. Under this model, one Sessions Court judge presides over the preliminary hearing, and if the case is committed to trial by judge alone, another Sessions Court judge tries the case. The same jurisdictional division continues today with judge-alone cases tried in the Chambre criminelle et penale of the Cour du Québec.

The second wave of reform was the merger of Superior Courts with County and District Courts, which began in Prince Edward Island in 1973 and was completed in Nova Scotia in 1992. The central trial court model of Canada's first century has been replaced by a mix of resident and travelling Superior Court judges with a broad array of civil, criminal, and family jurisdiction. The merger process was often beset by conflict, delay and even bitterness, but today's section 96 judges neither remember the conflict nor yearn for a return to the old days. Considering that all nine mergers required both federal and provincial legislation, their completion in less than twenty years is remarkable.[7] Today, an increasing proportion of civil and criminal cases once heard by County Court judges are now heard by Provincial Court judges (or in some provinces by part-time small claims adjudicators).

The third wave of reform is the creation of Unified Family Courts (UFCs) at the Superior Court level, beginning again in Prince Edward Island in 1973 and expanding to four Canadian cities in the mid-1970s as part of a federally funded pilot project. Nova Scotia is the seventh and most recent province to begin implementation of a UFC – a major step since its Family Court was still administered by the provincial social service ministry until the 1990s. Alberta has begun the process of legislating a unified family court, with strong provincial government support. Only British Columbia and Quebec have no plans to change the way family matters are distributed between their Superior and Provincial Courts.

The merger of Superior and County Courts was an all-or-nothing process in each province, while implementation of the UFC has been an incremental process within most provinces, often (but frequently not) resulting in provincial Family Court judges receiving section 96 appointments. This incremental expansion has generated federal-provincial negotiations and tensions not seen in earlier waves of reform; as a result, the federal government has been more involved than in the past in the provincial administration of justice.

In practice, provincial UFCs have operated as divisions of the Superior Court, with judges appointed directly to the Family Court bench rather than appointed to the Superior Court and assigned by a chief justice to sit in family law matters. Almost two decades ago, when a New Brunswick Family Division judge was interested in moving to the Court of Queen's Bench, a new appointee was given the Family Division vacancy, creating the potential for a two-tier status system in the section 96 courts, despite reformers' efforts to give family law equal status with civil matters. More recently, expansion of the Ontario Unified Family Court has stalled in the face of opposition by key section 96 judges to the subject-matter specialization it implies. Thus by 2004, Ontario's provincial government found itself filling vacant positions on the Ontario Court of Justice (the newest name for its former Provincial Court) in the field of family law, instead of continuing to phase out family court work by provincially appointed judges.

*Reorganization Rejected or Unrealized*

The most important and controversial reform proposal for the past quarter-century – neither implemented nor even piloted in a single province – is the unified criminal court. In the early 1980s New Brunswick developed a statutory framework that placed jurisdiction over all criminal cases in the Provincial Court. The plan's constitutionality was challenged, and a reference taken to the provincial Court of Appeal. That court concluded that the plan was constitutional, but the Supreme Court of Canada in *McEvoy v. New Brunswick*[8] unanimously disagreed in an unsigned judgment usually attributed to Chief Justice Bora Laskin. That judgment can read persuasively as constitutional doctrine, but was quite unexpected at the time, since the plan required concurrence of the federal Parliament, and previous cases in which legislation was held to violate section 96 involved provincial statutes alone.

In June 1990 provincial attorneys general, following the leadership of Ontario's Ian Scott (who had tabled legislation the year before), gave unanimous support to the principle of a unified criminal court at the Superior Court level. With federally appointed judges making up the unified court, constitutional objections in *McEvoy* would no longer apply. But opposition quickly emerged. While the proposal had the strong support of the Canadian Association of Provincial Court Judges (whose status and salaries would go up if they secured section 96 appointments), it had the strong opposition of federally appointed judges, whose workload would increase not only in volume but with a growing proportion of routine criminal proceedings. The Canadian Bar Association was mobilized, and the Court Reform Task Force, under respected B.C. Court of Appeal Justice Peter Seaton, reported its opposition in 1991.[9] The Canadian Judicial Council, made up entirely of federally appointed chief judges, asked me to complete a study on the subject, but specifically stipulated that no recommendations be included. When my report came before the full council in September

1991,[10] a resolution was immediately passed opposing the concept of a unified criminal court.

The only visible supporter of the unified criminal court among council members was New Brunswick Court of Queen's Bench Chief Justice Guy Richard. His championing of the proposal kept it alive in New Brunswick, but his retirement, coupled with a commitment by federal Justice Minister Alan Rock not to proceed with the change without the support of the New Brunswick bar and Queen's Bench judges, doomed the proposal. No requirement similar to Rock's for merger proposals had ever been made in the previous twenty years, and it would have prevented a number of them from being enacted. So New Brunswick Justice turned its attention to other initiatives.

Since then, the unified criminal court proposal received no provincial attention until January 2000, when Ontario Attorney General James Flaherty spoke in its favour. In the meantime, however, federal legislation authorized a single-level trial court for the new territory of Nunavut.[11] In retrospect, this step seems obvious and appropriate for the territory's small population, and it had strong support there. But this should not obscure the significance of the change; it required considerable effort by federal officials to canvass a wide range of federal statutory changes that would accompany any similar reform by the provinces. And it was only after a visit to Nunavut late in 1999 by Ontario's attorney general and deputy attorney general that the Ontario proposal was put forward.

A potential orphan amidst proposals for unified family courts and a unified criminal court are the small claims courts. Ontario's concept was that there should also be a unified civil court, but only New Brunswick has required Superior Court judges to hear small claims, and that experiment, begun in the 1980s, was abandoned by the late 1990s. Thus we now have civil cases heard in Provincial Courts in five provinces: British Columbia, Alberta, Saskatchewan, Newfoundland, and Quebec, with jurisdictional limits ranging from $5,000 to $30,000 in 2000, and five years later ranging from $5,000 to $70,000. At the same time, four other provinces have small claims heard by part-time adjudicators nominally attached to Superior Courts: Manitoba, Ontario, New Brunswick, and Nova Scotia. Provinces have in the recent past considered a variety of conflicting options; while one province considers shifting to lay adjudicators, another is urged to eliminate them. Thus no consensus has emerged on procedures or jurisdictional boundaries, and as Provincial Courts expand their civil jurisdiction, others may follow Quebec, which has a special procedure for civil claims under a smaller dollar limit, and then prohibits lawyers from appearing in those small-dollar proceedings. Despite the increased interest in civil justice reform in the 1990s, including a major Canadian Bar Association Civil Justice Task Force, there has been no overall examination of how best to organize the jurisdiction of civil courts.[12]

*Current Status of Provincial Trial Court Reorganization*

Three important changes (hinted at above) have emerged in recent years without any further formal reorganization of trial courts. These three patterns of change are likely to continue without explicit guidelines unless appropriate policies are developed and implemented.

First, Provincial Court systems that were traditionally characterized by the status differences between Superior Courts and courts staffed by provincially appointed judges are increasingly characterized by functional or subject-matter specialization. Superior Courts are increasingly dominated by civil cases, and Provincial Courts by criminal cases, so that federally and provincially appointed judges are differentiated by their subject-matter expertise and experience more than their status (or, if Ontario is a bellwether, their salaries). The spread of Unified Family Courts has accentuated that trend.

The major exceptions are Quebec and British Columbia, where Provincial Court judges do the widest range of work. Even these two provinces have not resisted the shift away from the generalist judge, and the Cour du Québec is divided by statute into three divisions or chambers (civil, criminal, and youth), with the civil division also having a unique jurisdiction over a wide range of appeals from provincial administrative tribunals.

Second, criminal matters are shifting from Superior to Provincial Courts. Legislation and practice, both federal and provincial, have encouraged Crown and defence counsel to opt for trial in Provincial Court. The combination of better-qualified, more effectively screened provincial appointees on one hand, and larger Superior Courts in which judges are more numerous and therefore less well known and less predictable on the other, means that defence counsel are less likely to encourage their clients to elect trial in a Superior Court. Conversely, the expansion of hybrid offences under the Criminal Code, and the increase to eighteen-month maximum sentences for summary conviction in a set of offences that frequently come to court, mean that Crown attorneys are more likely to opt for summary conviction proceedings in Provincial

Court, especially to preclude the accused from electing a trial by jury. Taken together, these changes have increasingly meant that Provincial Courts are becoming *de facto* unified criminal courts.

Third, the changes in Provincial Courts are generating new roles for subordinate judicial officers. As salaries and responsibilities of Provincial Court judges grow, both judges and governments have reason to shift routine matters to other judicial officers, notably justices of the peace (JPs). And as the jurisdiction of JPs expands, Provincial Court judges can move out of their less interesting work, and provincial governments can hire lay or legally trained officials at lower salaries. In Alberta, legislation authorizing new JP appointments was enacted in 1998.[13] And in the aftermath of the work of judicial salary commissions mandated by the Supreme Court of Canada in the PEI reference, similar developments are likely in other provinces; for example, existing JPs in Ontario are doing an increasingly wider range of preliminary work in criminal cases (e.g., first appearances, bail hearings).

In Canada's two largest provinces, this trend has also meant the fragmentation of criminal and quasi-criminal jurisdiction. In Quebec, Municipal Courts are available (with full-time judges in three large municipalities and part-time lawyer-judges in others) to hear summary conviction offences. By shifting those cases out of the Cour du Québec, its criminal caseload in Montreal was cut in half, from 28,000 cases in 1998 to perhaps 14,000 a year later. In Ontario, most provincial offences (by volume) have been shifted to courts administered by municipalities (which get to collect and keep the fine money), reversing a policy of thirty years' standing.

The criminal defence bar has even found itself supporting an expanded role for justices of the peace. In the early 1990s, Toronto criminal defence counsel favoured a pilot program in which JPs would conduct preliminary hearings – a plan seen as preferable to abolishing the procedure and feasible given the limited authority of the preliminary hearing judge.[14]

## Range of Future Options

This part will define four different options for trial court reorganization. Given renewed interest in a unified criminal court, these models will be presented in terms of their impact on criminal court processes. Note however that the focus on criminal court work leaves open the future organization of civil litigation, including small claims. The most likely outcome is the emergence of three streams of litigation (small claims, simplified or economical procedures, and full-dress litigation), parallel to Lord Woolf's report in England and implementation of the Woolf rules in April 1999. At the same time, this outcome begs the question of who will adjudicate small claims and simplified procedure cases, and whether Superior Courts will evolve a set of subordinate judicial officers whose role in civil cases parallels that of Provincial Court JPs in criminal cases.

*Option One: Trial Court Unification*

This option has been the dominant paradigm for reform of trial courts for over a century, rooted in the English *Judicature Act* of 1874 that created a unified Superior Court. It also goes back to the French Revolution and the replacement of local feudal courts by a framework of liberal professional adjudication that has come to be a fundamental part of the modern state.

In the United States, the concept of court unification has been extended beyond the Superior Courts so that a dozen American jurisdictions (eleven states and the District of Columbia) had some form of consolidated or unified trial courts by 1990.[15] However, with rare exceptions (Minnesota being the most ambitious), virtually every unified 'single level' trial court has some class of subordinate judicial officers to do the wide variety of routine tasks that require independence and professionalism, but not the higher salaries commanded by judges with the broad authority conferred by a unified trial court.

Even in current Canadian Provincial Courts, subordinate judicial officers exist in every province but one. New Brunswick alone has neither sitting nor signing justices of the peace, so Provincial Court judges must remain in their chambers until the arrest warrants ordered when accused persons have failed to appear in court are typed and ready for the judge's signature.

*Option Two: Two-Level Trial Court Structure*

While trial court unification is the dominant paradigm for reform, the two-level trial court is the dominant reality throughout the common law world. Exceptions go in the direction of even more levels: for example, Australian states have three levels of trial courts (the English Canadian model from 1867 to 1973), and the only state to abolish its District Court (Queensland) reinstated that court thirty years later. England itself has a mix of trial courts too numerous to count, and a variety of judges whose titles are separate from the courts on which they sit; somehow it is all supposed to work, or so they tell us.

Throughout the Commonwealth, countries of all sizes have a Superior Court and a Magistrate's Court (under those or other names). A decade ago, New Zealand shifted a chunk of the jurisdiction of its Superior Court to its District Court (citing Ontario's Zuber Report to support the shift), but maintained the two distinct trial courts – in a country with a total of three million people.[16] Much smaller countries in the Commonwealth, including island states in the Caribbean, have done the same; however, those Superior Courts typically combine trial with more extensive appellate jurisdiction.

While Canada maintains a two-level court structure, federal and provincial policy on court organization and jurisdiction, particularly in matters of criminal law, could at best be termed a policy of incremental change, and at worst a process of drift. Most provinces have moved to so high a degree of subject-matter specialization that Superior Court judges are no longer generalists, and their role in criminal matters has become little different from the role of central trial court justices before merger began in the 1970s.

*First New Option: Recognizing and Extending Specialization*

Rather than creating a unified criminal court, statutory changes could be made in the two-tier court structure that expand the responsibilities of Provincial Court judges in criminal cases without either violating the constitutional standard established in *McEvoy* or shifting appointment and remuneration of criminal court judges to the federal government.

This option would take two steps further to expand specialization. The first step would be the adoption of the Quebec model in other provinces, so that judge-alone trials following a preliminary hearing would be conducted by Provincial Court judges. Judge Bernard Grenier of the Cour du Québec made this recommendation in a study for the Law Reform Commission of Canada in the late 1980s.

The second step would be statutory authorization for Provincial Court judges to try criminal cases with a jury. Under *McEvoy*, jury trial jurisdiction could not extend to charges within the exclusive jurisdiction of the Superior Court (e.g., capital murder and offences such as 'alarming Her Majesty'), but it is likely to be constitutional for provincially appointed judges to sit with juries in a whole range of indictable offences. Historical research in Quebec and Ontario suggests that at the time of Confederation, judicial officers equivalent to post-Confederation magistrates did sit with juries, adding historical support to the constitutional argument.[17] While constitutional questions would surely be raised, I believe a process could be designed whereby provincially appointed judges, designated by a section 96 judge with appropriate administrative authority, could conduct jury trials consistent with the current constitutional strictures of section 96.[18] It is more likely that provincial authorities would hesitate not for constitutional reasons but out of concern that the use of juries in criminal cases might increase.

From the 1960s through the 1980s, many provincial governments gave a high priority to the development of provincial legal institutions as part of a general strategy of 'province building.'[19] In the 1990s this process of institutional development has been replaced by an emphasis on constraining the public sector, downsizing the public service (including court staff), and reducing the costs of government (and the cost of administering justice). In the process, provincial governments, including the government of Quebec, no longer seem to be exploring ways to expand the jurisdiction (and the authority and status) of the judges they appoint to the bench.

The option of expanding the criminal jurisdiction of Provincial Courts, while it would recognize the high degree of specialization already built into the practice of law, could also pose problems. So few criminal cases would be left within the jurisdiction of Superior Court judges that they would have less opportunity to maintain and hone their skills. Counsel experienced in criminal law might be unwilling to accept a section 96 appointment if too little criminal work were available. In turn, the subject-matter specialization would be divided by the source of the judge's appointment, so an able lawyer out of favour with one level of government or the other would either be unable to secure a judgeship or might be appointed to a court whose cases are far removed from his or her knowledge and practice. Given the sharp boundaries between the two courts, there would be little chance for judges to move between courts and sit on matters for which their skills and interests are better matched.

*Second New Option: Trial Court Integration*

A different approach would be to leave the two court levels intact, but manage the criminal caseload of the two courts as a single enterprise. In other words, Superior Court judges assigned to criminal work and Provincial Court judges in the same centre (perhaps the same court-house, but at least a location in close proximity) would work together as a single team, supported by trial coordination and court support personnel. Cases could be interchanged as the flow of work demanded. In the process, Provincial Court judges could be assigned a wider variety of work (including jury trials), and Superior Court judges with an interest in criminal work would be assured the opportunity to try cases that might otherwise not reach that court.

This option has two antecedents, one American and one English. In the United States, there is an increased emphasis on the administrative coordination of separate trial courts in the same community.[20] The trend began in California, where court coordination was initially authorized and later mandated by the state legislature. Legislative leaders had hoped to merge Superior and Municipal Courts in California's fifty-eight counties, but ran into voting rights issues arising from how judges would be elected in the largest, most populous counties. The legislation that first produced consolidation of the two levels included a judicial opt-in provision that required concurrent majorities of Superior and Municipal Court judges in each county. While this legislative solution slowly unfolded, the courts in most counties merged their criminal dockets well before merging formal jurisdiction.

Approaches to court coordination in California varied from county to county. Sacramento County was one of the earliest effective coordination projects, under the leadership of Municipal Court Judge Roger Warren, who was subsequently named president of the National Center for State Courts in Williamsburg, Virginia. Marin County, a wealthy jurisdiction north of San Francisco, established what it called a 'vertical felony panel' by which judges from both levels of courts worked together in the same courthouse (a distinctive building designed by Frank Lloyd Wright) to ensure that all courtrooms were covered and trial dates could be given earlier than when each court scheduled its cases separately. I even recall watching an experienced Superior Court judge sitting one afternoon in bail court after the last-minute collapse of his scheduled jury trial.

In fact, the widespread interchangeability of American trial judges is remarkably different from Canadian practice. Some analysts would

attribute the ability of judges to be assigned across levels of court to
state constitutional provisions that create a unified court system. Thus,
regional assignment judges in New Jersey have for fifty years transferred judges from one court to another within a single county or a
multi-county vicinage. In New York's unified court system, a limited
jurisdiction judge from New York City's Civil Court or Criminal Court
can sit 'by designation' in the Superior Court (i.e, Supreme Court) 'at
the pleasure of the Administrative Judge,' normally for a six-month
period during which the judge receives the higher salary given to a
Supreme Court justice.

Yet over twenty years ago, I found similar practices in the non-uni-
fied Georgia court system. Superior Court judges in Savannah would
ask for assistance from a State Court judge, who in turn sought assistance from the county Probate Court judge, who also sat as a
Recorder's Court judge. This pattern could be duplicated in jurisdictions that show a flexibility facilitated when judges interact with one
another regularly, and come to understand and respect their diverse
skills and common strengths.

The trial court integration option also resembles the English Crown
Court, created over thirty years ago following Lord Beeching's Royal
Commission on Assizes and Quarter Sessions.[21] A single criminal
court for indictable offences (the lay magistrates still handle intake
procedures and summary offences) is made up of judges with a wide
variety of formal ranks and titles. Over a decade ago, I visited the
Southwark Crown Court on the south bank of the Thames in London.
The judges who sat that week were drawn from High Court justices,
circuit judges, County Court judges, and even stipendiary (full-time
law-trained) magistrates. One judge had administrative responsibilities analogous to those of a senior judge in a provincial courthouse in
Canada, but the key personnel were the trial coordinators, who
worked in the courthouse but were permanent staff in the Lord Chancellor's Department. The status differences endemic to the English
judiciary, while having the potential to drive judges apart, are perhaps
counteracted most effectively by the practice throughout England of all
the judges who sit in a particular courthouse – regardless of their rank
and whether they are temporary or permanent – having lunch together
each day court is in session.

The late Chief Justice Nathan Nemetz of British Columbia talked
about the English Crown Court as a model for Canada as far back as
the 1970s, when his Supreme Court justices had few criminal cases,
and County and Provincial Court judges did all but a handful of the

criminal trials. His concern was mitigated initially by merger of Supreme and County Courts, but the continued devolution of criminal cases to Provincial Court make his concern relevant once again.

An integrated trial court is more feasible in Canadian provinces today than in the past, because the administration of Superior Courts and Provincial Courts has increasingly been integrated, so that support services for the two levels are often combined. However, except in British Columbia, trial coordination is the responsibility of executive branch officials, so that the development of effective management processes may be hindered by longstanding and unresolved tensions in the relationship between judges and court administration.[22]

Note also that each of the four options can (and is likely to) be accompanied by continuing growth of subordinate judicial officers, a trend cited above. In a number of provinces, giving added responsibilities to subordinate judicial officers (usually justices of the peace) could enhance their status and professionalism; however, without revamping selection processes, expected qualifications, and terms and conditions of employment, the overall quality of justice in criminal cases could be diminished. Expanding the role of JPs also raises administrative issues, since the supervision of those officials would necessarily expand the scope and complexity of many chief judges' responsibilities.

NOTES

1 In fact, at the time of Confederation, there were a number of English superior courts, and these were combined into a single court in the 1874 *Judicature Act*. Ontario followed suit in 1882. For a detailed historical overview, see Carl Baar *One Trial Court: Possibilities and Limitations* (Ottawa: Canadian Judicial Council, 1991), ch. 1. This report was published in French as *Un tribunal de premiere instance unique: limites et perspectives*.

2 I owe this observation to Peter H. Russell, *The Judiciary in Canada: The Third Branch of Government* (Toronto: McGraw Hill Ryerson, 1987), ch. 9. This remains the best general text on the Canadian judiciary.

3 See Perry S. Millar and Carl Baar, *Judicial Administration in Canada* (Montreal and Kingston: McGill-Queen's University Press, 1981), 326.

4 John McLaren, 'Maternal Feminism in Action – Emily Murphy, Police Magistrate' (1988) 8 *Windsor Yearbook of Access to Justice* 234; Elsie Gregory MacGill, *My Mother the Judge* (Toronto: Ryerson Press, 1955).

5 Alfred Watts, Q.C., *Magistrate-Judge: The Story of the Provincial Court of British Columbia* (Victoria: Queen's Printer, 1986), 79–82.

6 The Supreme Court of Canada at that time was more liberal in allowing these inroads into the jurisdiction of Superior Courts under section 96; cf. *Reference re: Adoption Act*, [1938] S.C.R. 398, 71 C.C.C. 110, [1938] 3 D.L.R. 497.

7 Although it should be noted that the British Columbia government sought merger in the late 1960s, but the chief justice of the B.C. Supreme Court was able to defeat the required federal legislation.

8 *McEvoy v. New Brunswick (Attorney General)*, [1983] 1 S.C.R. 704, 4 C.C.C. (3d) 289, 148 D.L.R. (3d) 25.

9 Court Reform Task Force (Seaton Report), *Court Reform in Canada* (Ottawa: Canadian Bar Association, 1991).

10 Baar, *One Trial Court*.

11 See *An Act to amend the Nunavut Act with respect to the Nunavut Court of Justice and to amend other Acts in consequence*, S.C. 1999, c. 3, assented to 11 March 1999.

12 Note the parallels to the English experience discussed by Ian R. Scott in his chapter in this volume.

13 Carl Baar, 'JPs Return to Alberta – but Not Quietly' (1998) 22 *Canadian Lawyer* 11–12.

14 The major empirical study of the preliminary hearing remains David G. Alford et al., *Some Statistics on the Preliminary Inquiry in Canada* (Ottawa: Department of Justice, 1984). For additional relevant data, see Carl Baar, 'Court Delay and Waiver of the Preliminary Hearing' (1992), 15 C.R. (4th) 261.

15 These states are surveyed in Baar, *One Trial Court*. More recently, California moved to a single-level trial court after a decade of voluntary coordination and consolidation discussed below, and Michigan piloted trial court consolidation in six counties. The resulting controversy is surveyed in six articles, 'Examining Court Consolidation in Michigan' in vol. 85 of *Judicature*, (November-December 2001), 115–39.

16 See New Zealand Law Commission, *Report No. 7: The Structure of the Courts*; (Wellington, 1989); and, The Hon. Thomas G. Zuber, *Report of the Ontario Courts Inquiry* (Toronto: Ontario Ministry of the Attorney General, 1987), ch. 6.

17 Professor Donald Fyson in the Department of History at Laval University has done research on the role of post-Conquest judicial officers in Quebec, and Professor Jim Phillips at the University of Toronto Law School is similarly well-versed in pre-Confederation practices in Ontario.

18 Even if the current Supreme Court is disinclined to accept Healy's arguments in his chapter in this volume, *McEvoy* should still not stand in the way of this option.

19 This argument was developed by Peter McCormick, 'Judicial Councils for Provincial Judges in Canada.' (1986) 6 *Windsor Yearbook of Access to Justice* 160.
20 Canadian provinces have increasingly integrated their court support services, but, unlike the American examples, this has not extended to integration of either the judiciary or the management of caseflow.
21 Of course, Ian Scott rightly emphasizes in his chapter that the Crown Court still left a two-tier criminal court structure operating in England and Wales for the past thirty years. But the original 1874 unification of superior courts in England later became the basis for consolidating superior and limited jurisdiction trial courts in the United States.
22 See most recently Robert G. Hann, Lorne Sossin, Carl Baar, Karim Benyekhlef, and Fabien Gelinas's report for the Canadian Judicial Council, *Alternative Models of Court Administration*, September 2006.

# 3 Superior Courts in the Twenty-first Century: A Historical Anachronism?

CHERYL MARIE WEBSTER AND ANTHONY N. DOOB

*In this chapter Cheryl Marie Webster, a new criminology scholar, teams up with Anthony Doob, one of Canada's leading criminologists, to provide a quantitative analysis of the distribution of criminal cases between Provincial and Superior Courts.*

*Statistical analyses of the work of Canadian trial courts have been difficult because the provinces are responsible for the administration of these courts. As such, there is no national authority that can impose a uniform way of keeping track of all of their work. In addition, there are methodological problems, which Webster and Doob discuss, in defining cases and measuring the work of any trial court. In this chapter, they use data collected from the provinces by the Canadian Centre for Justice Statistics on nearly one million criminal cases dealt with in the trial courts of six provinces and one territory for the fiscal years 1998–9, 1999–2000, and 2000–1. It is the most comprehensive and coherent effort yet attempted to compare the criminal trial caseloads of Provincial and Superior Courts.*

*The findings of these two scholars provide strong empirical evidence for the proposition that the Provincial Court has become the primary criminal court in Canada: 98 per cent of criminal cases are resolved in Provincial Courts. Although the Superior Courts' caseloads are heavily weighted towards the most serious cases, a majority of such cases are resolved in Provincial Courts. Webster and Doob show that one of the trends that may account for this phenomenon and which is evident over the three years studied is the increasing inclination of both prosecutors and defence lawyers in hybrid offence cases (i.e., cases in which the Crown can opt to proceed summarily, thus ensuring that the case remains in Provincial Court, or by way of indictment, whereby the accused can choose the court in which the case is resolved) to opt for trial in the Provincial Court.*

*In interpreting these findings as showing the primacy of Provincial Courts in handling criminal cases, it must be borne in mind that the Superior Court carries out appeal and supervisory functions in the criminal law area and deals as well with a number of special processes, such as police wiretap applications. The report of Ontario Superior Court judges presented in chapter 10 below gives a full account of the criminal law work of the Superior Court. Nonetheless, the question remains whether a court that handles such a small portion of the country's criminal caseload and whose judges are much less likely to have had extensive criminal law experience than those on the Provincial Court should continue to handle some of the most serious aspects of criminal justice.*

To assess with accuracy the actual distribution of business in criminal courts, we need statistical data.

Law Reform Commission of Canada, 1989

The system of two-tiered criminal trial courts in Canada has been evolving since its inception with Confederation. Although arguably appropriate to the circumstances in 1867, the distinctions between the Superior and Provincial Courts have become increasingly blurred with the dramatic growth in stature, jurisdiction, competence, and public importance of the latter judicial level. In fact, the cumulative effect of these changes has been described as one of the major court reforms in the last quarter-century.

This evolution in the role of the Provincial Courts in criminal matters and the apparent functional similarities between the two judicial levels have led several scholars, politicians, and practitioners[1] to question whether the historically entrenched court structure and hierarchy continue to fit the reality of today. With criticisms of inefficiency, complexity, and inequality, the current two-tiered court system has increasingly come under attack.

In response, calls for criminal justice structural reform have been heard with varying degrees of intensity and frequency. Proposed solutions have fluctuated between radical restructuring (i.e., unification) and more conservative internal reorganization (i.e., administrative centralization). However, one of the principal stumbling blocks to the eventual resolution of this debate has been a dearth of empirical data on the operation of the current adult criminal court system. Indeed, a substantial amount of current 'knowledge' surrounding the operation of criminal trial courts would appear to be based on anecdotal accounts, personal experiences, or presumptions drawn from the legal arrangements in the Criminal Code. This lack of empirical studies has been recognized as a serious obstacle to the identification of potential problems in the present two-tier system as well as the establishment of a measure by which to evaluate the effectiveness of possible solutions.[2]

This chapter will empirically examine several of the assumptions underlying the current debate on the reform of the criminal court structure. The focus of our study is on the role of the Superior Court vis-à-vis its Provincial Court counterpart in criminal matters. More specifically, we will explore potential distinctions between the caseloads of these two levels of court as well as identify several trends over time in the use of Superior Court. With these objectives, it is not our intent to ignore the sensitivity of the issues surrounding court structure reform nor to minimize the enormity of the project. Rather, we simply aspire to broaden the current debate beyond its present confines. By providing an empirical dimension to the analysis of the operation of the two-tiered trial court system, it is our hope to further document the nature and extent of some of its potential problems in order to better guide the determination of the most appropriate solutions.

## Methodology

The data that form the basis of this paper were purchased by the Federal Department of Justice from the Adult Criminal Court Survey project of the Canadian Centre for Justice Statistics (CCJS). Information on the operation of adult criminal courts has been collected in Canada for less than a decade and does not yet cover all criminal trial courts. As of early 2002, data for this chapter were available only for a three-year period in seven jurisdictions: Newfoundland and Labrador, Prince Edward Island, Nova Scotia, Ontario, Saskatchewan, Alberta, and the Yukon.[3]

Our unit of analysis is a 'case,' defined as one or more charges presented against an individual and disposed of in court on the same day.[4] Court data are exceedingly complex for many reasons. For example, multiple charges (that may or may not arrive in court on the same day and may or may not relate to the same incident) make the definition of a case both awkward and complicated as only one name or charge can be used to identify the entire case. As the most significant or serious charge defines the case, information is lost on the process and out-comes of the others.

Equally problematic is the fact that the charges associated with a case may change (in number and in nature) as it moves through the system. Precisely because a case in the adult courts is defined by CCJS at the end of the court process, any information on prior alterations in the charge(s) are not available with these data. For this reason, we are unable, for instance, to accurately identify all cases that are of the exclusive jurisdiction of the Superior Court. A case that begins as a first- or second-degree murder, but ends (in Superior Court) as a man-slaughter will be described in these data as a manslaughter. As such, we would have erroneously eliminated it as part of the core jurisdic-tion of the Superior Court.

Similarly, there are some instances for which we believe that the final description of the case may (incorrectly under this definition) be more reflective of the original charges than the final charges on which a per-son was found guilty (e.g., the result of a change which was not noted on the data file received from the province). Though occasionally both-ersome, these problems do not appear to us to be serious. Neverthe-less, this definition does mean that one must look to other sources of data to estimate the number of cases which are in the exclusive juris-diction of one court or another.[5]

In this chapter, we examine the data at various levels of aggregation. For some analyses, we pool across all cases in the seven jurisdictions; for others, we look at provincial differences,[6] and/or distinctions between individual offences (or offence categories).[7] In this way, we are able to discern potential systemic problems within the adult crimi-nal courts as well as those of a more isolated or local nature. Indeed, the existence of offence or jurisdiction-specific issues may mandate more procedural or administrative solutions than structural changes to the entire court system. In addition to this cross-sectional analysis, we also assess short-term trends occurring in recent years. More specifi-cally, we analyse three years of case information corresponding to the fiscal years beginning on 1 April 1998, 1999, and 2000.

For various technical reasons, we were not able to obtain complete data on all of the variables that CCJS currently possesses on these cases. Further, the information acquired does not contain detailed descriptive data (e.g., on the legal issues needed to be resolved) on those cases we analyse. Thus, it is important to remember that cases which might look to be the same can, in fact, be different. We could not alter the ways in which CCJS has grouped its information, so we were restricted by the categorizations that already existed (that is, we were not able to isolate all hybrid offences, as many of them were included within broader offence categories). Finally, missing data constituted a significant problem for a small number of the variables included in the dataset. Consequently, we could not look at several of the specifics of the cases.

In sum, the dataset analysed for this chapter comprises 929,622 cases representing all of those processed in Newfoundland and Labrador, Prince Edward Island, Nova Scotia, Ontario, Saskatchewan, Alberta, and Yukon during the fiscal years 1998–9 to 2000–1.

## Superior Court as a Distinct Level of Adult Criminal Trial Court

A study of the role of the Superior Court might logically begin with an examination of the proportion of all adult criminal court offences which are dealt with by this judicial level in comparison with that handled by the Provincial Court. To address this issue, we distinguish between three different types of cases. In the first instance, we refer to those cases which are apparently resolved in the Superior Court (the Superior Court caseload).[8] The second category is defined as those cases which enter Superior Court but subsequently re-elect back to Provincial Court where they are ultimately completed (the re-election caseload).[9] Finally, the last group constitutes those cases which never leave Provincial Court and are resolved at this level (the Provincial Court caseload).

Table 1 presents the proportion of cases completed in Provincial and Superior Courts. As can be seen on the left side of this table, we have broken down the data by jurisdiction, with each row representing data from one of the seven provinces. Across the top, we have listed the three routes by which a case is resolved: in Superior Court (after transferring from Provincial Court), in Provincial Court after re-election (having transferred to Superior Court and subsequently returning to Provincial Court for resolution), and in Provincial Court with no elections (having never 'visited' Superior Court).

From table 1, it is clear that the Superior Court deals with very few cases compared to the Provincial Court. Only 17,490 of the 929,622 cases in our database (1.9 per cent) were ultimately resolved in the Superior

Table 1
Proportion of cases completed in Provincial and Superior Courts by jurisdiction

| | | Caseload | | | |
| --- | --- | --- | --- | --- | --- |
| | | Superior Court | Provincial Court – re-election | Provincial Court only | Total |
| Nfld. & Lab. | Count | 338 | 3 | 20,854 | 21,195 |
| | Row per cents | 1.6% | .0% | 98.4% | 100.0% |
| PEI | Count | 108 | 0 | 4,761 | 4,869 |
| | Row per cents | 2.2% | 0% | 97.8% | 100.0% |
| Nova Scotia | Count | 717 | 157 | 47,582 | 48,456 |
| | Row per cents | 1.5% | .3% | 98.2% | 100.0% |
| Ontario | Count | 10,077 | 136 | 575,349 | 585,562 |
| | Row per cents | 1.7% | .0% | 98.3% | 100.0% |
| Saskatchewan | Count | 1,209 | 265 | 79,017 | 80,491 |
| | Row per cents | 1.5% | .3% | 98.2% | 100.0% |
| Alberta | Count | 4,959 | 688 | 179,242 | 184,889 |
| | Row per cents | 2.7% | .4% | 96.9% | 100.0% |
| Yukon | Count | 82 | 2 | 4,076 | 4,160 |
| | Row per cents | 2.0% | .0% | 98.0% | 100.0% |
| Total | Count | 17,490 | 1,251 | 910,881 | 929,622 |
| | Row per cents | 1.9% | .1% | 98.0% | 100.0% |

Court. This pattern holds across all seven jurisdictions with little variation. Said differently, the bulk of the adult criminal court caseload
(98 per cent) is being resolved exclusively in Provincial Court.[10]

Interestingly, the data presented in this table also shed light on the
extent to which cases move back and forth between the two levels of
court. Contrary to the notion that this practice occurs frequently,[11] very
few cases (1,251 or 0.1 per cent) in these jurisdictions in fact visit the
Superior Court before re-electing back to Provincial Court to be
resolved.[12] Again, these results are consistent across jurisdictions. This
finding is particularly significant in light of the current discussions
surrounding the system of elections and re-elections. This procedure
has been criticized for not only introducing unnecessary complexity to
the system but also permitting its manipulation by counsel (e.g.,
through the practice of 'judge-shopping' or as a delay tactic).[13] If, in
fact, these strategies are being employed, it would appear that they are
occurring in only a very small number of cases.[14]

A similar criticism has been raised with regard to the inefficiency of the two-tier trial court system. More specifically, it is argued that a substantial amount of duplication exists between the two levels of court, primarily due to their concurrent jurisdiction in a high percentage of Criminal Code offences.[15] This overlap is considered by some to constitute a needless expense and a waste of judicial and administrative manpower. As the Law Reform Commission of Canada points out, 'there would be no point in having multiple court levels if they all performed the same functions.'[16]

This argument has been countered, in large part, with the notion that Superior Court is, in fact, reserved to deal with specific types of offences or those of a particular nature (e.g., the most serious and/or complex cases). In fact, Seniuk and Lyon make reference to the belief that the more serious and complex cases are the ones brought before the Superior Court. Similarly, the Special Committee on Court Restructuring notes that 'the judges of the two divisions preside over cases that differ in ... type.'[17]

To examine the issue of the nature of the cases handled by the two levels of court and their various routes of resolution, we created a number of distinct offence categories.[18] Table 2 looks at these selected offences by the court in which they are ultimately completed. The data are presented as column percentages: the proportion of the three caseloads (Superior Court, Re-Elections, and Provincial Court) made up of each offence category. Thus, one would read this table in the following manner: 4.3 per cent of the cases resolved in Superior Court are murder, manslaughters, and attempted murders. Only 0.1 per cent of the Provincial Court caseload is composed of this aggregated offence category.

With respect to the make-up of the various court caseloads, table 2 shows that the re-election cases (that is, those that visit Superior Court but are completed in Provincial Court) are, generally speaking, similar to those that go to Superior Court and are resolved at this judicial level. Clearly, the dramatic difference (some of which is determined by restrictions on the kinds of cases that can be dealt with in Superior Court) is between the type of cases dealt with in Provincial Court and those that are either resolved in Superior Court or simply visit that level of court. For instance, while 14.7 per cent of the Superior Court caseload and 9.1 per cent of the re-election caseload are made up of cases of level I sexual assault, only 1.1 per cent of the Provincial Court caseload is composed of this particular offence.

Table 2
Proportion of cases completed in Provincial and Superior Courts by selected offences
(column per cents)

| Type of offence (most serious charge) | | Caseload | | | |
|---|---|---|---|---|---|
| | | Superior Court | Provincial Court – re-election | Provincial Court only | Total |
| Murder, manslaughter, attempted murder | Count | 747 | 14 | 1126 | 1887 |
| | Column per cents | 4.3% | 1.1% | .1% | .2% |
| Robbery | Count | 1,273 | 82 | 8,173 | 9,528 |
| | Column per cents | 7.3% | 6.6% | .9% | 1.0% |
| Sexual assault II & III | Count | 217 | 13 | 423 | 653 |
| | Column per cents | 1.2% | 1.0% | .0% | .1% |
| Assault II & III | Count | 1,769 | 138 | 39,213 | 41,120 |
| | Column per cents | 10.1% | 11.0% | 4.3% | 4.4% |
| Sexual assault I | Count | 2,566 | 114 | 9,917 | 12,597 |
| | Column per cents | 14.7% | 9.1% | 1.1% | 1.4% |
| Assault I | Count | 485 | 72 | 116,225 | 116,782 |
| | Column per cents | 2.8% | 5.8% | 12.8% | 12.6% |
| Other violent offences | Count | 1,715 | 95 | 31,834 | 33,644 |
| | Column per cents | 9.8% | 7.6% | 3.5% | 3.6% |
| Break and enter | Count | 1,007 | 106 | 25,609 | 26,722 |
| | Column per cents | 5.8% | 8.5% | 2.8% | 2.9% |
| Minor property | Count | 359 | 48 | 134,463 | 134,870 |
| | Column per cents | 2.1% | 3.8% | 14.8% | 14.5% |
| Fraud over | Count | 742 | 27 | 5,773 | 6,542 |
| | Column per cents | 4.2% | 2.2% | .6% | .7% |
| Other property | Count | 1,454 | 90 | 66,259 | 67,803 |
| | Column per cents | 8.3% | 7.2% | 7.3% | 7.3% |
| Driving offences | Count | 502 | 70 | 112,805 | 113,377 |
| | Column per cents | 2.9% | 5.6% | 12.4% | 12.2% |
| Drug possession | Count | 133 | 23 | 40,154 | 40,310 |
| | Column per cents | .8% | 1.8% | 4.4% | 4.3% |
| Drug trafficking | Count | 2,237 | 190 | 16,298 | 18,725 |
| | Column per cents | 12.8% | 15.2% | 1.8% | 2.0% |
| Other Criminal Code and federal statutes | Count | 2,284 | 169 | 30,609 | 305,062 |
| | Column per cents | 13.1% | 13.5% | 33.2% | 32.8 |
| Total | Count | 17,490 | 12,51 | 910,881 | 929,622 |
| | Column per cents | 100.0% | 100.0% | 100.0% | 100.0% |

Further, drug trafficking (including possession for the purpose of trafficking) constitutes another high-volume offence of the Superior Court caseload (12.8 per cent) but only a mere 1.8 per cent of that of the Provincial Court (and 15.2 per cent of the re-election cases). Similarly, levels II and III assault dominate the re-election caseload, representing 11.0 per cent of all its cases (and 10.1 per cent of the Superior Court cases) while they only comprise 4.3 per cent of the Provincial Court total caseload. Conversely, the Provincial Court caseload is largely comprised of minor property, level I assault, and driving offences – constituting, respectively, 14.8, 12.8, and 12.4 per cent of its total number of cases. These three types of offences represent, in each case, less than 3 per cent of the Superior Court caseload (and, at most, approximately 6 per cent of the re-election cases). Clearly, the small minority of cases being dealt with in Superior Court are not distributed across offence types in the same way as those handled by the Provincial Court. Simply put, the data in table 2 suggest that the more serious offences[19] make up a higher proportion of the Superior Court caseload than that of the Provincial Court.

The issue of the 'seriousness' of the cases being dealt with by each type of caseload is further explored in the following table. Table 3 reproduces the same data as the previous table except that we have presented them as 'row percents' – the proportion of each offence type that is resolved through each of the three court routes. This reconstruction allows us to make more direct comparisons between the various offence types (which differ in terms of the seriousness of the crime). In reading this table, we can see that 78.7 per cent of the level I sexual assault cases are resolved in Provincial Court (without ever visiting Superior Court). When combined with information presented in table 2, we can conclude that while level I sexual assault constitutes only 1.1 per cent of the total Provincial Court caseload, 78.7 per cent of the cases of this offence being dealt with in the adult criminal courts are resolved in Provincial Court.

Several points are noteworthy in regard to table 3. The more serious an offence is, the more likely it is to be completed in Superior Court. Potentially the clearest illustration of this affirmation is with the assault and sexual assault offences. As the following comparisons indicate, the percentage of cases which receive their final resolution in Superior Court decreases as the offence becomes less serious:

• 33.2 per cent of all cases of levels II and III sexual assault are dealt with in Superior Court as compared to only 20.4 per cent of level I sexual assault;

- 4.3 per cent of all cases of levels II and III assault are resolved in Superior Court as compared to only 0.4 per cent of level I assault.

Having said this, it is also important to note that Superior Court deals with fewer serious offences than does Provincial Court in absolute terms. For instance, while Superior Court resolves 39.6 per cent of all murder/manslaughter/attempted murder offences, Provincial Court is responsible for 60.4 per cent of this aggregated offence category (including the 0.7 per cent of re-election cases). Said differently, 747 cases of these offences were resolved in Superior Court in comparison with 1,140 cases (including re-elections) which were completed in Provincial Court. Clearly, one can assume that all cases within this broad offence classification which involved a trial or a plea of guilty on first or second degree murder were resolved in Superior Court.

A similar pattern is found for each of the offences that we examined. For instance, while Superior Court handles 33.2 per cent of the level II and III sexual assaults (217 cases), its provincial counterpart completes 66.8 per cent of them (64.8 per cent + 2.0 per cent), representing a total of 436 cases. In other words, Provincial Court deals with approximately twice as many cases of this category of serious offences. Even more impressive is the comparison that may be drawn with robbery. In dramatic contrast with the 1,273 cases of this offence handled by Superior Court (13.4 per cent of all robberies), Provincial Court resolves 8,255 of them (86.6 per cent of all robberies), more than six times as many.

In brief, although Superior Court is getting a non-trivial proportion of the most serious offences, in no offence grouping that we examined (other than, of course, first and second degree murder) does this court deal with more of them, in absolute terms, than does the Provincial Court.

Another possible distinguishing factor between the two levels of trial court involves the complexity of cases. Unfortunately, the only (obviously imperfect) measure that we have of complexity is whether or not the case involved single or multiple charges. This variable is problematic for a number of reasons. For instance, it may not capture aspects of complexity unrelated to the number of charges (for instance, the number of facts that are at issue). For example, a case in which the perpetrator was apprehended at the scene of the crime may be less complex than one in which his or her identity is a significant issue. Given the questionable face validity of this measure as a proxy for case complexity, we hesitate to draw any firm inferences based on differences between the various caseloads involving this variable.

Table 3
Proportion of cases completed in Provincial and Superior Courts by selected offences
(row percents)

| Type of offence (most serious charge) | | Caseload | | | |
|---|---|---|---|---|---|
| | | Superior Court | Provincial Court – re-election | Provincial Court only | Total |
| Murder, manslaughter, attempted murder | Count | 747 | 14 | 1,126 | 1,887 |
| | Row per cents | 39.6% | .7% | 59.7% | 100.0% |
| Robbery | Count | 1,273 | 82 | 8,173 | 9,528 |
| | Row per cents | 13.4% | .9% | 85.8% | 100.0% |
| Sexual assault II & III | Count | 217 | 13 | 423 | 653 |
| | Row per cents | 33.2% | 2.0% | 64.8% | 100.0% |
| Assault II & III | Count | 1,769 | 138 | 39,213 | 41,120 |
| | Row per cents | 4.3% | .3% | 95.4% | 100.0% |
| Sexual assault I | Count | 2,566 | 114 | 9,917 | 12,597 |
| | Row per cents | 20.4% | .9% | 78.7% | 100.0% |
| Assault I | Count | 485 | 72 | 116,225 | 116,782 |
| | Row per cents | .4% | .1% | 99.5% | 100.0% |
| Other violent offences | Count | 1,715 | 95 | 31,834 | 33,644 |
| | Row per cents | 5.1% | .3% | 94.6% | 100.0% |
| Break and enter | Count | 1,007 | 106 | 25,609 | 26,722 |
| | Row per cents | 3.8% | .4% | 95.8% | 100.0% |
| Minor property | Count | 359 | 48 | 134,463 | 134,870 |
| | Row per cents | .3% | .0% | 99.7% | 100. 0% |
| Fraud over | Count | 742 | 27 | 5,773 | 6,542 |
| | Row per cents | 11.3% | .4% | 88.2% | 100.0% |
| Other property | Count | 1,454 | 90 | 66,259 | 67,803 |
| | Row per cents | 2.1% | .1% | 97.7% | 100.0% |
| Driving offences | Count | 502 | 70 | 112,805 | 113,377 |
| | Row per cents | .4% | .1% | 99.5% | 100.0% |
| Drug possession | Count | 133 | 23 | 40,154 | 40,310 |
| | Row per cents | .3% | .1% | 99.6% | 100.0% |
| Drug trafficking | Count | 2,237 | 190 | 16,298 | 18,725 |
| | Row per cents | 11.9% | 1.0% | 87.0% | 100.0% |
| Other Criminal Code and federal statutes | Count | 2,284 | 169 | 302,609 | 305,062 |
| | Row per cents | .7% | .1% | 99.2% | 100.0% |
| Total | Count | 17,490 | 1251 | 910,881 | 929,622 |
| | Row per cents | 1.9% | .1% | 98.0% | 100.0% |

Having said this, it is still noteworthy that the two levels of court do, in fact, differ on this measure. While the Superior Court caseload continues to be very similar to that of the Re-Elections (both demonstrating almost identical proportions of single and multiple-charge cases), Provincial Court is less likely than Superior Court to have multiple-charge cases (44.0 versus 63.5 per cent) (data not presented). This higher proportion of multiple charges being heard by the Superior Courts holds across all of the offence groupings except murder/manslaughter/attempted murder (an anomaly which may have to do with the grouping of these offences) and break and enter. However, it is also important to note that Provincial Court still resolves the vast majority of the multiple-charge cases. Even for the more serious offences (for example, level II and III sexual assault, robbery, level II and III assault), the Provincial Courts hear more of the multiple charge cases than do the Superior Courts.

In sum, clear distinctions between the two levels of court may not be as apparent as one might have initially expected. The clearest distinction between the levels of court is that the Superior Court is being mobilized very infrequently for adult criminal court cases. When used, the Superior Court caseload is different from that of the Provincial Court only in terms of the relative proportion of each type of offence resolved. In absolute terms, Provincial Court continues to deal with more cases of every offence grouping that we examined than does Superior Court. Further, while the Superior Court caseload involves a relatively higher proportion of the more serious offences, Provincial Courts still resolve more cases, serious and less serious, than do the Superior Courts. Finally, although cases in Superior Court are more likely to be multiple versus single-charge in nature, Provincial Court ultimately deals with a substantially higher number of multiple-charge cases than does Superior Court.

When placed within the context of the notion of overlap between the two levels of trial court, these findings do, in fact, provide some support for this contention. Indeed, true specialization would arguably suggest that Superior Courts dealt with the majority of cases of a specific offence or nature. Putting aside the obvious exception of the exclusive jurisdiction offence of murder, we have not been able to identify a distinguishing criterion. It is true that the overall mix of cases that the two judicial levels hear is somewhat different (table 2). However, it is equally true that the Provincial Courts complete more cases of every offence that we examined than do the Superior Courts (table 3).

Having said this, several caveats to these conclusions may be raised. First, significant differences may still exist between these two levels of court that are not being captured by the variables in our dataset. For instance, a more refined measure of complexity (e.g., the type of issues raised, such as Charter arguments and motions) may indicate divergences in the caseloads of the Superior and Provincial Courts. A similar argument may be made with regard to the issue of seriousness. Given data limitations, we were only able to make comparisons between offences of differing degrees of seriousness (based on the maximum penalty that the crime could incur). A more sophisticated analysis should examine distinctions within categories of the same offence. It is possible that the more serious cases of a particular offence category are being dealt with more frequently by the Superior Court than by its provincial counterpart. Further, it is equally plausible that the case-processing done within the Superior Court – for which we also have no data – would indicate distinctions between these levels of court (e.g., in terms of the number, length and/or complexity of trials held). Moreover, we have no measures of other criminal law functions performed by the Superior Court (e.g., bail reviews, summary conviction appeals, or prerogative writs). Hence, the tentative conclusions which we have drawn in this chapter may be as much a reflection of the limitations in the number and type of variables in our dataset as they are of actual differences existing between Superior and Provincial Courts.

## Trends over Time in the Use of the Superior Court

The recent descriptions of the Provincial Court as the primary criminal trial court today appear to find corroboration in our analyses. Indeed, this level of court deals not only with the vast majority of all cases entering the criminal court system, but also with more cases within each offence grouping that we examined than does Superior Court. Further, while the relative proportion of serious or multiple-charge cases is higher in Superior Court, the Provincial Court still deals with more of them in absolute terms.

Moreover, the current dominance of the Provincial Court in criminal matters extends beyond the nature and volume of present caseloads. Indeed, it is also derived from trends over time. More specifically, the short-term trend in the use of Superior Court is not optimistic in terms of its obvious role within the criminal trial court system; as we have noted, it is used very infrequently. However, even within the short

Table 4
Proportion of cases completed in Provincial and Superior Courts by year (1998 to 2000;
PEI and Yukon excluded)

| | | Caseload | | | |
|---|---|---|---|---|---|
| | | Superior Court | Provincial Court – re-election | Provincial Court only | Total |
| 1998–9 | Count | 6,713 | 419 | 306,975 | 314,107 |
| | Row per cents | 2.1% | .1% | 97.7% | 100.0% |
| 1999–2000 | Count | 5,609 | 394 | 296,406 | 302,409 |
| | Row per cents | 1.9% | .1% | 98.0% | 100.0% |
| 2000–1 | Count | 4,978 | 436 | 298,663 | 304,077 |
| | Row per cents | 1.6% | .1% | 98.2% | 100.0% |
| Total | Count | 17,300 | 1249 | 902,044 | 920,593 |
| | Row per cents | 1.9% | .1% | 98.0% | 100.0% |

time period covered by these data (three years), this level of court use declined. This overall downward trend is clearly demonstrated in table 4 for the five provinces in which comparisons across years could be made with some confidence.[20]

While the Superior Court caseload constituted 2.1 per cent of the total number of adult criminal court cases resolved in these five provinces during the fiscal year 1998–9, it represented 1.9 per cent of the cases dealt with during the following year and only 1.6 per cent of those resolved in 2000–1. It is true that there was a general decline in the number of adult criminal cases being brought to court over this three-year period. However, the proportional decline in the Superior Court caseload was substantially greater than that in the Provincial Court. By 2000 the Superior Court criminal caseload in these five provinces had declined by 26 per cent, whereas the Provincial Court caseload had declined by less than 3 per cent. The proportion of re-election cases remained the same over the three-year period (0.1 per cent). In brief, the reduction in Superior Court criminal caseload is, in relative terms, dramatic.

Clearly, these findings lend some empirical support to recent claims that the Superior Court may effectively be going out of the criminal law business. Specifically addressing the situation in Ontario, it has even been suggested that a de facto transfer of criminal law jurisdiction has occurred from the Superior Court which has resulted in a single criminal court – the Provincial Court. Whether or not one can, in fact, conclude that the Superior Court has, for practical purposes, become largely irrelevant in Ontario for criminal cases, it can clearly be demonstrated that the decline in its use is not restricted to this province. The data indicate that this trend is a characteristic of all five jurisdictions analysed in this report.

The difficulty with these findings is that they relate only to three years of consecutive data. Therefore, it is problematic to conclude that the decline in the use of Superior Court reflects part of a long-run trend rather than simply short-term or temporary fluctuation.[21] Said differently, the reduced use of this level of court could merely indicate random variation over time and not a more permanent characteristic of the Superior Court today. Although only additional data collected over time will provide a more reliable measure of the long(er) term trends in the use of the Superior Court, an examination of several of the potential explanatory factors for the decline may provide some insight into the foreseeable future of this level of court for criminal matters.

To this end, we examine three possible explanations. While we look at each of these hypotheses individually, it is important to note that they are neither mutually exclusive nor an exhaustive list of all plausible accounts of the decline in use of the Superior Courts. On the contrary, they simply reflect the limited number of variables in our dataset. Further, we do not evaluate the relative strength of each of them in explaining the declining use of this judicial level. Finally, we are not suggesting causal relationships or using statistical estimates to predict future trends. Rather, we are simply exploring several of the current trends within the criminal justice arena and their possible impact on the use of the Superior Court.

The first explanation is rooted in the general trends in crime. More specifically, it is possible that relatively fewer cases are coming into the criminal court system which are eligible to go to the Superior Court. Table 5 examines this hypothesis. In order to correctly interpret this table, the large residual category at the bottom of the table entitled 'all other offences' (accounting for approximately 67 per cent of the cases) needs some explanation. As noted at the beginning of this paper, we were limited in this dataset to only about thirty specific offence categories. Thus, the categories of 'hybrid' and 'indictable' in the table below refer only to the subset of offences in our data that are clearly identifiable as hybrid and indictable.[22] As such, they might be seen as a non-random selection of these two offence classifications. Within the 'residual' category, there are large numbers of hybrid and indictable offences that we were not, for this purpose, able to identify. Hence, the 'selected' hybrid and indictable offences should be seen as being merely examples of these offence types.

As table 5 suggests, our first hypothesis finds some empirical support. Of those offence classifications eligible for Superior Court (that is, homicide/attempted murder as well as selected indictable and hybrid offences), small declines exist in their proportion of the overall adult criminal caseload. More specifically, a smaller proportion of homicide/attempted murder cases (from 0.22 per cent to 0.18 per cent, or 704 to 565 cases, of all cases in the criminal courts) were coming into the courts in 2000 than in 1998. A similar trend occurs for selected indictable offences (a decline from 3.7 per cent of the total caseload to 3.5 per cent, from 11,848 cases to 10,797 cases) and for specific hybrid offences (29.9 per cent to 29.4 per cent, from 94,871 cases to 90,194). The largest decline occurred with the offence grouping of murder/manslaughter/attempted murder, falling 139 cases (from 704 to 565 cases) or 19.7 per cent in the three-year period. In comparison, the overall criminal caseload only declined 3.2 per cent (from 317,267 to 306,972 cases) over the same period of time.

Hence, it seems likely that one of the factors related to the decline in the use of Superior Court is the reduction in the proportion of serious crimes which are entering the court system. Indeed, these data suggest that the cases being dealt with by the criminal courts within these seven provinces in 2000 were less likely to be ones that could go to Superior Court than those which were coming into the criminal courts in 1998. Said differently, a reduction in the pool of cases eligible for Superior Court would appear to be occurring. Consequently, if current crime rates for serious offences continue to fall, as they have done over the past decade one would expect to see a further decline in the use of the Superior Court.[23]

It would seem worth noting that the findings presented in table 5 concerning homicide/attempted murder cases are particularly telling given that this offence includes part of the core criminal jurisdiction of the Superior Court. Of the nine offences over which this level of court has exclusive jurisdiction, murder is the only one which is prosecuted with any frequency. As table 5 shows, the number of homicide/attempted murder cases is small and has been declining over time. The question which logically arises is whether it makes sense to maintain

Table 5
Selected offence classifications by year (1998–2000)

| Type of offence (most serious charge) | | Year | | | |
| --- | --- | --- | --- | --- | --- |
| | | 1998–9 | 1999–2000 | 2000–1 | Total |
| Murder, manslaughter, attempted murder | Count | 704 | 618 | 565 | 1887 |
| | Column per cents | .2% | .2% | .2% | -2% |
| Selected indictable | Count | 11,848 | 11,217 | 10,797 | 33,862 |
| | Column per cents | 3.7% | 3.7% | 3.5% | 3.6% |
| Selected hybrid | Count | 94,871 | 90,448 | 90,194 | 275,513 |
| | Column per cents | 29.9% | 29.6% | 29.4% | 29.6% |
| All other offences | Count | 209,844 | 203,100 | 205,416 | 618,360 |
| | Column per cents | 66.1% | 66.5% | 66.9% | 66.5% |
| Total | Count | 317,267 | 305,383 | 306,972 | 929,622 |
| | Column per cents | 100.0% | 100.0% | 100.0% | 100.0% |

a separate criminal court in part to deal exclusively with an offence which constitutes such a tiny proportion of the total adult criminal caseload.[24]

The second explanation that we examined for the decline in the use of the Superior Courts is derived from Crown elections. More specifically, the Crown attorneys, in their decisions regarding how to proceed in the cases of hybrid offences, could be choosing more often to proceed summarily than by indictment. By doing so, the Crown eliminates the possibility of a case going to Superior Court, further reducing the number of cases eligible for this level of court.

Table 6 indicates that the Crown's decision does, in fact, contribute to the decline in the use of the Superior Courts. We broke down our 275,513 cases of selected hybrid offences into those that went by indictment and those that proceeded summarily (and a residual category, disproportionately from Nova Scotia and Alberta, in which the Crown election could not be identified).

In table 6, the percentage figures relate to the proportion of total caseload (not shown in the table) for that year constituted by the identified cases. In 1998 our selected hybrid-indictables (i.e., those selected

Table 6
Crown elections for selected hybrid offences as a proportion of total caseload by year
(1998–2000)

| Result of Crown election for selected hybrid offences | | Year | | | |
| --- | --- | --- | --- | --- | --- |
| | | 1998–9 | 1999–2000 | 2000–1 | Total |
| Selected hybrid-unknown | Count | 7,842 | 8,057 | 7,510 | 23,409 |
| | Per cent of all cases for that year | 2.5% | 2.6% | 2.4% | 2.5% |
| Selected hybrid-summary | Count | 71,939 | 70,901 | 72,090 | 214,930 |
| | Per cent of all cases for that year | 22.7% | 23.2% | 23.5% | 23.1% |
| Selected hybrid-indictable | Count | 15,090 | 11,490 | 10,594 | 37,174 |
| | Per cent of all cases for that year | 4.8% | 3.8% | 3.5% | 4.0% |

hybrid offences in which we could identify a Crown election to proceed by indictment) accounted for 4.8 per cent of the total criminal court caseload in our seven provinces. By 2000, those selected hybrid offences proceeded by indictment accounted for only 3.5 per cent of the criminal caseload. In contrast, hybrids proceeded summarily accounted for 22.7 per cent of the criminal court caseload in 1998 and 23.5 per cent of the caseload two years later. Hence, an increase in the proportion of hybrid cases which are not eligible for Superior Court is coupled with a decline in the proportion of those which could, in fact, opt for this higher level of court. The combination of these two phenomena could constitute yet another factor in the explanation of the decline in the use of the Superior Court.

We subsequently examined the data in table 6 in a different manner. More specifically, we looked at the change in the proportion of selected hybrid cases that clearly proceeded by indictment across the three years (excluding those cases where the Crown election was not recorded). The results are shown in table 7. Because of a high proportion of missing data in Alberta (22.8 per cent) and Nova Scotia (46.3 per cent) on Crown elections, we have excluded these two provinces from this analysis. For purposes of clarity, we have also eliminated

Table 7
Crown elections for selected hybrid offences by year (1998–2000)
(Alberta and Nova Scotia excluded)

|  |  |  | Crown election where known | | |
| --- | --- | --- | --- | --- | --- |
|  |  |  | Summary | Indictable | Total |
| Year | 1998–9 | Count | 55,660 | 13,510 | 69,170 |
|  |  | Row per cents | 80.5% | 19.5% | 100.0% |
|  | 1990–2000 | Count | 55,333 | 10,185 | 65,518 |
|  |  | Row per cents | 84.5% | 15.5% | 100.0% |
|  | 2000–1 | Count | 56,464 | 9,094 | 65,558 |
|  |  | Row per cents | 86.1% | 13.9% | 100.0% |
| Total |  | Count | 167,457 | 32,789 | 200,246 |
|  |  | Row per cents | 83.6% | 16.4% | 100.0% |

the relatively small number of cases from the remaining five jurisdictions in which we could not identify the Crown election.

Clearly, a substantial reduction in the proportion of hybrid-indictable offences occurred over our three-year period (from 19.5 to 13.9 per cent). This trend was also analysed across jurisdictions (not presented). The reduction shown in table 7 is due to declines in the proportion of selected hybrid cases which proceeded by indictment in only three of the five provinces examined (Ontario, Saskatchewan, and Yukon). A similar reduction was not found in Newfoundland and Labrador and Prince Edward Island. As was the case for the preceding table, Nova Scotia and Alberta were also excluded from this analysis because of a high rate of cases in which the Crown election was not recorded.

To explore this reduction in the number of hybrid cases proceeded with by indictment in more detail, we looked at this pattern across individual selected hybrid offences. The data indicate that the decline over time in the selected group of identifiable hybrid-indictable cases was due, in large part, to level II assault.[25] This offence was hybridized in 1995. From 1998 to 2000, the proportion of cases of this offence in which the Crown elected to proceed by indictment declined from 83.7 to 47.9 per cent. This substantial decrease in the proportion of hybrid-indictable level II assault offences would have clearly contributed to the reduction in the pool of cases eligible for the Superior Court.

This finding is of particular relevance to criminal procedure reform. The past ten years have seen the reclassification of a number of Criminal Code offences.[26] One of the dominant trends in this reform process has been the hybridization of indictable offences. In addition, Parliament has recently set the maximum sentence available for certain hybrid offences (e.g., level I sexual assault and level II assault) that proceed summarily at 18 months in prison rather than the 'standard' summary conviction maximum of six months. Indeed, these legislative practices have been accepted and/or adopted by consecutive parliaments for more than a decade. Clearly, these presumably permanent changes in the nature of offences reflect Parliament's belief that the current structure of the Criminal Code is more appropriate or desirable for modern society.

Within this context, our results shed light on the impact of this specific reform process on the two levels of criminal court. In particular, the recent hybridization of level II assault is associated with a substantial decline in the proportion of cases which are eligible for the Superior Court.[27] Said differently, the (collateral) effect of this legislative process seems to be the reduction of the Superior Court caseload. Indeed, it appears that the relative perceived value of this level of court for Crown attorneys is being overtaken by other interests. For instance, the importance or desire of proceeding by indictment may have decreased in hybrid offences with the increase in the maximum sentence for a case proceeded summarily from six months to 18 months. This possibility would certainly provide a plausible explanation for Seniuk and Lyon's observation that the Crown's choice in hybrid offences is 'more often than not ... the Provincial Court.'[28] Particularly when combined with the present trend toward greater hybridization of Criminal Code offences, this structural change in the nature of offences suggests a continued decline in the use of the Superior Court.

The third explanatory factor addressed in this chapter for the reduction in the use of the Superior Court is rooted in the defence election. More specifically, it is possible that the accused have become less willing to choose this level of court, even when it is available to them. In order to test this hypothesis, we looked only at those cases which we could identify as being eligible for either level of court (see table 8). To this end, we examined only selected indictable offences (except murder) and hybrid cases for which the Crown proceeded by indictment. Hence, all 157,554 cases shown in table 8 apparently could either have gone to Superior Court or remained in Provincial Court.

Table 8
Accused elections for those cases eligible for Superior Court across years (1998–2000)
(PEI and Yukon excluded)

| | | | Caseload | | | |
|---|---|---|---|---|---|---|
| | | | Superior Court | Provincial Court – re-election | Provincial Court only | Total |
| Year | 1998–9 | Count | 5,245 | 322 | 52,511 | 58,078 |
| | | Row per cents | 9.0% | .6% | 90.4% | 100.0% |
| | 1999–2000 | Count | 4,125 | 286 | 45,959 | 50,370 |
| | | Row per cents | 8.2% | .6% | 91.2% | 100.0% |
| | 2000–1 | Count | 3,705 | 324 | 45,077 | 49,106 |
| | | Row per cents | 7.5% | .7% | 91.8% | 100.0% |
| Total | | Count | 13,075 | 932 | 143,547 | 157,554 |
| | | Row per cents | 8.3% | .6% | 91.1% | 100.0% |

From table 8, the accused appear to be electing the Superior Court less frequently over time. Indeed, we can see that for those cases which were eligible to be tried in Superior Court, fewer were actually completed there in 2000 than in 1998 (7.5 versus 9.0 per cent). An alternative way of describing these data is that the number of cases that we could identify as being eligible for Superior Court and in which the accused actually elected that court fell from 5,245 in 1998 to 3,705 in 2000 – a drop of 29.4 per cent. The corresponding decline in Provincial Court cases was only about half of this figure (14.2 per cent).

Our data show that this generalization holds in Newfoundland and Labrador, Nova Scotia, Ontario, and Alberta, but not in Saskatchewan. These findings largely parallel those previously identified with respect to the Crown election. Indeed, it may not only be the Crown attorney's perceptions of the usefulness or benefits of the Superior Court which seem to be changing. The relative increased value attributed to the Provincial Court also appears to extend to the defence.

Various explanations may be put forward to account for this alteration in the perceived advantages of Superior Court vis-à-vis other interests. From a tactical perspective, the requirement of full disclosure may have made the discovery function of the preliminary inquiry less important, reducing the number of elections to Superior Court as a means of evaluating the Crown's evidence. From a more historical stance, improvements in the quality of the Provincial Court bench may have made the Superior Court less distinctive. From an administrative point of view, certain jurisdictions have officially begun to discourage the informal practice of 'judge shopping' at the Superior Court level. From a more pragmatic approach, various legal aid incentives may disincline particular segments of the accused population from seeking resolution of their cases in the Superior Court.

In brief, we may be witnessing yet another example of changes in the administrative and the structural procedures of the adult criminal court system which could, in fact, be rendering the recourse to Superior Court less necessary or attractive. Indeed, it seems that the relative perceived value of this level of court for the defence is also being overridden by other interests. Given that many of the proposed reasons underlying this pattern of preference constitute structural or administrative alterations which are unlikely to change over time (e.g., legal competence of the Provincial Court bench or disclosure requirements), it is improbable that we would witness significant shifts in the pattern of defence election in the near future.

**Conclusions**

The terms 'superior' and 'inferior' have traditionally been used to describe the two-tiered adult criminal trial courts in Canada. While defensibly accurate at the time of Confederation, these designations have recently been increasingly criticized. Beyond the troubling possibility that these descriptors may be perceived by the general public as a reflection of judicial hierarchy based on competence to try criminal cases, importance of the work performed or the social class of the accused, they also suggest that clear empirical distinctions may be drawn between these two levels of court.

Particularly with regard to their present caseloads, this supposition would appear to be largely misleading. Indeed, caseload distinctions in the seven jurisdictions that we examined would seem to be minimal. More specifically, a substantial number of cases before the Superior Court do not appear to be materially different from indictable offences heard in Provincial Court. While the Superior Court does, in fact, deal with a higher proportion of serious offences than does its provincial counterpart, as well as more multiple-charge cases than those with a single charge, the Provincial Court completes a significantly greater number of these same cases in absolute terms. Further, despite the fact that the distribution of cases in Superior Court by offence is different from that found in Provincial Court, this latter level of court still handles more cases of every offence grouping that we examined.

Ironically, the most pronounced distinction between these levels of court that we were able to identify resides in the roles that they may foreseeably play in the future in criminal matters. While the extensive caseload of the Provincial Court, both in nature and number, bodes well for its continuation as the primary criminal trial court for both summary and indictable offences, the short-term trend for the Superior Court appears much less optimistic. Clearly, the very infrequent use of this level of court has been declining even further over the most recent years. We have identified three independent explanations for the decline. While rates of serious crime are difficult to predict, current structural changes in criminal law in combination with an apparent, generalized decrease in the perceived relative net value of Superior Court by various criminal justice players certainly suggest that a reversal in the current declining role of Superior Court within the adult criminal trial court system would be unlikely.

Despite alleged dangers of statistical analyses as well as inherent limitations of our dataset, we believe that our findings raise provocative questions regarding the current system of the two-tiered criminal trial courts in Canada. Indeed, the changing nature and volume of criminal work performed by the two levels of court would appear to support, if not dictate, the need for a discussion of court reform. While this call for dialogue does not necessarily mean the endorsement of a unified criminal court, it clearly emphasizes the urgency to explore new strategies to ensure that the criminal court structure continues to reflect the modern roles of the Superior and Provincial Courts in Canada.

NOTES

This study was supported in large part by the federal Department of Justice. We wish to thank the department and, in particular, Howard Bebbington, for their support of this research. In addition, we are grateful to Howard Bebbington and the Honourable David Cole for their extensive advice and valuable suggestions on numerous earlier versions of this paper. The views expressed or implied in this chapter do not necessarily reflect those of the Department of

Justice or those people who have provided us with comments on earlier drafts. Additional support was received from the Social Sciences and Humanities Research Council of Canada from a grant to Anthony N. Doob and a doctoral fellowship to Cheryl Marie Webster from the Fundaçao para a Ciência e a Tecnologia.

1  Ontario Conference of Judges' Subcommittee on Court Reform, 'Criminal Court Reform in Ontario: The Attorney General ABs Call for a Dialogue and the Response of the Ontario Superior Court Judges Association.'

2  Law Reform Commission of Canada, *Trial within a Reasonable Time: A Working Paper Prepared for the Law Reform Commission of Canada*; Working Paper 59 (Ottawa: Government Services, 1994); Committee of Criminal Court Administration, Canadian Bar Association (Ontario), 'Submission to Ontario Courts Inquiry' (Toronto: The Association, 1986), 25; and David Alford, Paul Chumak, Lise Cloutier, David Johnson, and David McKercher, 'Some Statistics on the Preliminary Inquiry in Canada' (Ottawa: Department of Justice, 1984).

3  The reasons for the absence of the other jurisdictions vary. As of the time of this study, no data were collected by CCJS for New Brunswick, Manitoba, and British Columbia. In addition, complete three-year coverage was not available for the Northwest Territories and Nunavut. Finally, data for Quebec did not include the municipal courts which dispose of an estimated 20 per cent of the charges for the province.

4  The Special Committee on Court Restructuring recommended the standardized use of cases as the unit of analysis when examining Superior and Provincial Court caseloads. As noted in the Report of the Ontario Superior Court of Justice (see ch. 10 below) at 13, the 'comparison of the number of charges laid in Provincial Court with the number of indictments added or completed in Superior Court both distorts and misleads.'

5  As an illustrative example, police and youth court statistics may be used to estimate the number of murders. From the former data source, it would appear that a total of 213 adults were charged with first- and second-degree murder during the 1998 calendar year in the seven jurisdictions under study. The corresponding numbers for 1999 and 2000 are 179 and 185 respectively (CCJS, 1999, 2000, 2001). From the latter statistics, one notes that few youths are transferred to adult court in Canada. For example, only fifty-two youths across all of Canada were transferred to adult court (eighteen of whom were in these seven jurisdictions) in 1999–2000. Of these eighteen cases, only eight of them were for murder.

6 Due to incomplete coverage of Superior Court data for the Yukon and Prince Edward Island for the full three years under study, we did not include these jurisdictions in any analysis of provincial caseload comparisons over time.

7 As the Special Committee on Court Restructuring, reminds us (at 13), there is a real danger in treating a 'murder' and 'accommodation fraud' in the same way when comparing the caseloads of the two levels of criminal court. Heeding this warning, our analyses also examine differences across similar offences. However, it still should be emphasized that two cases consisting of the same offence (for example, two robberies) could, in fact, be very different in seriousness as well as legal complexity.

8 A case was defined as having been completed in the Superior Court if its final appearance was in this level of court or (in the case of jurisdictions in which Superior Court activity is not available) if the last notation for the case was that it had been sent to Superior Court.

9 For those provinces for which information on Superior Court case processing was not available, a minimal amount of error may be introduced with our categorization of the Superior Court and re-election caseloads. More specifically, it is possible that a small number of the cases identified as Superior Court caseload may not yet have been resolved in Superior Court before the end of the fiscal year. As such, they may have eventually re-elected back to Provincial Court at the beginning of the following year. In these cases, our estimates of the Superior Court caseload may be slightly inflated while the Provincial Court re-election caseload may be underestimated to a small degree.

10 If we add the re-election cases which are ultimately completed in Provincial Court, the percentage of cases resolved at this level of court increases to 98.1 per cent.

11 Law Reform Commission, *Trial within a Reasonable Time*, 65.

12 With reference to this movement between levels of court, CCJS detected a number of 'anomalous' cases within the Superior Court caseload which apparently showed multiple elections before ultimately being resolved (presumably) at this judicial level. Given that the Criminal Code contains no provision prohibiting an accused who has re-elected once from re-electing a second time, we might interpret these cases as having initially gone to Superior Court and subsequently re-elected back to Provincial Court before returning to Superior Court for resolution. If this assumption is correct, the value of 0.1 per cent as the proportion of cases moving between the two levels of court may constitute a slight underestimation.

A less interesting explanation is that the definition of a case (charges grouped at the end of the process) may create this anomaly by joining charges that 'moved' across levels of court on different dates before finally being resolved on the same date.

13 See Law Reform Commission, *Trial within a Reasonable Time*; Carl Baar: *One Trial Court: Possibilities and Limitations* (Ottawa: Canadian Judicial Council, 1991); Hon. T.G. Zuber, *Report of the Ontario Courts Inquiry* (Toronto: Ontario Ministry of the Attorney General, 1987); and E. MacKaay *The Paths of Justice: A Study of the Operation of the Criminal Courts in Montreal* (Montreal: Groupe de Recherche en Jurimetrie, Université de Montréal, 1976).

14 Interestingly, re-elections do not appear to be employed with the same frequency across non-summary offences. Clearly, more research is needed to better understand this criminal procedure.

15 Gerald T.G. Seniuk and Noel Lyon, 'The Supreme Court of Canada and the Provincial Court of Canada' (2000) 79 *Canadian Bar Review* 77. The cases over which the Provincial Court presently has jurisdiction comprise at least 99 per cent of all Criminal Code offences. Equally revealing is the significant change in the number of offences which fall under the exclusive jurisdiction of the Superior Court. Whereas in 1892, 136 offences could only be processed in Superior Court, only nine are not currently shared with the Provincial Court. Of these, only 1 (murder) is prosecuted with any frequency.

16 Law Reform Commission of Canada, *Working Paper 59, Toward a Unified Criminal Court* (Ottawa: Ministry of Supply and Services, 1975), 27.

17 Seniuk and Lyon, 'The Supreme Court,' 96; *Report of the Ontario Superior Court Judges*, 16.

18 Several of the categories identified in table 2 constitute aggregated groupings of offences rather than individual offences. With regard to the aggregated offence category of 'minor property,' the cases contained in this group constitute all offences of the absolute jurisdiction of the Provincial Court that we were able to identify. Interestingly, one may note that 0.3 per cent of these cases are classified as part of the Superior Court caseload (table 3). One possible explanation for this apparent anomaly is, of course, that the case is defined by the most serious charge existing at the *end* of the processing of the case. For instance, a case could have begun as a theft over $5,000 and elected to be tried in Superior Court. However, the accused could have ultimately been found guilty of a 'theft under' rather than a 'theft over.' As such, this case – completed in Superior Court – would be described by the former offence (theft under). In addition, it is important to remember that tables 2 and 3 present the total caseload for each level of

court. As such, several of the offences (e.g., murder or minor property) can only be resolved by one of the levels of court. Since our purpose in presenting these data is to examine total caseloads for each judicial level and not the court which handles the greatest proportion of those cases which could have been resolved by either level, we have not isolated the offences of concurrent jurisdiction.

19 We are measuring the seriousness of an offence by the maximum penalty that may be handed down for a conviction.

20 Because complete Superior Court data for Prince Edward Island and the Yukon were not available for all three years under study, a peculiarity in the coding of the cases going to this level of court may slightly overestimate the numbers of cases at this judicial level in the second and/or third years. For this reason, we have not included estimates of the relative caseloads across years for these two jurisdictions. Although the same anomaly is possible for Alberta, we believe that the small rate of error – if one, in fact, exists – would be constant over time. As a consequence, we have excluded Prince Edward Island and the Yukon from table 4 as well as from any other tables involving caseload comparisons across years.

21 Some partial data do, in fact, suggest that the decline in the use of Superior Court has been occurring over the entire last decade. Appendix A of the report submitted by the Ontario Conference of Judges' Subcommittee on Court Reform presents data from Ontario on criminal proceedings added to, disposed of, and pending on the Superior Court trial list for the years 1992–2000. In each case, a consistent decline in absolute numbers is shown. To illustrate the magnitude of change, there were 10,943 proceedings (apparently referring to cases) added to the trial list in 1992. This number dropped to 3,781 in 2000.

22 Our category of 'selected indictable' is composed of all cases of: robbery with a firearm, all other classifications of robbery, levels II and III sexual assault, level III assault, arson, theft over, fraud over, possession of stolen property over, and impaired driving causing bodily harm. Our classification of 'selected hybrids' is comprised of all cases of: level I sexual assault, levels I and II assault, mischief to property over, and impaired driving and refusal to blow. Although these broad categories of indictable and hybrid offences are not, by any means, exhaustive, they do capture the majority of the high volume crimes of each group. As such, they should provide a reasonably reliable estimate of the general trends of these classifications.

23 While there would not appear to be any compelling reasons at present to suspect that current crime rates for serious offences will significantly increase in the near future, we are reluctant to eliminate this possibility as

an unlikely event. Indeed, the ability of criminologists to predict crime rates or even identify their strongest explanatory factors has not been met with overwhelming success. Having said this, there have also been no recent indications of consistent increases.

24 Because CCJS data use an end-date definition of their cases (i.e., cases are defined by the charges that are still active at the end of the adult court process), some initial murder charges dealt with in Superior Court but which were subsequently altered, such as the accused pleading to a lesser charge or the original charge being modified by the Crown after a plea bargain, would not be captured by the court data described here. For this reason, it appeared to us more sensible to examine all of the cases of this broader category even though only a subset of them are in the exclusive jurisdiction of the Superior Courts. Despite our inability to identify with any confidence only the murder cases, we do know from the police and youth court statistics presented in note 5 that there is likely to be no more than approximately two hundred first or second degree murder cases each year pooled across these seven provinces. This would constitute roughly 0.07 per cent of the total criminal court caseload.

25 For reasons having to do with data quality, we were unfortunately not able to examine changes in Crown elections for another high-volume, recently hybridized offence – break and enter of a non-dwelling.

26 See, for instance, Bill C-42 (S.C. 1994, ch. 44) and Bill C-17 (S.C. 1997, ch. 18).

27 We are not necessarily implying that a causal relationship exists between the hybridization of offences and the reduction in the proportion of cases being dealt with in Superior Court. Given that we were not able to rule out the possibility that other factors may have contributed to this decline, we are merely emphasizing that these variables appear to be correlated.

28 Seniuk and Lyon 'The Supreme Court,' 96.

# 4 Constitutional Limitations upon the Allocation of Trial Jurisdiction to the Superior or Provincial Court in Criminal Matters

PATRICK HEALY

*Since the Constitution assigns the power to make criminal law exclusively to the federal Parliament, it is the federal Parliament that determines in which courts criminal cases will be tried. Parliament does this through provisions of the* Criminal Code. *Over the years, through amendments to the* Criminal Code, *Parliament has greatly reduced the crimes that can be tried only in Superior Courts. Today the Code designates only ten offences that must be tried in a Superior Court. The most important of these is murder. The others are such uncommon matters as treason, alarming Her Majesty, intimating Parliament, and piracy. The Code also still requires that jury trials (for any offence) be conducted by a Superior Court judge. The constitutional question that Patrick Healy, one of Canada's most respected constitutional scholars, examines in this chapter is whether Parliament could go all the way and empower Provincial Court judges – exclusively or concurrently with Superior Court judges – to try all criminal offences and conduct jury trials.*

*In 1983, in the* McEvoy *case, the Supreme Court of Canada answered the question in the negative. Here Professor Healy revisits that case and carefully considers the cogency of its reasoning. His conclusion is that* McEvoy *was wrongly decided. The Supreme Court's principal reason for denying the federal Parliament the power to bestow full criminal jurisdiction on a Provincial Court was the need to preserve a residue of criminal jurisdiction exclusively in the hands of judges who had full judicial independence. Healy points out that since Provincial Court judges are acknowledged by the Supreme Court itself to enjoy the same degree of independence as Superior Court judges, the Court's reasoning no longer holds water. While Professor Healy accepts that Superior Courts have an inherent and constitutionally protected core jurisdiction, he does not think that this core includes trial of certain criminal offences or limits the criminal jurisdiction that Parliament can assign to Provincial Courts.*

*Healy suggests that a reference case with questions much better framed than those in McEvoy be taken to the Supreme Court. If this were done, and the constitutional cloud created by McEvoy were cleared away, an alternative model of consolidating criminal trial court jurisdiction would be opened up. Instead of having to elevate Provincial Court judges to the Superior Court and having them paid and appointed by Ottawa, Provincial Court judges appointed and paid by the provinces could hear all criminal cases and conduct jury trials. If Parliament wished, Superior Courts might continue concurrently to exercise some of their criminal trial responsibilities.*

At issue are constitutional constraints upon the creation of a unified criminal court and the allocation of jurisdiction over jury trials to the Provincial Court. The purpose of this article is not to test whether either of these options is desirable or preferable. The aim is solely to ascertain whether Canadian constitutional law imposes limitations that would prevent the creation of a unified criminal court or the allocation of jurisdiction over jury trials to the Provincial Court.[1] Thus this article is focused upon Parliament's legislative authority to assign jurisdiction over criminal offences to the Superior and Provincial Courts.

A unified criminal court could mean several things: a single Superior Court in the province, a single Provincial Court, or a court of mixed jurisdiction with judges appointed jointly by federal and provincial authorities.[2] These permutations, and others, need not be considered here. There is no doubt that exclusive trial jurisdiction in all criminal matters could be allocated to the Superior Court of the province. It will suffice here to determine whether exclusive jurisdiction over all matters of trial, including jury trials, could be allocated to the Provincial Court. If this hypothesis can be sustained, it must follow that the Constitution permits considerable flexibility in the allocation of trial jurisdiction in criminal matters and flexibility in the creation of a unified criminal court.

More precisely, then, the two questions under consideration are whether there is a constitutional imperative to the effect that some criminal offences must be reserved to the Superior Court for trial and, further, that jury trials cannot be allocated to the Provincial Court.

In brief, the conclusion in this article is that no constitutional principle bars the allocation of exclusive jurisdiction over all criminal offences to the Provincial Court, including jury trials. No explicit constitutional rule in Canadian law would prevent this. The same result follows from an examination of cases and historical principles. It is argued below that decisions of the Supreme Court of Canada, wherein it is affirmed that in criminal matters the Superior Courts retain an irreducible core jurisdiction *for purposes of trial*, cannot be sustained except as an expression of policy and judicial preference. These decisions are infirm because they lack historical foundation and they rest upon an anachronistic model of jurisdiction and judicial independence that has been overtaken by modern developments in Canadian judicature.

If the first conclusion is too broad, a second and narrower conclusion would be that the Superior and Provincial Courts could be given concurrent jurisdiction over any criminal offence. This is substantially the position that now obtains in Canadian law under the *Criminal Code*[3] by virtue of sections 468 and 552. The former allows the Superior Court to hear any indictable offence, including those otherwise allocated to the jurisdiction of the Provincial Court. The latter defines the court of criminal jurisdiction as the Superior Court in all places except Quebec and Nunavut, where the court of criminal jurisdiction is the Cour du Québec and the Court of Nunavut respectively.[4] This view of concurrency is reinforced in criminal matters, though not as an expression of constitutional principle, by the number of indictable offences in which the accused has a right of election to be tried in the Superior Court with a jury, the court of criminal jurisdiction or the Provincial Court.[5]

Finally, it would appear that there is no constitutional impediment to bar the allocation of jurisdiction over jury trials to the Provincial Court. Such jurisdiction was exercised for many years after Confederation in the District and County Courts. Judges of these courts were appointed pursuant to section 96 of the *Constitution Act, 1867*, but District and County Courts were not Superior Courts. Historically they were descendants of courts empowered by royal commission to exercise some of the jurisdiction that would otherwise be exercised by Superior Courts[6] but they were not, by that same commission, empowered to exercise all of the authority of a Superior Court. While these courts were created under section 96, and not as Superior Courts, there is no coherent principle to the effect that jurisdiction over a jury trial must be exercised by a court constituted under section 96, as opposed to a Superior Court. The grant of jurisdiction over jury trials to District and County Courts can be seen as an allocation of jurisdiction to an inferior court exercising a statutory jurisdiction.[7] There is no reason why such an allocation could not be made today to the Provincial Court.

## Authorities

The central point is whether there is an 'irreducible core jurisdiction' of the Superior Court that prevents allocation of all trial jurisdiction in criminal matters to the Provincial Court, including jurisdiction in jury trials. Three cases in the Supreme Court of Canada affirm the concept of an irreducible core jurisdiction in criminal matters.[8] The jurisprudence does not clearly identify or demarcate that jurisdiction but affirms its existence. Further, the cases concerned with criminal jurisdiction form part of a larger body of jurisprudence that is concerned with constitutional limitations on jurisdiction in other matters.[9] All of this jurisprudence collectively endorses what has been called in Canadian constitutional law 'the Lederman thesis,' based upon a celebrated article published by Professor W.R. Lederman in the *Canadian Bar Review* in 1956.[10] Attention will be given here first to the authorities and then to the Lederman thesis.

### McEvoy v. Attorney General of New Brunswick

*McEvoy* appears to stand for a proposition of constitutional law that in criminal matters there is an irreducible core jurisdiction, for purposes of trial, in the Superior Court. While no attempt is made in the decision to define that jurisdiction, there are only two possibilities by which to define it. One is that the Superior Court has exclusive jurisdiction to consider offences expressly reserved to the 'superior court of criminal jurisdiction,' and the other is jurisdiction over jury trials. That is, trial jurisdiction must be reserved to the Superior Court for the indictable offences enumerated in section 469 of the *Criminal Code*, or jury trials must be reserved to the Superior Court, or both.[11]

*McEvoy* went to the Supreme Court on appeal from the advice of the Court of Appeal of New Brunswick in a reference under the *Judicature Act*.[12] Seven judges of the Supreme Court delivered a unanimous opinion that was signed by 'The Court.' The three questions referred to the court were these:

> Can Parliament confer exclusive jurisdiction to try all indictable offences under the *Criminal Code* on a new court whose judges are appointed by the province?
>
> Can Parliament do this if the new provincial court has concurrent jurisdiction with the New Brunswick Superior Courts?

Can the New Brunswick Legislature constitute and appoint the judges to the new court if that court has either exclusive or concurrent jurisdiction?[13]

The Court of Appeal answered all three questions affirmatively[14] and the Supreme Court of Canada answered all three negatively. The reasons of the Supreme Court demand attention.[15]

The questions posed in *McEvoy* were abstract in the sense that they were stated for examination in the absence of any legislative proposal, by a competent federal or provincial authority, for the actual creation of a unified criminal court in New Brunswick. The court quoted a summary of the proposal stated by the Attorney General of New Brunswick:

> The proposal envisages a new court constituted to accept and to exercise complete criminal jurisdiction: Dealing exclusively with all criminal law matters, including criminal code offences, other federal offences and provincial offences. This court would replace the present Provincial Court and its judges would be appointed by the Lieutenant-Governor in Council. It would not be constituted by the Legislature as a superior court and it would exercise statutory jurisdiction only.
>
> Amendments to the Criminal Code and other federal statutes would be requested of the Parliament of Canada to confer jurisdiction in criminal matters upon the new court. The implementation of the proposal thus is conceived as a blending of the authority of the two legislative bodies. (p. 715)

Apart from this, there were no details concerning the establishment of such a court or the allocation of jurisdiction to it.

The Supreme Court deplored the absence of details and a more specific context within which to answer the three questions, and for this reason half of the court's opinion was given to determining whether the questions referred were not specific enough to warrant answers. On this point the conclusion was stated thus:

> While we deprecate the practice of bringing before the Court as important constitutional questions as are raised in this case on extremely flimsy material, we would not abort the appeal on this ground. We believe for the reasons which follow that the Court has enough of the essential features of the proposed scheme to be compelled to the conclusion that all three questions must be answered in the negative. (pp. 714–15)

In brief, the reason given for this conclusion was that section 96 of the *Constitution Act, 1867* does not allow Parliament or the legislatures, or the two acting jointly, to eliminate the criminal jurisdiction of the Superior Courts over indictable offences. The thrust of this conclusion was, apparently, that there must be a Superior Court of criminal jurisdiction in each province that tries at least some indictable offences. The substance of this conclusion must be considered.[16]

The Supreme Court expressed in *McEvoy* the view that the power to appoint judges to the superior courts under s. 96 of the *Constitution Act, 1867* is a constitutional requirement to establish such courts, which implies an irreducible principle of Canadian constitutional law, unaffected by the distribution of legislative competence, that there must be such courts in each province with criminal jurisdiction. This point is developed in five paragraphs:

> What is being contemplated here is not one or a few transfers of criminal law power, such as has already been accomplished under the *Criminal Code,* but a complete obliteration of Superior Court criminal law jurisdiction. Sections 96 to 100 do not distinguish between courts of civil jurisdiction and courts of criminal jurisdiction. They should not be read as permitting the Parliament of Canada through use of its criminal law power to destroy Superior Courts and to deprive the Governor General of appointing power and to exclude members of the Bar from preferment for Superior Court appointments.
>
> Parliament can no more give away federal constitutional powers than a province can usurp them. Section 96 provides that 'The Governor General *shall appoint* the Judges of the Superior, District, and County Courts in *each* province.' The proposal here is that Parliament transfer the present Superior Courts' jurisdiction to try indictable offences to a provincial court. The effect of this proposal would be to deprive the Governor General of his power under s. 96 to appoint the judges who try indictable offences in New Brunswick. That is contrary to s. 96. Section 96 bars Parliament from altering the constitutional scheme envisaged by the judicature sections of the *Constitution Act, 1867* just as it does the provinces from doing so.
>
> The traditional independence of English Superior Court judges has been raised to the level of a fundamental principle of our federal system by the *Constitution Act, 1867* and cannot have less importance and force in the administration of criminal law than in the case of civil matters. Under the Canadian constitution the Superior Courts are independent of both levels of government. The provinces constitute and maintain the Superior Courts; the federal authority appoints the judges. The judicature sections

of the *Constitution Act, 1867* guarantee the independence of the Superior Courts; they apply to Parliament as well as to the Provincial Legislatures.

Both sides of the proposal under review are flawed. Parliament cannot in effect give away the Governor General's s. 96 appointing power under colour of legislation vesting jurisdiction to try all indictable offences in a provincial court. New Brunswick cannot exercise an appointing power in respect of courts with s. 96 jurisdiction under colour of legislation in relation to the constitution, maintenance and organization of courts with criminal jurisdiction.

Nor is much gained for the proposed new provincial statutory Court by providing for concurrent Superior Court jurisdiction. The theory behind the concurrency proposal is presumably that a Provincial court with concurrent rather than exclusive powers would not oust the Superior Courts' jurisdiction, at least not to the same extent; since the Superior Courts' jurisdiction was not frozen as of 1867, it would be permissible to alter that jurisdiction so long as the essential core of the Superior Courts' jurisdiction remained; s. 96 would be no obstacle because the Superior Court would retain jurisdiction to try indictable offences. With respect, we think this overlooks the fact that what is being attempted here is the transformation by conjoint action of an inferior court into a superior court. Section 96 is, in our view, an insuperable obstacle to any such endeavour.[17]

Thus, because the Constitution requires the establishment of Superior Courts, and does not distinguish between civil and criminal jurisdiction, there must be some criminal jurisdiction in the Superior Courts. It will be noted – again – that nothing in these reasons is said to define the scope of criminal jurisdiction in the Superior Courts that is implied by section 96. That is – again – the Court asserts the existence of that jurisdiction but does not enumerate its contents. Indeed, the Court acknowledges that Parliament has validly allocated broad parts of criminal jurisdiction to the inferior courts and that in 1867 the superior and inferior courts had concurrent jurisdiction over many indictable offences.[18] Nevertheless, the Court asserts, the legislative authority in the provinces to establish the Superior Courts and the power of the governor general to appoint judges in those courts cannot be compromised by allowing Parliament to allocate all criminal jurisdiction to an inferior court established by the province. To do so would imply that Parliament can 'give away' a power granted to the governor general and that the provincial legislatures could exercise such powers by creating a court that would have the jurisdiction traditionally held by a Superior Court.[19]

The last paragraph in the passage quoted above is difficult to follow but its meaning rests on the assertion that the allocation of all jurisdiction over criminal offences to the Provincial Court is an attempt to transform the Provincial Court into a Superior Court. It also rests on the assertion that the judicature provisions of the *Constitution Act, 1867*, notably the power of appointment, presuppose an ascertainable substantive jurisdiction in the Superior Courts. The proposal advanced by New Brunswick expressly stated that the allocation of jurisdiction would be entirely statutory and that the unified criminal court would not be constituted as a Superior Court. That is, it would not be given the attributes of a Superior Court. The assertion by the Supreme Court would thus appear to have little but pyrrhic force because it says that Parliament can allocate almost, but not quite, everything to the Provincial Court.[20] And then it fails to say what the reserved remainder might be. This is scarcely a convincing argument, based upon history, principle or policy, against a theory of concurrency. It is an argument that section 96 of the *Constitution Act, 1867* is more than a power of appointment and implies a substantive definition of the jurisdiction of Superior Courts in civil and criminal matters. But, even then, it does not provide a coherent exposition of such a substantive definition.

However, of special note in the passages quoted above is the third paragraph. There it will be seen that a reason given for preserving a criminal jurisdiction in the Superior Court is that sections 96 to 100 of the *Constitution Act, 1867* guarantee the independence of the Superior Court. The Supreme Court states that the Superior Courts are independent of either level of government and that the independence of the courts 'cannot have less importance and force in the administration of criminal law than in the case of civil matters.'[21] Buried in this language is a proposition that liability for indictable offences, or at least some indictable offences, must be tried in an independent court. This is not the same as saying that such offences must be tried in the Superior Court, and the ramifications of this proposition are developed below. In brief, however, the argument is this: if the Provincial Court is now recognized as an independent and impartial court, as opposed to an inferior tribunal that is not an independent court, there can be no objection to the allocation of criminal jurisdiction at trial.

The strength of the reasons in *McEvoy* would be increased if the court had defined the irreducible scope of criminal jurisdiction in the criminal courts. As it did not, this leaves two possible conclusions concerning the reasons. One is that those reasons are incomplete and can only be made complete by a ruling that does define the irreducible scope of criminal jurisdiction over offences for trial in the Superior Courts. There is no such ruling in *McEvoy* or, seemingly, any other case.

The other possible conclusion that arises from *McEvoy* is that the Supreme Court was wrong, not when it said that the Constitution precludes abolition of the Superior Courts, but when it said that jurisdiction for the trial of some indictable offences cannot be allocated to the Provincial Court. Unless it can be shown that the Superior Courts have under the *Constitution Act, 1867* or the Charter an irreducible and defined jurisdiction to try indictable offences, it is submitted that the better view of *McEvoy* is that it was wrongly decided.

Why? Canadian law has always, even before Confederation, divided criminal jurisdiction between the Superior and inferior courts, and it is incorrect to suggest that all indictable offences lay within the jurisdiction of the Superior Court at Confederation. (In *McEvoy* the Supreme Court expressly acknowledged this.[22]) This division is now reflected in the distinction between the 'superior court of criminal jurisdiction' and the 'court of criminal jurisdiction,' as defined in section 2 of the Criminal Code. Before and since 1867 the division of criminal jurisdiction has not been symmetrical in the sense, for example, that all indictable offences are heard in the Superior Court and summary conviction offences heard in the Provincial Court. Inferior courts have heard some indictable offences before and after 1867, but here again the distribution of this jurisdiction has been uneven.

At this juncture it is necessary to review the current allocation of criminal jurisdiction in the Code and to note some essential points concerning the evolution of that allocation. Although there is and has been a bewildering array of terms for different courts in different provinces, there has always been an elementary distinction between the Superior Court and an inferior court, the latter being (by whatever name) any court other than the Superior Court. The focus of attention here is on the jurisdiction over indictable offences.

Under the current scheme, section 468 declares that a Superior Court may try any indictable offence. Section 469 provides that only a Superior Court may try offences enumerated therein.[23] For the rest, section 553 stipulates a list of offences within the absolute (not exclusive) jurisdiction of the Provincial Court and section 552 identifies the court of trial for all other indictable offences tried without a jury.[24] That court is now the Superior Court in all provinces except Quebec, where it is the Cour du Québec.[25] In addition, section 536 allows the accused to elect trial by jury, trial by judge alone, or trial in the Provincial Court for all indictable offences except those listed in sections 469 and 553. Thus, according to this scheme, an inferior court may in principle hear any indictable offence except that which is listed in section 469 or that which is tried by jury.[26] As a matter of practice, it is only section 552 that allocates trial jurisdiction to the Superior Court in jurisdictions other than Quebec. The history of trial jurisdiction over indictable offences discloses an important fact. Until recently the predecessors to section 552 gave jurisdiction over indictable offences tried without jury to inferior courts and had done so since the original codification.[27] Thus the allocation in section 552 to the Superior Courts is relatively novel and the allocation to the Cour du Québec in section 552 is more consistent with established jurisdiction. So too is the definition of a court of criminal jurisdiction in section 2.

As the Code stands now, the only inferior court with criminal juris- diction is the Provincial Court. This was not always the case because, as already noted, there were previously several criminal courts with jurisdiction over indictable offences tried without jury, most notably, the magistrates' courts. The definition of a court of criminal jurisdic- tion was first introduced in the Code in 1953 to distinguish the magis- trates' jurisdiction from that of all other inferior courts over indictable offences. This was also the effect of section 552. The 'court of criminal jurisdiction' is defined in section 2 of the *Criminal Code*:

(a)   a court of general or quarter sessions of the peace, when presided over by a superior court judge,

(a.1)  in the Province of Quebec, the Court of Quebec, the municipal court of Montreal and the municipal court of Quebec,

(b)   a provincial court judge or judge acting under Part XIX, and

(c)   in the Province of Ontario, the Ontario Court of Justice.

It will be noted therefore that, according to the scheme of the Code, a Provincial Court is, in principle and in every jurisdiction, competent to try any indictable offence other than those enumerated in section 469. As a practical matter, given the terms of section 552, in most jurisdic- tions the trial court for indictable offences tried without a jury upon election of the accused is the Superior Court. But in principle a 'court of criminal jurisdiction' has jurisdiction to try anything except those offences listed in section 469. This can include, obviously, the Provin- cial Court, and only the list in section 552 prevents this. That is the effect of the definition of a court of criminal jurisdiction in section 2 of the Code and the introductory clause of section 469. Since the Provincial Court is now the only inferior court with criminal jurisdiction, none of this statutory complexity is now strictly necessary. The essential point is that the jurisdiction of the Superior Court and the inferior courts over indictable offences tried without jury has been, in principle and in practice, concurrent from before Confederation.

What has changed since Confederation has been the *distribution* of jurisdiction over offences between the Superior Court and inferior courts. Many offences that were within the exclusive jurisdiction of the Superior Court have been removed from it by successive amendments of section 469. The range of indictable offences within the absolute jurisdiction of the Provincial Court (section 553) increased over time. Some indictable offences have been reclassified as hybrid offences and some have been reclassified as summary conviction offences. In short, there has been a progressive expansion of the jurisdiction of inferior courts in criminal matters, including indictable offences. The only exception, leading to expansion of the Superior Courts' jurisdiction over indictable offences, has been the amendment of section 552 that defines a judge for trial over indictable offences tried without jury as a judge of the Superior Court in every province except Quebec. As noted, this is a modern development and has nothing to do with constitutional constraints upon the allocation of trial jurisdiction.

Section 553 of the Code declares that Provincial Court judges have absolute (not exclusive) jurisdiction over the offences listed therein and section 552 declares who shall be a competent judge for all other indictable offences that are tried without a jury. Two points are especially noteworthy in this scheme for the allocation of jurisdiction. First, in all provinces but Quebec, indictable offences in which the accused elects trial by judge alone are tried by a judge of the Superior Court of the province. In Quebec, indictable offences except those tried with a jury are tried before a judge of the Cour du Québec. Second, in Nunavut the Court of Justice is given the jurisdiction of a Superior Court of criminal jurisdiction and a court of criminal jurisdiction.

Hence, the starting point would seem to be that Parliament may validly allocate jurisdiction over all indictable offences tried without a jury to the Provincial Court, unless there is a peculiar historical anomaly within the principles of constitutional law that restricts this proposition to the courts of Quebec. But there is not, because in other provinces before the amendment of what is now section 552, jurisdiction was commonly allocated to inferior courts.

As noted above, the Superior Courts do not have, and did not have before Confederation, exclusive jurisdiction over indictable offences. If they did, the allocation of indictable offences to the absolute jurisdiction of the Provincial Court in section 553 (or to any inferior court) was unconstitutional from the outset. No suggestion to this effect has ever been sustained.[28] Further, the Superior Courts have no constitutional monopoly over trial of indictable offences in which the accused elects to be tried by judge alone. If they did, the allocation of that jurisdiction to the judges of the Cour du Québec was unconstitutional. No suggestion to this effect has ever been sustained. Finally, it must be noted that the provision of the Code that is now section 469 reserves to the Superior Court of criminal jurisdiction a list of enumerated offences. Over time the number of offences thus enumerated has been reduced by Parliament from dozens to ten. If there were a constitutional principle that reserved all of the offences first enumerated in the section to the Superior Court, on the basis that they were within the exclusive jurisdiction of the Superior Court in 1867, every subsequent amendment to reduce the number of listed offences would have been unconstitutional. These amendments reduce the exclusive jurisdiction of the Superior Court to the vanishing point. If the jurisdiction of that court was *irreducible*, it must follow that these amendments were invalid. No such argument has been sustained.

In the absence of historical analysis of the criminal law and criminal jurisdiction, the Supreme Court of Canada's conclusions in *McEvoy* are reached on the basis that they are implied by the judicature provisions in sections 96 to 100 of the *Constitution Act, 1867*. In the course of its reasons, however, the Court asserts a perplexing position. It asserts that there might be no objection to incremental erosion of the Superior Court's jurisdiction, but that outright 'ouster' or 'abolition' would be unconstitutionally invalid. This would appear to be inconsistent with the principle that there is an 'irreducible core jurisdiction.' If it is irreducible, it cannot be eroded incrementally or any other way. Further, if it is irreducible, it must lie in the offences listed in section 469; but if that list has been abbreviated to ten offences, the jurisdiction is reducible and, for most practical purposes, has been reduced to murder. Either that reduction is unconstitutional or the supposed constitutional constraint has no substance in defining the jurisdiction of the Superior Court over offences.

What, then, can the irreducible core jurisdiction of the Superior Court mean in criminal matters? Some assistance can be drawn from basic principles. In the Canadian legal system a Superior Court is a court of general and inherent jurisdiction while an inferior court is a statutory creation of limited jurisdiction. A Superior Court thus has all jurisdiction except that which is lawfully taken away from it by statute; an inferior court has no jurisdiction except that which is specifically given to it by statute. In criminal matters, therefore, the irreducible core jurisdiction of a Superior Court for purposes of trial must refer, at least in part, to trial jurisdiction over matters not otherwise assigned to a court by statute. This concept would have been a necessary component in Canadian law for as long as there existed common law crimes or for as long as there was no comprehensive statutory allocation of jurisdiction over offences. After 1950, however, common law crimes were abolished[29] and thereafter it could be stated with confidence that all crimes were prescribed by the legislature and assigned by it to either the Superior Court of criminal jurisdiction or a court of criminal jurisdiction. In short, with the abolition of common law crimes, there remained no necessary foundation for a Superior Court of general and inherent jurisdiction for the trial of specified offences.[30] By definition, there were no such offences and there could be no such jurisdiction. In the end, this would mean that in modern times the only irreducible core jurisdiction would refer to the power of review over inferior tribunals.

If *McEvoy* is correct, the structure of criminal jurisdiction since Confederation has been unconstitutional and the reallocation of jurisdiction by amendments of sections 469 and 552 has also been unconstitutional. There are, however, grounds upon which to question the soundness of *McEvoy*. First, the Court itself deplored the obligation to decide a matter presented on such a thin record. Second, the opinion contained no historical analysis. Third, the opinion takes no account of more recent developments in Canadian judicature, notably the evolution of the Provincial Court.

When the principles in *Reference re: Residential Tenancies Act* are applied to criminal matters, as they were in *McEvoy*, they dictate that the judicature provisions of sections 96 to 100 of the *Constitution Act, 1867* imply a substantive criminal jurisdiction in the Superior Courts. It means that an implicit aspect of the judicature provisions trumps the express and exclusive jurisdiction of Parliament over the criminal law. Perhaps it is correct that the judicature provisions have a determinative effect on aspects of substantive jurisdiction in non-criminal matters. Perhaps it is even correct that these provisions might have some limited effect on some aspects of jurisdiction in criminal matters, but not in the allocation of jurisdiction over offences to the Provincial or Superior Court. In principle, the judicature provisions are necessary for the allocation of a substantive jurisdiction that is either part of the general and inherent jurisdiction of a Superior Court or where a matter is otherwise not allocated to a specific court. For practical purposes, however, this can refer in criminal matters only to the power of review by the Superior Courts by way of prerogative relief: all other aspects of substantive jurisdiction are comprehensively defined by Parliament in the Code.

### Reference re: Young Offenders Act, s. 2 (P.E.I.)

In 1991 the Supreme Court was asked for its advice concerning the allocation of jurisdiction over criminal offences to divisions of the various Provincial Courts that were typically called Youth Court. The Court concluded unanimously that this allocation was constitutionally valid, although the reasons given for this conclusion were not unanimous. Lamer C.J.C. spoke for a majority of five judges, while Wilson J. and La Forest J. delivered concurring reasons. The reasons of La Forest J. differ significantly from those of the chief justice.

Lamer C.J.C. took the position that the validity of the legislation had to be determined by application of the criteria stated in *Reference re: Residential Tenancies Act*. He began with the proposition that Parliament's legislative authority over criminal law and procedure implies a power to allocate jurisdiction over offences to specific courts, including courts established by the provinces. The generality of this proposition is qualified by section 96 of the *Constitution Act, 1867*, which has been interpreted to mean that neither Parliament nor a provincial legislature may allocate to an inferior court or administrative tribunal exclusive jurisdiction over any matter within the exclusive, or 'core,' jurisdiction of the Superior Courts at Confederation. Whether or not some matter lies within that exclusive or core jurisdiction will be determined substantially by an initial characterization of the matter in question. Here, according to the chief justice, the matter was properly characterized as jurisdiction over young persons charged with criminal offences.[31] As this matter was not at Confederation within the exclusive jurisdiction of the Superior Courts, Parliament could validly allocate that jurisdiction to the Provincial Court.

The crux of this conclusion is that at Confederation there was no matter defined as criminal jurisdiction over young persons. The same conclusion is stated, with great emphasis on the historical novelty of a specialized criminal jurisdiction over young persons, in the concurring reasons of Wilson J.

La Forest J. also delivered concurring reasons that underscored the importance of the *Young Offenders Act* in providing a comprehensive statutory scheme for criminal jurisdiction over young persons. This, he said, was sufficient for the validity of the act. As noted, however, the reasons of La Forest J. also differ significantly from those of Lamer C.J.C. and Wilson J. In his view the test of jurisdiction developed in *Reference re: Residential Tenancies Act* was not 'fully applicable.' Indeed, he said that the only part of that test that can apply to an ordinary court, as opposed to an administrative tribunal, is the first part concerned with the jurisdiction of the Superior Courts over the matter in question at the time of Confederation. This would mean that if the Superior Courts did not have exclusive jurisdiction over the matter in 1867 there could be no constitutional impediment to the allocation by Parliament of jurisdiction to the Provincial Court. La Forest J. thus took the view that the test developed in *Reference re: Residential Tenancies Act* was only fully applicable in instances where Parliament or a legislature allocated jurisdiction to an administrative tribunal rather than the ordinary courts. The reasons for this view are not elaborated but, as will be seen below, it is a point of great importance.

There is a difference between jurisdiction over the offence and jurisdiction over the offender. While it might be true that there was no specialized criminal jurisdiction over young persons in 1867, it is not true that there was no criminal jurisdiction over young persons in 1867.[32] That jurisdiction would have been exercised by the ordinary courts having jurisdiction over the offence at that time. If a young person was charged with an offence within the exclusive jurisdiction of the Superior Court, that court would have jurisdiction over the young person. Similarly, if some other court had jurisdiction over the offence at that time, that court would have jurisdiction over the young person. In short, the court with jurisdiction would be defined by the ordinary law governing jurisdiction over the offence and not by age. It follows therefore that the statutory scheme affirmed by the Supreme Court in *Reference re: Young Offenders Act, s. 2 (P.E.I.)* was one in which Parliament decided to redefine criminal jurisdiction over offences charged against young persons.

This redefinition included, in the main, an allocation to the Provincial Court of jurisdiction over offences that were previously within the exclusive jurisdiction of the Superior Court. Strictly speaking, this is not a contradiction of *McEvoy* because the *Young Offenders Act* did not purport to extinguish the exclusive jurisdiction of the Superior Court. The act did allocate offences that were previously within the exclusive jurisdiction of the Superior Court to the Provincial Court and, in doing so, effectively created a concurrent jurisdiction over those offences in the Provincial Court for a specified group of alleged offenders. The characterization of this arrangement as concurrency is reinforced in the act itself by those provisions that allow for transfer to adult court. If concurrency of this kind is permissible for a subset of alleged offenders, there is no reason why it should not be permissible for all offences.

A final point concerning *Reference re: Young Offenders Act, s. 2 (P.E.I.)* is that it weakens considerably the force of *McEvoy*. The earlier case appeared to assert that in criminal matters there is an irreducible jurisdiction at trial in the Superior Court over certain offences. The later case contradicts this by holding that the Provincial Court may be given jurisdiction over offences charged against young persons, including murder and attempted murder. This is, on any account of the matter, a reduction of the jurisdiction of the Superior Court because it takes away from the exclusive jurisdiction of the Superior Court. The position created by *Reference re: Young Offenders Act, s. 2 (P.E.I.)* would appear to be that Parliament can give jurisdiction to the Provincial Court over any offence provided that it does not extinguish the jurisdiction of the Superior Court over the same offences. This would seem to provide support, at least in part, for the very notion of concurrency that was rejected by the Supreme Court in *McEvoy*.

## MacMillan Bloedel Ltd. v. Simpson

In this case the Supreme Court was required to determine whether Parliament could, in section 47(2) of the *Young Offenders Act*, allocate exclusive jurisdiction to the Youth Court to try cases of contempt *ex facie* allegedly committed by young persons. The Court ruled, over the dissenting reasons of four judges, that Parliament could grant this jurisdiction to the Provincial Court but that it could do so only on the basis that this jurisdiction is concurrent with that of the Superior Court. That is, the jurisdiction of the Provincial Court could be concurrent with that of the Superior Court, but not exclusive. The reason given by the majority was that jurisdiction over contempt *ex facie* was one of the inherent powers of the Superior Court and, as such, part of its core jurisdiction that could not be diminished without amendment of the Constitution.

Lamer C.J.C. gave reasons for the majority and it is instructive to review them because they focus on the meaning that should be given to the core jurisdiction of the Superior Courts in criminal matters. The answer, according to the majority, is that the core jurisdiction of the Superior Court is synonymous with its *inherent* jurisdiction. It is immediately obvious that this is quite different from jurisdiction over offences, which Parliament can allocate in its exercise of authority under section 91(27) of the *Constitution Act, 1867*. As explained above, jurisdiction over offences is not a matter of inherent jurisdiction and for this reason cannot be considered one of the historic distinguishing features of a Superior Court.

In his reasons Lamer C.J.C. acknowledged the difficulty in defining the inherent jurisdiction of Superior Courts but he drew a general conclusion that 'powers which are "hallmarks of superior courts" cannot be removed from those courts' (para 35). He adopted a four-fold classification of the inherent powers of a Superior Court as developed in an article by Keith Mason:

(i)   ensuring convenience and fairness in legal proceedings;
(ii)  preventing steps being taken that would render judicial proceedings inefficacious;
(iii) preventing abuse of process; and
(iv)  acting in aid of Superior Courts and in aid or control of inferior courts and tribunals.[33]

Lamer C.J.C. thus adverted specifically to the power of a Superior Court to control its own process, to enforce its orders, to exercise supervisory control over inferior bodies, and to exercise original jurisdiction over justiciable disputes that are not otherwise allocated to the jurisdiction of a particular decision-making body. All of this, of course, has nothing to do with the jurisdiction of a court over any criminal offence or class of offences.

The approach taken by the chief justice in *MacMillan Bloedel Ltd.* is significantly more refined than that expressed in *McEvoy* or *Reference re: Young Offenders Act, s. 2 (P.E.I.).* By equating the core jurisdiction of a Superior Court with its inherent jurisdiction, he says in effect that the irreducible jurisdiction of the Superior Court is defined by its historic attributes or characteristics and not by a specified subject-matter. On this point the Court would appear to be unanimous, but the dissenters go further and assert that there is no argument of principle or policy that would bar Parliament from allocating jurisdiction over contempt *ex facie* to the Provincial Court. In taking this position, the dissenters refuse to accept the proposition that there is a core of jurisdiction in the Superior Court that cannot be taken away from it by an express legislative decision. The point of disagreement between the majority and the minority has not been reconsidered, much less settled, since *MacMillan Bloedel Ltd.* For present purposes this does not matter because, whether there is or is not an irreducible core of jurisdiction in the Superior Court, that core does not include a defined set of criminal offences or classes of offences.

The latter cases affirm that Parliament can allocate to the Provincial Court offences that have traditionally been within the jurisdiction of the Superior Court. They would appear to affirm that such jurisdiction may be concurrent in the sense that the Superior Court and the Provincial Court could try the same matter. This is consistent with section 468 of the Code and with the distribution of jurisdiction in section 552. A final question is whether the Provincial Court could be given exclusive jurisdiction over all criminal offences. The answer, it is submitted, is affirmative. Even if there is a core jurisdiction in the Superior Court, *MacMillan Bloedel Ltd.* makes plain that this core does not define jurisdiction over offences. It defines powers that are historic attributes or characteristics of a Superior Court. The allocation of subject-matter jurisdiction therefore remains a matter of policy for the determination of Parliament.

**The Lederman Thesis**

The decisions reviewed above lie among a cluster of cases concerning the broad proposition that some matters can only be adjudicated in and by Superior Courts, and therefore that there are limits upon Parliament and the legislatures when they purport to create decision-making bodies that have adjudicative functions. The broad proposition is known in Canadian constitutional law as the Lederman Thesis.

The Lederman thesis is found in a 1956 article entitled 'The Independence of the Judiciary.' In it Professor Lederman argued that only the Superior Court of the province, to whom judges were appointed under section 96 of the *Constitution Act, 1867*, provided the characteristics of an independent judiciary in Canada. Those characteristics were, notably, fixed salary, security of tenure, and independence. Inferior courts and administrative tribunals did not have these characteristics.

Professor Lederman also noted that one of the characteristics of a Superior Court is that it is a court of general and inherent jurisdiction. From this, he said, it followed that there are characteristics of a Superior Court that cannot be eroded or transferred to an inferior court or administrative body. Such bodies could only act within a jurisdiction defined by statute and with such powers as were granted for that purpose. Without general or inherent jurisdiction, they could not grant prerogative relief and they had no powers to control their process.

It is important to clarify what Professor Lederman did and did not say in the assertion of his thesis. He denied the existence of a principle of government that would allow for a neat separation of powers among the judiciary, the legislature, and the executive branches. Instead, he said, there is only a functional distinction between the creation of law and the application of law. As for the latter, he said that sections 96 to 100 of the *Constitution Act, 1867* necessarily imply that some matters for adjudication must lie within the jurisdiction of the Superior Court of the province and cannot be transferred to a provincially appointed court or tribunal. More specifically – and this was the thrust of his concern – he said that some matters over which the provinces had legislative jurisdiction under section 92 would necessarily have to lie within the adjudicative jurisdiction of the Superior Court, as distinguished from a provincial tribunal.

How does his argument run toward this conclusion and, second, what is the meaning of that conclusion? At the risk of excess, it would be better to observe the construction of the argument in Professor Lederman's own words.

Sections 96 to 100 have been judicially construed to impose a separation of powers at the provincial level in favour of the provincial superior courts. So we must ask what is the test delineating the separation or defining the limits of the guarantee ... A further detailed review of the cases is not necessary or possible in this article, but, as I consider the guarantee of jurisdiction to provincial superior courts to be *necessarily* implied in sections 96 to 100 of the B.N.A. Act, some reasons for my position need to be given.

[O]ne must first dispose of a false explanation frequently offered to justify such a separation of powers. We must reject the idea that natural law or legal science gives us a neat threefold material division of governmental functions into the legislative, the administrative and the judicial. If such a division were possible as a matter of substance, then a guaranteed separation of powers could be based upon it. One would merely need to insist that only courts could exercise the judicial function, only legislatures could legislate, and so on ... [N]o such threefold division exists ... [N]o functional test exists.

[F]unctionally, there is only the distinction between law-making and law-applying, and even between these two there is a twilight zone. The primary law-making or legislative power in Canada resides in representative legislatures, though they delegate some limited powers of this nature to subordinate tribunals and officials. The law-applying power is assigned to a great variety of persons variously described as administrative, executive or judicial officers or tribunals. Primarily the judicial tribunal or court merely offers one system or method of applying laws. Administrative or executive officers and tribunals offer other and different systems or methods of applying laws. The question of guaranteed jurisdiction for superior courts as against administrative tribunals comes to this: Are there some laws which the legislature concerned must entrust for interpretation and application exclusively to superior courts?

Now to reason in this way is not to discount the status of the courts, particularly the superior courts. What we must seek is understanding of the real basis of their importance. The superior courts, because of their unique combination of institutional characteristics and procedural practices, occupy a primary and central place in the total law-applying process. The prototype for the superior court is supplied by the English central royal courts after the Act of Settlement. It is this history alone that defines for us the essential institutional and procedural characteristics of these tribunals.

We must consider the guarantee of jurisdiction to the provincial superior courts in Canada in these terms. What law-applying tasks should be a monopoly of the superior courts? What legislative schemes are by their nature such that they should be entrusted for interpretation and application to the superior courts, to the exclusion of administrative tribunals or executive officials? This is a matter of substantive jurisdiction to interpret and apply certain types of laws, legislative schemes or statutes, and here also the English example has operated and is indispensable. In other words, the standard way to create a superior court has been and is to follow the English model in substantive jurisdiction as well as in the appointment, tenure and payment of judges. In this regard, both before and after 1867 in British North America, our judicature statutes have recited that the local superior court is to have in its territory jurisdiction equivalent to that enjoyed by the English central royal courts of common law and chancery. So, there is typical superior-court jurisdiction just as there are typical superior-court institutional characteristics.

But Mr. Willis and Professor Laskin, if I understand them correctly, have argued that when a provincial legislature passes laws within section 92 of the B.N.A. Act, it should have a fully free choice as to the institutional arrangements to prevail for the administration of those laws. That is, they seem to say that a provincial legislature should be free to assign or re-assign the law-applying power and task concerning any law within the scope of section 92 to a provincial administrative tribunal or executive official, rather than to a provincial superior court. Moreover, they assert, there is nothing in the normal meaning of words in sections 96 to 100 of the B.N.A. Act to dictate a different result ... Thus they argue in favour of a purely institutional test of the position of a superior court for purposes of these sections ...

At the most, an exclusive institutional test like this would mean that the whole of the interpretation and application of laws within section 92 of the B.N.A. Act could be withdrawn from provincial superior courts and vested in provincial administrative (that is, non-curial) tribunals or provincial minor courts. Mr. Willis seems to think there are enough political and practical inhibitions to prevent this extreme result, but I do not share his faith. There have been several famous (or notorious) feuds between certain provincial governments and certain federal governments. Often different political parties are in control at Ottawa and in provincial capitals. I should fear that at times a provincial government, if it were free to do so, would commit at least some important laws within section 92 for administration to non-curial tribunals *just to place provincial appointees in control of the law-applying process*, regardless of how desirable curial administration in the superior-court sense might be for that type of law. ...

This other test is based squarely on the typical jurisdiction in substance of superior courts rather than on the typical institutional characteristics of superior courts. It is the nature of the law-applying task in issue that is crucial. One focuses on the statute or legislative scheme to be applied and asks – Is this statute of such a nature that clearly it ought to have a superior-court administration rather than a non-curial administration? If the answer is affirmative, then the statute in question must be committed to a provincial superior court for authoritative interpretation and application to the persons and circumstances contemplated by it. If the answer is negative, only then may the province commit the law-applying task to a non-curial provincial tribunal.[34]

Before entering upon a critical discussion, given the length of this quoted passage, it is useful to identify several salient points in it.

Professor Lederman distinguishes between law-making and law-applying but acknowledges that between them there can be some overlap in the responsibilities of public institutions and officials. Despite this overlap, he says that there must be some guarantee of jurisdiction reserved to the Superior Courts if those courts are to be immune from extinction by the legislative allocation of law-applying functions to administrative tribunals or executive officials. To determine the scope or content of that guaranteed jurisdiction, Professor Lederman notes two possible tests. One is whether legislation intended that an administrative tribunal should use the adjudicative procedure of a Superior Court and be headed by a person whose terms of appointment are comparable to those of a Superior Court judge. The inadequacy of this institutional test is that it would not prevent a legislature from removing all jurisdiction from the ordinary courts. Thus Professor Lederman proposes a second test based upon the typical jurisdiction of a Superior Court. If the law-applying function in question is one that 'ought to have a superior-court administration rather than a non-curial administration,' it must be given to the court as opposed to a non-curial tribunal. This functional or substantive test is thus based upon the subject-matter for adjudication and is not frozen by the attribution of jurisdiction as it was known in 1867.

The starting point in Professor Lederman's discussion is that only the Superior Court of the province meets the test of an independent judiciary. At the time that he wrote, neither administrative tribunals nor Provincial Courts could meet this test. Thus the basic distinction in Professor Lederman's argument is between an adjudicative body that meets the test of an independent judiciary and an adjudicative body that does not. This is, in modern terms, a distinction between an independent court and a body that is not an independent court. From the premise that the Superior Court of the province is the only model for an independent court in Canadian government, he argues that a province could not vest adjudicative jurisdiction over some matters in something other than an independent court so as to avoid the jurisdiction of the Superior Court. In short, it is Professor Lederman's argument that some matters must be adjudicated by independent courts. It is *not* his argument that some matters must be adjudicated in the Superior Court, although this appears to be part of his argument solely because at the time of writing the only independent court was the Superior Court.

The Lederman thesis was an analysis of the constitutional significance of an independent judiciary within the peculiar arrangements of Canadian federalism established by the *Constitution Act, 1867*. It was a bold thesis that synthesized many strands of constitutional and administrative law and linked them to the signal principle of the independence of the judiciary. The thesis was partly exposition and partly argument due to the absence of any express statement in the *Constitution Act, 1867* concerning the independence of the judiciary. More specifically, the thesis was concerned with aspects of Canadian judicature that could only be implied by the text of the Constitution. For all its brilliance – and it was brilliant – the thesis was constructed from the materials of constitutional and administrative law that Professor Lederman could see and reasonably foresee at the time of writing. Those materials not only inform the thesis but limit it. Nobody should be surprised that, just as those materials limit the thesis, the thesis itself should require reconsideration in view of developments in constitutional, administrative, and other matters.

The Lederman thesis was constructed and advanced at a time when there was no provincial court that is comparable to the Provincial Court as it has evolved in the past thirty years. The provincial courts in 1956 were typically described as 'minor provincial courts' and their business was conducted by lay magistrates who could lay no more claim to the exercise of judicial functions than provincially appointed administrative tribunals. Lederman thus rightly made a distinction between subject-matter jurisdiction that must properly be reserved to the Superior Court and that which might be given to a provincial tribunal, whether it was a court of lay magistrates or an administrative tribunal. He was right because the Superior Court provided the only model for *an independent court* and there was no provincial court that could offer a notion of judicature similar to that in sections 96 to 100 of the *Constitution Act, 1867*, based upon security of tenure, fixed salary and independence.[35]

This is a matter of historical significance that cannot be passed over quickly. For a very long time, and certainly in 1956, the orthodox view was that the magistrates' courts ('minor provincial courts') exercised their limited jurisdiction under the supervision of the Superior Court. This meant that such courts could be supervised by judicial review or by means of appeal, typically appeal *de novo*. Perhaps, then, it was accurate to describe those lower courts as 'inferior' because their judges lacked formal training and all of the qualities associated with a court of record and an independent judiciary. Perhaps it was accurate or sound at the time to say that these courts required supervision by the Superior Court. But all this changed radically with progressive reform of the Provincial Court and its establishment as an independent court of record. The incidence of judicial review of a trial in Provincial Court is nil, as is the incidence of appeal *de novo*. The Superior Courts exercise no power of judicial review over a trial conducted within the jurisdiction of the Provincial Court, and their appellate role is limited to summary conviction matters.

The Lederman thesis was adopted in the *Reference re: Residential Tenancies Act* and *McEvoy* and other cases, but it was adopted and has been applied since in a manner that overstates the significance of the Superior Court and understates the significance of the Provincial Court. To repeat, there was in 1956 no provincial court comparable to what is known today. Magistrates were appointed at pleasure and most had no legal training. The Provincial Court today is a court that cannot be compared with or assimilated to an administrative tribunal, at least in criminal matters.[36] Thus the Lederman thesis, on its own terms, must be modified today to take account of the modern Provincial Court. The Supreme Court of Canada has not yet expressly modified this thesis but, for all practical purposes, has already implicitly done so.

In brief, the Provincial Court has become an independent court that conforms to almost all of the functional characteristics of a Superior Court and, more specifically, is governed by principles of judicature that are similar in principle to those stated and applied to the Superior Courts under sections 96 to 100 of the *Constitution Act, 1867*. The modalities are not identical, obviously, but in all essential aspects the Provincial Court most closely resembles the Superior Court and bears less or even little resemblance to an administrative tribunal.[37] There can be no doubt whatever of this evolution of the Provincial Court. It is an independent court in every sense as much as the Superior Court.

A modified version of the Lederman thesis would be that as a matter of constitutional principle there are some matters that are properly within the jurisdiction of courts, as opposed to administrative tribunals, but it is now a matter of legislative preference whether that court is the Superior Court or the Provincial Court. The modification lies in saying that there are some matters that must be reserved to the courts rather than to the Superior Court alone. This modified thesis is an adjustment that reconciles two irreconcilable trends in the jurisprudence of the Supreme Court: one epitomized by *McEvoy* and the other epitomized by the *Provincial Judges Reference*.[38]

The problem with *McEvoy* is that it cannot be reconciled with the original allocation of jurisdiction to inferior courts in Quebec because, on the principles stated in *McEvoy* itself, that allocation would have to be considered unconstitutional if the subject-matter would otherwise and previously have been within the jurisdiction of the Superior Courts. Moreover, *McEvoy* would force the conclusion that successive amendments of section 469 were also unconstitutional because they successively subtracted jurisdiction from the Superior Courts.

If the modified Lederman thesis is sound, it is nevertheless important not to overstate it. In particular it is important not to suggest that this version of the thesis would permit abolition of the Superior Court or of all its jurisdiction in criminal matters. Even if the Provincial Court is now firmly established as an independent court, and even if in all other material aspects it has characteristics that are comparable to those of a Superior Court, it remains distinct from the Superior Court in one material respect. The Provincial Court is not established or maintained under judicature provisions of the *Constitution Act, 1867*. Accordingly, its existence is not guaranteed. It can be abolished by statute and, if it is not abolished, its substantive jurisdiction can be altered or varied by the legislature. It is this point that allows clarification and restatement of the irreducible core jurisdiction of a Superior Court.

The point of constitutional principle is that the Superior Court is ineradicable in the structure of Canadian judicature. It cannot be eliminated and thus its jurisdiction, unlike that of the Provincial Court, cannot be entirely destroyed. If the Provincial Court were abolished tomorrow, and with it any jurisdiction assigned to it by statute, the Superior Court would remain. But it does not follow from the ineradicable nature of the Superior Court that it must be given exclusive trial jurisdiction over specific offences. It means one of two different things. It might mean that the Superior Court must be given by statute a concurrent jurisdiction with the Provincial Court in any place where the Provincial Court is given jurisdiction over an offence listed in section 469. Or it might mean that, in the absence of an assigned jurisdiction to the Provincial Court, the Superior Court has jurisdiction.

Substantial support for a modification of the Lederman Thesis can be found in a sequence of cases concerning the independence and impartiality of judges appointed by the province. These were cases based upon constitutional principles derived from the interpretation of section 11(d) of the Charter. It is unnecessary to review the entire sequence of these cases because the essential points can be found in the *Provincial Judges Reference*.[39]

In this case the Supreme Court held unanimously that section 11(d) of the Charter provides a constitutional guarantee that all courts having jurisdiction over criminal offences must be independent and impartial. By a majority the Court went further and asserted that the Constitution guarantees the independence of a wide variety of courts and tribunals. In reaching this conclusion, Lamer C.J.C. stated that the independence of the Provincial Court was impliedly guaranteed by the preamble to the *Constitution Act, 1867* in the phrase that declares that Canada should be governed by 'a Constitution similar in Principle to that of the United Kingdom.'[40] As this text is concerned solely with the allocation of jurisdiction at trial over criminal offences, it is unnecessary to embark upon a consideration of this wider conclusion in the *Provincial Judges Reference*. It will suffice for present purposes to note that the Court leaves no doubt that the Provincial Court is in criminal matters an institution that possesses the three characteristics of an independent court: security of tenure, financial security, and administrative independence.

In effect the Court decided that section 11(d) provides a guarantee of judicial independence that is similar in principle but not identical to that provided to the Superior Courts in sections 96 to 100 of the *Constitution Act, 1867*. The Court declared that this view is compelled by the Charter (at least in all cases in which a person is charged with an offence), justified in principle by the remainder of the Constitution, and reinforced by provincial statutes for the organization and discipline of Provincial Courts.[41]

The same conclusion was affirmed in *Therrien v. Québec*. At issue in that matter was, among other things, the validity of the procedure established in Quebec for the removal of a provincially appointed judge. At no point did the Supreme Court reject or modify in substance the reasons given in the *Provincial Judges Reference*. In several parts of its opinion the Court expressly affirmed the proposition that judges of the Provincial Court enjoy a form of independence that is similar in principle to that afforded the Superior Court. To this the Court added that judges of the Provincial Court, like those of the Superior Court, occupy 'a place apart' in which they must command the confidence and respect of the public. This place apart is that occupied by all members of an independent judiciary.

## Jury Trials

There remains the question of jurisdiction over jury trials. The argument against giving jury trials to the Provincial Court is based upon the first part of the test in *Reference re: Residential Tenancies Act;* that is, if only the Superior Court could conduct a jury trial in 1867, only a Superior Court can conduct a jury trial now. However, this is a narrow formulation of principle that fails to account for many relevant considerations, most notably the reduction in the incidence of jury trials, the allocation of jurisdiction to a judge sitting without a jury, and the reclassification of offences.

An example will illustrate the point. The number of offences within the exclusive jurisdiction of the Superior Court has been gradually reduced and most of these remain offences in which the accused has an election as to mode of trial: trial by judge and jury, trial by judge alone, or trial by Provincial Court judge.[42] In Quebec the latter two options mean the same thing except that the second option implies the right to a preliminary inquiry. There can be no sustaining principle for this arrangement unless it is accepted that the quality of justice in any of these modes of trial is equally acceptable. The significance of trial by jury lies in the jury presided over by a judge who is properly qualified to sit in an independent court – not in the fact that the judge is a member of the Superior Court.

Once again, therefore, trial jurisdiction must be assessed to account for the evolution of the courts themselves. It is established that the Provincial Court is for constitutional purposes an independent court, and as it cannot now be sensibly argued that Provincial Court judges know less law or have inferior judgment, there can be no objection in principle to a jury trial conducted by a Provincial Court judge. Moreover, it has long been held that the Superior Court has no supervisory power to review the trial of a case in Provincial Court; that is now a question for appeal in indictable or summary conviction matters.

A further point concerning jurisdiction over jury trials is whether this is a matter affected by issues arising from sections 96 to 100 of the *Constitution Act, 1867*. Jury trial is a mode of trial and, if the argument is that a jury trial must be conducted by a Superior Court judge, it must follow that Superior Court judges have exclusive jurisdiction over a mode of trial – as distinct from a substantive offence. If this were strictly accurate, it would imply that a matter previously within the exclusive jurisdiction of the Superior Court with a jury could not be tried in any other way, and thus that amendments or reclassifications of offences to allow an election by the accused have been unconstitutional. The better view, it is submitted, is that the Charter would prevent abolition of trial by jury in criminal matters but that nothing in the Constitution as a whole dictates that a jury trial must be conducted in the Superior Court.[43]

There is another historical factor of importance concerning jurisdiction in jury trials. Before and after Confederation this jurisdiction was exercised not only by the Superior Courts but by the district and county courts. Judges of these courts were appointed, until the abolition of the courts, under section 96 of the *Constitution Act, 1867*. They were not Superior Courts of general or inherent jurisdiction. They were the descendants of pre-Confederation courts that were empowered by a royal commission to exercise some of the jurisdiction of the Superior Court in criminal matters, notably trial jurisdiction in relation to some felonies and treasons. After 1867 these courts continued to conduct jury trials but at no point, before or after Confederation, were these Superior Courts; nor has it ever been considered that these courts had the unique characteristics of a Superior Court. It follows that there is no general historical principle that jurisdiction over jury trials could only be exercised by a Superior Court.

## Conclusion

The organizing principles of Canadian judicature have changed significantly in the past thirty years. For present purposes the essential principles can be distilled in the following propositions:

- The Superior Court of the province cannot be abolished and the unique characteristics of a Superior Court cannot be attributed to any other court or tribunal.
- Neither jurisdiction over criminal offences nor mode of trial in criminal matters is a unique characteristic of the Superior Court and

sections 96 to 100 of the *Constitution Act, 1867* cannot limit the authority of Parliament under s. 91(27) to allocate jurisdiction over offences to the Superior or Provincial Court.

- Some matters must be adjudicated in an independent and impartial court. There is no exhaustive or comprehensive list of matters that must be tried in an independent and impartial court, but criminal liability for offences is one of those matters.
- All criminal offences must be tried by an independent and impartial court.
- The court of trial may be either the Superior Court or the Provincial Court.
- The mode of trial in the court of trial may be by jury or judge alone.

These conclusions follow from the preceding discussion in this text. Assuming that they are sound, Parliament may create in the Superior or the Provincial Court a unified criminal court. It also follows that a unified criminal court need not have the same features in each province, which means that in one province it might be designated by Parliament as the Superior Court and in others as the Provincial Court.

A final constitutional question arises concerning the allocation of jurisdiction at trial in a unified criminal court. If Parliament were to allocate jurisdiction over all offences to the Provincial Court, must it do so by preserving a concurrent jurisdiction in the Superior Court? For all of the reasons considered earlier in this text, it is submitted that the answer to this question is negative. In short, the allocation of trial jurisdiction is not constrained by an irreducible jurisdiction in the Superior Court and thus it is a matter of legislative preference relating to section 91(27) of the *Constitution Act, 1867*. A concurrent jurisdiction in the Superior and Provincial Court is not required, but there might be some practical advantage to preserving it in a provision such as section 468 of the Code.

If there were sufficient interest in the matter, one way to test the arguments and conclusions advanced in this text would be to refer a constitutional question for the advice of the courts. The reference might be something like this:

Does the Parliament of Canada have legislative authority under section 91(27) to provide for a unified criminal court in a province or territory by enacting the following amendments to the *Criminal Code*?

- Amend section 468 by deleting the word 'superior,' thus leaving only a 'court of criminal jurisdiction';
- Amend the definition of a 'court of criminal jurisdiction' to designate, for each province and territory, whether that court is the Superior Court or the Provincial Court;
- Repeal section 469 and the definition of 'superior court of criminal jurisdiction' in section 2;
- Amend section 552 to say that 'judge' has, in each province and territory, the same meaning as a 'court of criminal jurisdiction' defined in section 2.

For greater certainty, these amendments (and all consequential amendments arising therefrom) would allow Parliament to designate for each province and territory whether trial jurisdiction over indictable offences not in the absolute jurisdiction of the Provincial Court would lie in the Superior court or the Provincial court, and they would allow Provincial and Territorial Courts designated as courts of criminal jurisdiction to conduct jury trials.

This question might be improved but at least it is more precise than the matters considered in *McEvoy*.

NOTES

All my thanks to M.O.H.
This essay is an abbreviated version of the original. The original of this essay first published in (2003) 48 *Criminal Law Quarterly* 31.

1 The idea of a unified criminal court has been mooted for some time. The possibility was discussed in M. Lalonde, 'The Future of a Unified Criminal Court' (1980) 4 *Provincial Judges Journal*, 3. See also the Law Reform Commission of Canada, *Toward a Unified Criminal Court*, Working Paper 59 (Ottawa: Public Works and Government Services Canada, 1989).
2 The third of these possibilities could also include a national court of criminal jurisdiction created under the authority of section 101 of the *Constitution Act, 1867*. This option was considered by the Law Reform Commission, and more recently in Gerald Seniuk and Noel Lyon, 'The Supreme Court of Canada and the Provincial Court in Canada' (2000) 79 *Canadian Bar Review* 77.
3 R.S.C. 1985, c. C-46 (as am.).

4 The Court of Nunavut is a unified criminal court that could be created as such because Nunavut, not being a province, was for constitutional purposes a jurisdiction within a unitary state.

5 This is so with all indictable offences except those listed in sections 469 and 553: see the right of election in section 536 of the Code. The same point applies to hybrid offences in which the Crown must elect between indictable and summary procedure; if the Crown elects indictable procedure, the matter might be tried in a Superior Court or in a Provincial Court, depending upon the definition of the 'court of criminal jurisdiction' in the province or territory and, of course, depending upon the election of the accused.

6 For example, courts of oyez and terminer and of gaol delivery. Sir James Fitzjames Stephen in *A Digest of the Law of Criminal Procedure in Indictable Offences* (London: Macmillan, 1883), article 16, includes the courts of oyez and terminer and gaol delivery among the superior courts of criminal jurisdiction in England. See also his *History of the Criminal Law* (London: Macmillan, 1883), Vol. I ch. 4–6 passim, esp. p. 97 *et seq*. This view was apparently confirmed in section 538 of the *Criminal Code* as enacted in 1892 by 55–56 Vict., c. 29.

7 Although appointed under section 96, the district and county courts were inferior courts because they did not have the characteristics of a Superior Court. Any court that is not a Superior Court is better viewed as an inferior court. Among other things it had no jurisdiction to grant prerogative relief. Moreover, it did not have general and inherent jurisdiction. It is self-evident, of course, that the term 'inferior court' in no way signifies a qualitative assessment of its competence. While that might have been a tenable view many years ago, it is unsustainable today.

8 *McEvoy v. Attorney General of New Brunswick*, [1983] 1 S.C.R. 704, 4 C.C.C. (3d) 289, 148 D.L.R. (3d) 25; *Reference re: Young Offenders Act, s. 2 (P.E.I.),* [1991] 1 S.C.R. 252, 62 C.C.C. (3d) 385, 77 D.L.R. (4th) 492; *MacMillan Bloedel Ltd. v. Simpson*, [1995] 4 S.C.R. 725, 103 C.C.C. (3d) 225, 44 C.R. (4th) 277. These cases are reviewed below in turn.

9 See, for example, *Reference re Adoption Act*, [1938] S.C.R. 398; *Ontario (Attorney General) v. Victoria Medical Building Ltd.*, [1960] S.C.R. 32; *Reference re: Jurisdiction of Magistrate's Court Act*, [1965] S.C.R. 772, 55 D.L.R. (2d) 701; *Seminary of Chicoutimi v. Quebec (Attorney General)*, [1973] S.C.R. 681 *sub nom. Seminaire de Chicoutimi v. Chicoutimi (City)*, 27 D.L.R. (3d) 356; *Quebec (Attorney General) v. Farrah*, [1978] 2 S.C.R. 638, 86 D.L.R. (3d) 161, 21 N.S.R. 595; *Crevier v. Quebec (Attorney General)*, [1981] 2 S.C.R. 220, 127 D.L.R. (3d) 1, 38 N.R. 541; *Reference re: Residential Tenancies Act*, [1981] 1 S.C.R. 714 *sub nom. Residential Tenancies Act, 1979 (Re)*, 123 D.L.R. (3d) 554; *Reference re: Sec-*

*tion 6 of the Family Relations Act*, [1982] 1 S.C.R. 62, 131 D.L.R. (3d) 257, [1982] 3 W.W.R. 1. For discussion see Peter Hogg, *Constitutional Law of Canada*, 4th ed. (Toronto: Carswell, 1997), 190–97 and 505–11.

10  W.R. Lederman, 'The Independence of the Judiciary' (1956) 34 *Canadian Bar Review*, 769.

11  A central point must be clarified and emphasized here. This discussion is concerned only with the jurisdiction of courts over the subject-matter of offences. This is what is meant by 'trial jurisdiction' or 'jurisdiction for purposes of trial.' There is no issue concerning the existence of Superior Courts and there is no issue concerning their jurisdiction in matters of judicial review and prerogative relief. It is accepted as a matter of constitutional principle that Superior Courts cannot be eliminated from Canadian judicature. Subject to possible reform and replacement by an alternative statutory scheme for appeal or review of a Provincial Court, it is also accepted that the jurisdiction of a Superior Court to review the decisions of the Provincial Court cannot be eliminated. The sole question is whether there are some offences over which the Superior Court must be given exclusive or concurrent jurisdiction for purposes of trial.

12  *Judicature Act*, R.S.N.B. 1973, c. J-2 (as am.).

13  *McEvoy*, 709.

14  (1981), 127 D.L.R. (3d) 214, 62 C.C.C. (2d) 165, 36 N.B.R. (2d) 609 (C.A.).

15  See the articles by Robin Elliot: 'Is Section 96 Binding on Parliament?' (1982) 16 *U.B.C. Law Review*, 313 and 'New Brunswick Unified Criminal Court Reference' (1984) 18 *U.B.C. Law Review*, 127.

16  Hogg, *Constitutional Law*, 506–11.

17  *McEvoy*, 719–21.

18  *Ibid.*, 717.

19  The Court thus implicitly approves an assertion, rejected by the New Brunswick Court of Appeal, by Willis, 'Section 96 of the British North America Act' (1940) 18 *Canadian Bar Review* 517 at 523: 'It is *ultra vires* a provincial legislature "to take away [the whole of] the jurisdiction of a Court presided over by a Judge appointed by Federal authority and transfer that jurisdiction to a Judge (or other officer) appointed by the Provincial Executive" for such legislation is an indirect method of appointing a Judge of a Superior, District or County Court.' Not only does the Supreme Court approve this assertion; it extends it to Parliament, thus denying the conclusion of the Court of Appeal that the matter is properly characterized as being within Parliament's authority under section 91(27) of the *Constitution Act, 1867*.

20  See Hogg, *Constitutional Law*, 508.

21  *McEvoy*, 720.

22  *Ibid.*, 717.
23  This is the only provision of the Code that expressly reserves exclusive trial jurisdiction to the Superior Court. There is no provision of the Code that expressly reserves jurisdiction over jury trials to the Superior Court.
24  In principle, then, a prosecutor has the discretion to prefer a charge for an offence listed in section 553 before the Superior Court, but this is done rarely.
25  This has been the case only since 1985, by amendment of section 552: see section 553 (magistrates), section 552 (court of criminal jurisdiction) and section 469 (superior court of criminal jurisdiction).
26  It may be noted that section 473 of the Code permits offences listed in section 469 to be tried before a judge of the Superior Court, sitting alone, upon the consent of the accused and the Attorney General.
27  The evolution of this jurisdiction is apparent in the history of what is now section 552, which is traced in *Crankshaw's Criminal Code of Canada* (1993, as revised), vol. 3: 19–1 to 19–8.
28  This point was acknowledged in *McEvoy.*
29  This was the effect of *Frey v. Fedoruk,* [1950] S.C.R. 517, 97 C.C.C. 1, 10 C.R. 26.
30  There is a further irony here, which is that if the general and inherent jurisdiction of the Superior Courts over common law crimes is an essential constitutional characteristic of such courts, the abolition of that jurisdiction must have been constitutionally invalid. This conclusion is seemingly compelled by the theory, adopted in *McEvoy* and other cases, that sections 96 to 100 of the *Constitution Act, 1867* imply an irreducible trial jurisdiction of the Superior Courts.
31  This characterization is odd in at least one respect, which is that it is based upon jurisdiction over the offender rather than the offence. It is this novelty that allows the Chief Justice to assert that the matter is not constrained by the allocation of jurisdiction in 1867. It will be apparent that the identification of some element of novelty is an elastic and flexible exercise. Indeed, it may be said that as the Provincial Court did not exist in 1867 with the attributes that it now has, there might be no impediment to allocation of criminal jurisdiction to it generally, and not only in respect of jurisdiction over young offenders. This point is made and explored by Seniuk and Lyon, 'The Supreme Court.'
32  Whether there was a specialized jurisdiction or procedure for dealing with young offenders is a matter for further consideration. In 1869 Parliament passed *An Act Respecting the Trial and Punishment of Juvenile Offenders* (32–33 Vict., c. 33) and *An Act Respecting Juvenile Offenders within the Province of Quebec* (32–33 Vict., c. 34). It would be of interest to ascertain how these enactments consolidated pre-Confederation law or differed from it.

33 Citing Keith Mason 'The Inherent Jurisdiction of the Court,' (1983) 57
   *A.L.J.* 449.
34 Lederman, 'Independence of the Judiciary,' 1168–70.
35 In 1956, as today, the *Constitution Act, 1867* contains no provisions on judicature that apply to the Provincial Court.
36 This point was asserted unambiguously by the Supreme Court in *R. v.
   Valente*, [1985] 2 S.C.R. 673, 23 C.C.C. (3d) 193, 49 C.R. (3d) 97.
37 One can leave aside the difficult question whether administrative tribunals
   more closely resemble courts. It is of some interest, however, to note what
   appear to be three distinct phases in the evolution of the Lederman Thesis.
   The first, stated by Lederman himself, was the contrast between the irreducible core of the Superior Court's jurisdiction and that of provincial tribunals, including both administrative bodies and 'minor provincial courts.'
   The second, presented here as the modified Lederman Thesis, concerns the
   contrast between independent courts and administrative tribunals. The
   third, yet uncertain, concerns claims that some administrative tribunals
   might have some characteristics of a court.
38 *Reference re: Independence and Impartiality of Judges of the Provincial Court of
   Prince Edward Island*, [1997] 3 S.C.R. 3, 118 C.C.C. (3d) 193, 150 D.L.R. (4th)
   577, *sub nom. Reference re: Provincial Court Act and Public Sector Pay Reduction
   Act (P.E.I.), s. 10*, supp. reasons [1998] 1 S.C.R. 3, 121 C.C.C. (3d) 474, 155
   D.L.R. (4th) 1, motion for directions refused July 9, 1998, motion to extend
   period of suspension granted [1998] 2 S.C.R. 443 (hereafter the *Provincial
   Judges Reference*). This decision is reviewed in Gerald Seniuk, 'Judicial
   Independence and the Supreme Court of Canada' (1998) 77 *Canadian Bar
   Review* 381.
39 This conclusion was firmly criticized by Jean Leclair and Yves-Marie Moris-
   sette 'L'indépendance et la Cour suprême: Reconstruction historique dou-
   teuse et théorie constitutionnelle de complaisance' (1998) 36 *Osgoode Hall
   Law Journal* 485. See also the discussion in Seniuk and Lyon, 'The Supreme
   Court.'
40 In the criminal context it is not possible for the provinces to usurp the
   authority of Parliament in the allocation of criminal jurisdiction over
   offences. Under section 91(27) only Parliament can make this allocation.
   Moreover, the *Criminal Code* contains a comprehensive scheme for this purpose that excludes the necessity of any residual doctrine that jurisdiction
   lies in the Superior Court. That is, the allocation of jurisdiction is made
   entirely within a statutory scheme established by Parliament. It has been
   argued that a core of jurisdiction in the Superior Court is a constitutional
   imperative in Canadian federalism so as to preclude the possibility that the

provinces might usurp the jurisdiction of the Superior Court by the creation of provincial courts and tribunals and by the allocation to them of a jurisdiction that would otherwise lie in the superior court. This argument has no merit whatever in criminal matters because the attribution of jurisdiction over offences lies exclusively with the legislative authority of Parliament and is determined in a comprehensive statutory scheme for this purpose in the *Criminal Code.*

41  [2001] 2 S.C.R. 3, 155 C.C.C. (3d) 1, 200 D.L.R. (4th) 1. See also *Moreau-Bérubé v. New Brunswick (Judicial Council)*, [2002] 1 S.C.R. 249 and *Her Majesty in Right of the Province of New Brunswick v. Mackin,* [2002] 1 S.C.R. 405.

42  If trial by jury in civil matters were also considered a constitutional imperative, the abolition of this mode of trial in Quebec would have to be unconstitutional.

43  If trial by jury in civil matters were also considered a constitutional imperative, the abolition of this mode of trial in Quebec would have to be unconstitutional.

# PART TWO

## Comtemporary Projects of Trial Court Reform

# 5 Reform of the Trial Courts in Quebec

HUGUETTE ST-LOUIS

*The province of Quebec's distinctive character has always been evident in its judicial system. Unlike the common law provinces, Quebec did not rely on federally appointed County or District Court judges to administer justice at the local level. Instead it had a highly decentralized Superior Court and an extensive network of courts presided over by provincially appointed judges. The judges of Quebec's lower criminal court, the Court of Sessions, had security of tenure and professional qualifications commensurate with those of federally appointed judges decades before this development occurred in the rest of Canada. Similarly, Quebec has exceeded the other provinces in expanding the civil jurisdiction of its provincially appointed judiciary. Clearly, Quebec has endeavoured to retain as much control as possible over its justice system.*

*In this chapter, Huguette St-Louis, at the time of writing chief justice of the Court of Quebec, shows how the court over which she presided consolidates these tendencies in the evolution of Quebec's court system. The Court of Quebec's criminal and civil jurisdiction exceeds that of any Provincial or Territorial Court, save the Nunavut Court of Justice. In the criminal area, it tries all cases except jury trials. The monetary limit of its jurisdiction in civil cases is being raised from $30,000 to $70,000. It has been a pace-setter in the trial of small civil claims, instituting a less formal and more accessible system of adjudication that functions without the participation of professional lawyers. The Court of Quebec also has a large jurisdiction in administrative matters. Approximately forty provincial laws give the court an appellate jurisdiction in many matters, including appeals from the Rental Board, the Commission d'acces a l'information, and provincial income tax appeals. Court of Quebec judges compose Quebec's Professions Tribunal and Human Rights Tribunal.*

*The Court of Quebec is not far from having a comprehensive trial jurisdiction that covers all of the functions of inferior and superior courts. Assuming Patrick Healy's argument presented earlier in this book stands up and there is no constitutional bar to legislatures assigning Superior Court functions to a court whose judges are provincially appointed, Quebec would be expected to be the first province to give its Provincial Court full trial jurisdiction. If this occurs, it will be interesting to see what happens to Quebec's Superior Court with its federally appointed judges and the extent to which it continues to exercise a concurrent jurisdiction with the Court of Quebec.*

I am one of those who believe that the courts are not static institutions. On the contrary, they must adapt to the expectations of the system's users. In an article published in 2000 in the *Canadian Bar Review,* Judge Gerald Seniuk and Professor Noel Lyon showed that the development of the Provincial Courts raises many problems, not the least of them being the tendency of the system to evolve in a way that no longer fits the constitutional framework.[1] In this context, and in light of concrete examples and the reflections of experts, we must be particularly attentive to this issue.

The Court of Quebec, in its current form, is a relatively recent institution. Nevertheless, it is rooted in the history of Quebec, more specifically, in the *Quebec Act* of 1774.[2] This act, which came into effect in 1775, re-established French civil law and formally implemented British criminal law. The Court's genealogy can in fact be traced to this period, before the *Constitution Act* of 1867. With the *Quebec Act*, the Court of Quebec shares its ancestry with the Superior Court and the Court of Appeal.

That being said, I intend to discuss the 1988 reform of the Quebec provincial trial courts, which resulted in the unification of three separate courts, thereby creating the Court of Quebec. At the time, I was a member of one of these courts, having been appointed to the Provincial Court in 1984.

## A Wind of Change

As elsewhere in the world, the 1960s marked a turning point for Quebec, with a wind of change sweeping new ideas across the province. We refer to this period as the Quiet Revolution. No sector of social life was left untouched. The economy, healthcare, work, education, culture, and the role of the state, were all profoundly affected. Although not a sociologist, I believe we witnessed the birth of a new Quebec society, one that was much more open, focused on the future, and more confident in its abilities.

In the area of justice, this was also a turning point, a period of questioning institutions as they existed and of innovations stemming from the new social realities. For example, 1971 saw the adoption of the *Crime Victims Compensation Act*, of the *Act to Promote Access to Justice (Small Claims)* and of the *Legal Aid Act*.[3] In 1975 Quebec established a Charter of Human Rights and Freedoms.[4] In 1978, Quebec adopted the *Automobile Insurance Act*[5] which instituted a regime of no-fault insurance, and in the same year also created the Judicial Council. In fact, a large number of significant laws came into effect during the 1970s and 1980s, under the impetus of the collective questioning initiated several years earlier.

Quebec did not have a justice department until 1965, matters of justice being handled up to then in a somewhat less structured manner. The creation of a department proved to be a turning point for justice. The Department of Justice subsequently assumed responsibility for all issues relating to justice. It led, among others, to the publication in 1975 of a very important working paper, whose impact was (and still is) determinant on the types of reforms to be undertaken. This document, entitled 'La Justice contemporaine,' proposed for the first time a comprehensive vision of the justice system and the adoption of concrete measures to improve it and make it more accessible.[6] The measures included the unification of the provincial trial courts.

However, it was not until 1988, thirteen years later, that the National Assembly adopted an act following up on this recommendation.[7] The Court of Quebec was thus created through the unification of the Provincial Court, the Court of the Sessions of the Peace, and the Youth Court, and the disappearance of the Court of Justices of the Peace. In the speech he gave on adopting the act creating the Court, the justice minister told members of the National Assembly that the goal of the unification was to promote a justice system that was 'more efficient and more adapted to the needs and expectations of the 'justiciables' (that is, those who use the courts). This act, was intended to simplify the system, reduce the number of courts, counter the dispersion of jurisdictions and improve the mobility of judges.

Before the unification of these courts, Quebec had seven courts of justice, namely the Court of Appeal, the Superior Court, the three courts I just mentioned, the municipal courts, and the Court of Justices of the Peace. In addition, Quebec litigants could be called to appear before the Supreme Court of Canada and the Federal Court. Although the number of courts by itself did not complicate matters, it must be said that for the litigant, understanding the judicial system was not an easy task, each court having its own jurisdiction, organization, and distinct practices.

The first court to be part of the unification was the Provincial Court. This court exercised jurisdiction in civil and administrative, as well as criminal and penal matters. In addition, it had a significant appellate jurisdiction with respect to decisions rendered by boards or bodies that were not part of the judicial system. Lastly, this court also heard small claims cases. In criminal and penal matters, the court's judges also had the same jurisdiction as judges of the Court of the Sessions of the Peace, and in certain circumstances ruled on proceedings brought for violations of municipal ordinances or by-laws, as well as certain provisions of the Criminal Code. Its jurisdiction in criminal and penal cases was mostly exercised where, in a given region, there was neither a Court of the Sessions of the Peace nor a Municipal Court.

The Provincial Court was an independent court, having its own structure based on the existence of two appeal divisions – one in Montreal, the other in Quebec City – which in fact meant two quasi-independent administrative units. The court was composed of approximately 150 judges.

The second court to be part of the unification was the Court of the Sessions of the Peace. This court heard criminal and penal cases with the possibility of appeal. In criminal matters, it sometimes had exclusive jurisdiction, and sometimes concurrent jurisdiction with the Superior Court. In fact, only jury trials were outside its jurisdiction. The judges of this court also ruled on suits brought for breach of provincial laws. Like the Provincial Court, the Court of the Sessions of the Peace had its own structure, based on the existence of two appeal divisions. It was composed of approximately sixty judges.

The third court to be part of the unification was the Youth Court. This court exercised its jurisdiction under the federal *Young Offenders Act* and Quebec's *Youth Protection Act* and *Adoption Act*. It also heard cases involving the breach of a provincial law committed by a minor. This court had its own unique structure. It was composed of approximately forty-five judges.

Prior to 1988, these three courts were completely independent of each other and even had practically autonomous divisions within their own structure. To further simplify things, certain jurisdictions could be exercised concurrently. Each of these courts had its own judges in authority and even a bicephalous management arising from the compartmentalization of appeal divisions in Montreal and Quebec City. Each division had its own management system, its own policies and its own rules of practice.

For litigants and lawyers, the system was unnecessarily complex, requiring them to be familiar with different standards, often within the same court, and to deal with numerous different individuals. An understanding of every facet of the system was a heroic feat, since, as we all know, ignorance is no excuse! The situation resulted in unnecessary delays, the judges of one court being able to hear only cases within the jurisdiction of the court to which they belonged. For example, a judge of the Court of the Sessions of the Peace, hearing a criminal case outside a large urban centre could not hear a civil case, regardless of its importance. Worse yet, a Provincial Court judge who went to hear a civil case in a region where the Court of the Sessions of the Peace was sitting could not hear a criminal case, even if he had jurisdiction. The litigant then had to wait for the right judge from the right court.

It goes without saying that these three independent structures made unified management and resource planning difficult, if not impossible. I would add that this situation in some way 'diluted' judicial power with respect to executive power, each of the chief judges having to do the best they could for the benefit of the court of which they assumed control. The situation was also characterized by an absence of mobility and versatility of judges. The result was far from promoting consistency of thought and action for the courts in question. It was necessary to act. Hence, the creation of the Court of Quebec.

## Court of Quebec

The act creating the Court of Quebec brought together and harmonized the jurisdictions of these three constituent courts. Accordingly, the Court of Quebec comprises the Youth Chamber, the Civil Chamber, and the Criminal and Penal Chamber. At the time, it also included the Expropriation Chamber which was later abolished. Obviously, a new structure had to be defined. The 1988 act stipulated that the Court would comprise two regional divisions, Montreal and Quebec City, with each regional division comprising the three above-named Chambers.

In 1988, management of the court was assumed by a chief judge, assisted in each regional division by a senior associate chief judge. This judge was in turn assisted by seven associate chief judges – that is, three in Quebec City and four in Montreal, of which I was one. The nineteen coordinating judges, residing in the county seats of the main judicial districts, completed the team. All these judges had the same assignment power delegated by the chief judge. It is easy to imagine that at times the puisne judges did not know which chief to bow to!

The structure set up by the 1988 unification and the management functions of the judges were reviewed in 1995. On the basis of past experience, it became obvious that the objectives pursued when the court was created in 1988 could not be entirely achieved unless changes were made. For example, it appeared that maintaining the two regional divisions of Montreal and Quebec City, both totally independent of each other, ran counter to the unity of the court and the consistency of its practices. Also, the presence of ten chief judges having powers of assignment and deciding court policies did little to ease communication between themselves and the puisne judges, nor the participation of the latter in the decisions and policies of the court. In effect, communication between the chief judge and the puisne judges was hampered by an overly cumbersome structure.

Major changes were needed to optimize the effects anticipated by the 1988 unification. This is why the chief judge at the time asked the legislature to simplify the organization of the court while keeping in mind the following objectives:

- pursue the unification already initiated;
- reduce differences between regional divisions, both with respect to judicial practice and administrative practice;
- promote the development of a feeling of belonging by judges;
- promote the participation of judges in drawing up the court's policies;
- promote the consultation of all judges on judicial and administrative practices and encourage their involvement and participation in the various activities of the court; and, lastly
- consolidate regional self-sufficiency.

Essentially, the regional divisions of Montreal and Quebec City were abandoned and the number of senior associate chief judges was reduced to one. The number of associate chief judges was reduced to three one for each Chamber of the Court (Civil, Youth, and Criminal and Penal) and they no longer have a power of assignment but act as advisors in their respective jurisdiction. Lastly, the number of coordinating judges was reduced from nineteen to ten, a number corresponding to the current judicial regions.

In this structure, the power of assignment stems directly from the chief judge to the coordinating judge. In fact, the new structure was intended to refocus organization of the court around the chief judge and the coordinating judges so as to simplify the management of the court's judicial activities and improve participation of the judges in all regions. Since 1995, issues confronting the court are discussed at meetings held five times a year, which bring together the chief judge and the coordinating judges, thereby enabling better two-way communication. All judges now receive a copy of the minutes of these meetings. Also, the chief judge, senior associate chief judge, and associate chief judges hold regular meetings. Since 1996, all the judges have held an annual meeting at which they are encouraged to participate in workshops on topics of a more administrative nature that are of direct interest to them.

The creation of the Court of Quebec has significantly changed the judicial landscape in Quebec. Overnight, the court has in effect become the largest judicial body in Quebec, be it in terms of jurisdiction, the number of cases heard, the number of points of service or the number of member judges. The court has 270 judges working across the province at fifty-four points of service on a permanent basis and at forty-four others on a temporary basis. With the exclusion of cases heard by the municipal courts, it hears more than 80 per cent of Quebec court cases. That means 99 per cent of criminal cases, 100 per cent of penal cases (there are some one hundred jury trials a year), 99 per cent of youth protection, delinquency and adoption cases, and 79 per cent of civil cases, including small claims files (otherwise 71 per cent). Legislation has been introduced in the National Assembly to raise the monetary ceiling of the Court of Quebec's jurisdiction in civil cases from $30,000 to $70,000. This will bring the percentage of civil cases in the province dealt with by the Court of Quebec to well over 79 per cent.[8]

## Objectives Attained?

The Court of Quebec is a young institution which, in some respects, is constantly evolving. However, one may wonder whether thirteen years later, the unification has attained its objectives. Although the process has no doubt been fruitful, nonetheless there remains some way to go. As a matter of fact, although the court's current structure facilitates communication, it must be said that it is very difficult to satisfy everyone, even though there has never been so much information available to judges or so many consultations held to seek their views. Some judges fear that better organization is synonymous with bureaucratization of the judiciary. Clearly, I do not share their view. On the contrary, I believe that the better organized the judiciary, the stronger it will be towards the executive, thereby asserting its judicial independence.

This new entity was given its member judges the means to better administer justice. Accordingly, since 1988, a policy has been adopted to even out workloads and define the correct balance between each assignment (time sitting/time deliberating). This measure has resulted in greater equity in the division of tasks to be accomplished. The court is also committed to attaining target deadlines so as to better meet the expectations of litigants. In fact, these deadlines are generally respected, except for specific problems. For example, the court encourages judges to be versatile, that is, be able to hear cases in all areas that fall under the court's jurisdiction. This versatility is found primarily outside the large urban centres. The volume of cases in the major cities in all jurisdictions is so high that such versatility is not as essential there.

The sheer strength of numbers and the fact that the judges are now appointed for the entire province and with jurisdiction in all areas enables the court to administer justice more uniformly in all regions and in all fields. For example, in case of vacancies, we have transferred positions from one region to another, or from one Chamber to another when the needs required it. The court is therefore now able to effectively 'manage' the positions of judges based on the real needs of litigants. Versatility, administrative consistency, and mobility of judges throughout the province also enable the court to better deal with specific situations.

Accordingly, the creation of the court has enabled it to organize itself better, and to sustain its judicial activity more adequately and efficiently. This had not been possible with the three separate organizations from which it is issued. The organization of a court of justice involves the participation of judges. This involvement comes specifically through various committees where the numerous problems related to the court's activities and the overall exercise of judicial function are discussed. The participation of judges in these committees improves communication and discussions between from different regions and from different chambers, as well as between puisne judges and judges in management positions. Over time, this participation promotes the development of a feeling of belonging to the court and pride in being part of it. These committees deal with issues such as training, computerization, legal documentation, the presence of media in the courtroom, rules of practice, case flow management, and so on. The unification, through the discussions it has allowed between judges, also promoted the standardization of legal practice between regions.

I would also like to stress that unification has enabled the implementation of a major, varied, structured training program which I believe is something to be envied. At the request of judges working as coaches, we have even released one judge full time to assume responsibility for tracking the program, ensuring it meets the needs of judges, proposing topics that could be the subject of seminars, recruiting resource persons, and so forth. This program is functioning well and although it remains to be developed, we can say that judges, for the most part, actively participate and draw major benefits from it. It is clear that the situation prior to 1988 would not have enabled the implementation of a training program of such quality.

## Conclusion

I believe the experience acquired since 1988 has shown the positive advantages of unification and justified those who were promoting it at the time. In light of this positive experience, and following the same logic, I believe it would be appropriate to continue this process. Evidently, however, this exercise presents its challenges, three of which spring to mind: the implementation of true administrative independence for the courts; recognition of the constitutional status of Provincial Courts; and the implementation and integration into judicial activity of a justice one might call 'Justice.com.'

The first challenge to be addressed is true administrative independence. The relevance of administrative independence stems first and foremost from the control that the executive exercises over the resources it allocates to the judiciary. Not only does it determine the level of these resources, but it manages them and directs the personnel assigned to the court. It goes without saying that this status of dependency, this administrative subordination of the judiciary to the executive, is a source of considerable friction which affects the operation of the court. To ensure the separation of powers, implement the institutional independence recommended by the Supreme Court, and ensure better administration of justice, we have to set up an effective regime for the court's administrative independence.

The second challenge, clearly unavoidable, is the constitutional issue. It is extremely well documented and to be convinced, one need only read the paper by Seniuk and Lyon and other contributions to this book. More recently, in the preface to attorney Luc Huppé's book entitled *Le régime juridique du pouvoir judiciaire*[9] (*The Legal Regime of Judicial Power*), former Supreme Court Justice Louis-Philippe de Grandpré wrote the following:

> Barely fifty years ago, the provincial courts had only very minimum jurisdiction, with only the Court of the Sessions of the Peace having jurisdiction in penal cases by delegation of federal powers. At the time, in civil cases, there was the Circuit Court, whose members were named by the federal government. The jurisdiction of this Court was minor, with all major cases going to the Superior Court, the major trial court inherited from Great Britain through changes to the constitutional acts culminating in 1867. The past fifty years have brought us the Court of Quebec, whose jurisdiction is immense. This major reorientation is clearly politically correct, but one might wonder whether it is legally correct. That's a subject that will have to be addressed one day.

Personally, I would go even further and say that the unification of the trial courts is unavoidable and will happen one day. This would be in the best interest of the society, in terms of consistency, efficiency, and inherent costs. In my opinion, our experience shows that in Quebec we are ready to unify the Superior Court and the Court of Quebec into one court of first instance, in the best interest of the administration of justice and of the public in general. So how do we achieve this? I do not have the formula. The obstacles are numerous and varied in nature, but, with effort, they can certainly be overcome. We must strive to find the solutions.

The final challenge of unification is rooted in technological advances. Since Gutenberg invented the printing press in 1440, there has been no greater innovation in the realm of knowledge and communication than the advent of the internet. It is clear that the courts, the judiciary, and the legal community will be deeply transformed by this revolution. Not only must we integrate and master these new technologies, but we must now contemplate the new parameters of virtual courts, both in a local context and as part of the global village. This will be no small task.

NOTES

1 Gerald Seniuk and Noel Lyon 'The Supreme Court of Canada and the Provincial Court in Canada.' (2000) 79 *Canadian Bar Review* 77.
2 14 George III, c. 83 (U.K.).
3 *Crime Victims Compensation Act*, R.S.Q. 1971, c. I-6; *An Act to Promote Access to Justice (Small Claims)* S.Q. 1971, c. 86 which amended the Code of Civil Procedure of Quebec, R.S.Q. 1977, c. C-25; *Legal Aid Act*, R.S.Q. 1971, C. A-14.
4 *Quebec Charter of Human Rights and Freedoms*, R.S.Q. 1975, c. C-12.
5 *Automobile Insurance Act*, R.S.Q. 1977, c. A-25
6 Jérôme Choquette *Justice Today* (Quebec: Gouvernement du Québec, 1975).
7 *Court of Justice Act*, R.S.Q., c. T-16.
8 The legislation was passed on 8 June 2002 (*An Act to reform the Code of Civil Procedure*, S.Q. 2002, c. 7).
9 Luc Huppé, *Le Régime juridique du pouvoir judiciaire* (Montreal: Wilson and Lafleur, 2000).

# 6  Trial Court Restructuring:
## A Court Administrator's Perspective

MARIAN TYSON

*In this chapter, Marian Tyson, brings the insights and concerns of a profes-
sional court administrator to bear on the court restructuring debate. The success of any court reform, as much as the best possible performance of the
existing structure, depends on skilled, dedicated, and knowledgeable court
administrators. The emergence of court administration as an important jus-
tice-system profession has significantly increased Canada's capacity to
improve the services offered by our courts.*

*Speaking at the time as the president of the Association of Canadian Courts
Administrators, Tyson, understandably, did not align herself or her association with either side of the unification debate. Instead, she stresses the importance of identifying the practical objectives of structural change and assessing
reform proposals in terms of those objectives.*

*Tyson also draws on her experience with the day-to-day operations of the
court system to remind us of important changes that have been occurring in
the trial court system. One is the devolution of judicial or quasi-judicial functions to non-judges – prothonotaries and part-time adjudicators in the civil
courts, JPs in the criminal courts. Another related development is the drive for
less cumbersome and more accessible procedures. Restructuring of the trial
court system will have difficulty succeeding in a practical sense if it ignores
these trends.*

*In a setting where there is clearly a lack of consensus within the judiciary
on amalgamation of the courts themselves, Tyson underlines the advantages to
be gained by amalgamating administrative and physical facilities. Her discussion indicates that improvements in the coordination of court services and use
of court houses can offer consumers of justice a 'one-stop' system that significantly enhances Canadians' access to justice.*

As the current president[1] of the Association of Canadian Court Administrators (ACCA) and a senior court administrator from the province of Nova Scotia, my comments on trial court restructuring will reflect the practical administrative dimensions of the subject.

ACCA has on its board a broad range of people from across the country, including people who are senior in court administration in each of the provincial and territorial jurisdictions. As a group and individually, we have a very keen interest in court reform. When government makes a decision respecting a particular reform, to a large extent it is our staff and offices who have to make the plan work. As a group, ACCA is well positioned to participate in the dialogue respecting reform options and to provide key input to our governments across the country on reform options.

When we start to think about court reform it is useful to keep a number of things in mind. Canada has witnessed a great deal of change in its court systems in recent years and we have, I believe, throughout the country excellent court administrative staff. Successful court reform depends on having in place the supports and the tools needed to make reform options work.

It is also useful to keep in mind the big picture of what's going on in the justice system as a whole and how trial court reform fits into that picture. For example, we have criminal procedure reform under way and family court unification at various stages across the country. We are introducing technology that will have an enormous impact on the courts and their administration. And, as all of us working in the system know, an increasing number of self-represented litigants are appearing in our courts and at our counters. These trends and changes have an impact on reform, any kind of reform, and we need to take all of them into account when considering reform options.

Governments can only do so many things at one time. We must deal not only with competing demands for dollars but also for the time and resources needed to steer reforms through and make them work. Governments often find it easier to do the things that clearly need to be done and on which there is consensus. So when we see strongly divergent views, as is the case with trial court reform, and in particular criminal court reform, with, for example, a large number of Superior Court judges on one side of the issue and a large number of provincial judges on the other side, and strong groups such as the Canadian Bar Association, the Canadian Judicial Council, and the Law Reform Commission supporting one position or the other, it isn't any wonder that after about twenty years of working at the subject so little progress has been made. Indeed, David Hancock, the attorney general in Alberta, in his paper says that we have actually been working on this for thirty years.[2]

In my twenty-seven years of working with government, I have observed that governments will often postpone deciding an issue with the hope that one of two things will occur. The first is that somehow the parties or the stakeholders will get together and actually resolve the issues so that government will not have to make a decision one way or the other. Or secondly, that the problem will just disappear and government will not have to make any decision on the matter. The latter is exactly what we saw happening ten or so years ago when every provincial attorney general in the country in the mid-1990s came out in support of Criminal Court unification. At that time three jurisdictions were prepared to go ahead with a pilot project.

Nevertheless, there was fairly strong opposition on the part of the Superior Court judges, supported by the Canadian Judicial Council and the Canadian Bar Association. New Brunswick was quite persistent because at that time it had a chief justice who was interested in trying it out. But in the end, lacking the full support of the federally appointed judges that was considered necessary, New Brunswick abandoned its initiative. When it gave up, everybody gave up. Since then, the whole issue has been shelved and has only recently come back to life.

The challenge now is to agree upon a process that will enable discussion and principled debate to occur and will be geared toward resolution of changes which are in the interest of the public and the justice system as a whole. What it really comes down to is figuring out how to take self-interest out of the issue so that we can actually focus on working out which solutions are best for the justice system.

In assessing which reform options are most useful, we need to know why we are looking at reform. What are the objectives of reform? The reasons often given for trial court unification are that it will reduce delay, eliminate confusion and simplify the process. Eliminating hierarchy, reducing costs, avoiding duplication are the kinds of reasons we have heard and we have found to some extent to be applicable in family court unification. They are the reasons that I have also heard advanced for criminal court reform. We need to determine, first, whether these reasons point to serious problems in the area of criminal trial courts proposals, and secondly, whether the proposal that we are considering will effectively address these problems or whether it will create more problems than it solves, and whether there are better alternatives.

Various kinds of trial court reform are currently in progress. Administrative and legislative reforms now under way have significant implications for structural reform. Reforms of civil and family trial courts are moving forward, whereas the criminal court reform seems to be somewhat stalled. In civil court reform (and in fact in all areas of the justice system), responsibility and decision-making are being pushed down to lower levels. In our Superior Courts, senior non-judicial office holders are exercising decision-making power. In Nova Scotia, for instance, prothonotaries can now issue orders formerly issued by judges. Court staff have the power to waive court fees in accordance with regulations. The registrar of bankruptcy, a part-time official, has performed judicial duties along with his registration work, holding court one day a week.

While in some provinces small claims courts are part of the Provincial Court system or operate under the aegis of the Superior Court, in Nova Scotia they are independent free-standing courts. Our small claims court is staffed by part-time lawyers who serve as adjudicators and sit in the evenings. The recently passed *Justice Administration Amendment (2002) Act* increased the jurisdiction of small claims courts in civil suits from $10,000 to $15,000.[3]

In Nova Scotia our small claims court has recently taken on taxation of costs that were formally done by taxing officers in accordance with the *Barristers and Solicitors Act*. The legislation now before the House transfers, among other things, residential tenancy appeals and commercial appeals to the small claims court. So we have an expanding small claims court presided over by lawyers who are part-time and paid by the hour. I believe similar arrangements exist in some other jurisdictions.

The principal difference between Supreme Court trials and the small claims court trial processes is that the Supreme Court's (which is what we call over Superior Court) are process-heavy. In the Superior Court there are interrogatories, discoveries, pre-trial briefs, pre-trial hearings, post-trial briefs, interim applications, notice of trial, notice of readiness for trial, notice of expert witnesses, and so on. These complex proceedings provide all the safeguards needed to enable the parties, usually it is to be hoped, with the assistance of their lawyer, to work their way through the system and get to a result. In the small claims court, however, at least as it operates in Nova Scotia, there is very little in the way of process. Although there is now some pressure to increase the process, no agreement has been reached on this matter. Thus, we simply have people filling in an application, getting a court date, appearing before the small claims court personally or with a lawyer and making arguments. The small claims adjudicator provides an oral or written decision which is usually short and must be rendered within sixty days.

The small claims court and Superior Court have concurrent jurisdictions in cases involving $10,000 or less. This gives litigants a choice: if they want full process, they can file their action in the Supreme Court, or they can choose the small claims court with virtually no process. Nowadays more and more people are opting for the latter. The dilemma I think is that lawyers are professionals and if they are appearing in any court (but, in particular, the Supreme Court) they feel that they should be well prepared and judges expect them to be so. However many, if not most small, claims litigants, cannot afford to pay the legal expenses associated with the full process. And so we seem to have a dilemma. Litigants are better off with a lawyer than without a lawyer and therefore it is preferable for them to appear in court with a lawyer. However, if they appear in our Supreme Courts with a lawyer, then our judges expect the full preparation and are very critical of lawyers who are not fully prepared. To overcome such an all-or-nothing situation, we should be looking at something between the small claims court and the full process – a streamlined process in which lawyers do not need to do briefs, there is no discovery, and judges give oral or short decisions.

The same trend is evident in our Family Court, where decision-making is being pushed down to senior court officers. These staff members are now issuing orders and requiring disclosure. Also, in the family area, there are a number of programs intended to divert people from court and help them resolve their problems out of court. And of course, we have the unified court process and that experience in the family law area.

In the criminal courts we see the same trend in terms of devolving responsibilities to justices of the peace. Some commentators have advocated using lay judicial officers or lay justices of the peace. In Nova Scotia we have moved in the opposite direction. A hundred JPs scattered throughout the province were issuing search warrants, some of which in this Charter era have become very complicated. We were concerned that JPs who lacked any legal training, indeed who had very little training of any kind, were dealing with such complex matters. We were also concerned that being out in the communities and knowing the local police very well they would be more inclined to grant the police orders than might be the case if the police had to appear before judges or legally trained JPs. In fact, we saw some evidence that this was happening. So Nova Scotia has gone in the other direction and created a smaller number of JP centres staffed by legally-trained justices of the peace.[4] They sit in four-hour or eight-hour shifts, and a JP is on call for emergencies overnight.

Turning now to the possibility of a unified criminal court, county court amalgamation and family court unification point to two different approaches. If we were to follow the County Court amalgamation model, we would have a situation where all judges of the Provincial Court become members of the Supreme Court all at once. Alternatively, if the piecemeal elevation in the family division of the Superior Court is the model, the federal government will begin by making a limited number of appointments elevating provincially appointed judges to the Superior Court. There are problems with proceeding piecemeal. In the Family Court amalgamation, if not all judges are elevated, we could have a situation in which judges who are excellent in family law, but who may not be very interested or suitable for criminal court work, end up in the Provincial Court doing criminal law because that is really the only option left for them. We have a shrinking Family Court, which raises issues about sufficient coverage of the courts, and systems and processes, which is confusing and can result in inconsistencies.

At the present time, uncertainty about whether the federal government will find the funds to complete family court amalgamation and uncertainty about which judges will be elevated and which will not are producing a great deal of stress. Meanwhile the province has to determine whether it should appoint more Family Court judges and more Provincial Court judges. (Unlike the other provinces, Nova Scotia's Family Court is separate from its Provincial Court which is a criminal trial court.) It is difficult to manage a court system effectively amidst so much uncertainty.

We started out to improve the system by combining two systems into one. We wanted to reduce delay. We wanted to avoid duplication. We wanted to avoid hierarchy. We had two levels of trial courts, we were going to have one – but in fact we now have three! In this condition of incomplete reform, the public is faced with a more complex and confusing system than that in place before we started. Moreover, programs are operating in the family division areas that do not exist in other areas because of the money saved by the elevation of Family Court judges to the Family Division of the Supreme Court, and that is problematic. If we are going to proceed with criminal court unification, I would urge that, to avoid all of these problems, we follow the County Court amalgamation model.

In considering criminal court reform, the models include having all of the Provincial Court judges who are elevated or appointed to the Superior Court become members of its general pool of judges eligible for doing all of the Superior Court's work, or instead become members of a specialized criminal division similar to the family division of the Supreme Court. Carl Barr has identified four options for criminal court reform.[5] One is complete unification of the Provincial and Superior Courts into a single court, recognizing that everywhere, other than New Brunswick, justices of the peace would continue to do some minor criminal work under the direction of the Superior Court. His second option is a two-level trial court structure, which is essentially what we have now. Baar points out that the two-level trial court is the dominant reality through the common law world, and the exceptions go in the direction of even more levels – which is an interesting observation. His third option is to expand the responsibilities of Provincial Court judges in criminal cases, as Quebec has been doing to cover all criminal matters including jury trials. He believes (and as Patrick Healy argues[6]) this could be done without violating the constitutional standard established in *McEvoy*, and without shifting the appointment and remuneration of these judges to the federal government. Baar's fourth option is to leave the two court levels intact, but to manage the criminal caseload as a single enterprise so that we would have Superior Court judges and Provincial Court judges in the same buildings or buildings that are close and supported by the same staff. Working together as a team, the two groups of judges would handle all of the criminal work. The advantage of such an arrangement is that Provincial Court judges would have a broader variety of work and Superior Court judges who are interested in criminal work would have the opportunity to continue to work in that field.

Baar's fourth alternative should prompt us to consider how we can achieve some of the goals of court restructuring through administrative reforms that are already taking place. Administrative reform might mean different levels of trial courts sharing buildings, staff, equipment, courtrooms, technology, and so on. In Nova Scotia we are moving in this direction. In most areas other than our main metro area, judges are now using the same building. Also, we have staff who are multifunctional supporting all of the courts, so that a court reporter will work in the Supreme Court or the Family Court or Provincial Court. Although this sharing of resources and support systems is not yet one hundred percent complete, it is getting very close. In terms of the executive branch, one manager manages the whole operation. There is no ownership of courtrooms: although judges may use the same courtroom most of the time, they are able to use whatever courtroom and technology is available.

This merger of facilities and management works well when all the courts are in one building. However, it works less effectively when courts are operating in separate buildings, even if they are close. For example, in Sydney, Nova Scotia, when all of the courts except the Family Court were in one building, even though the Family Court was just down the street from the main courthouse, it was difficult to manage and train staff who had to run back and forth between the buildings and difficult to share courtrooms. Once the Family Court was moved into the same building as the other courts, the merged system of court administration began to work well. Integrating court administration and services works well in smaller areas and certainly saves money. The public is better served when court services are available on a one-stop shopping basis. Court staff are able to answer questions about all of the courts, direct people to the appropriate courtrooms or offices rather than having them start off at the wrong place, as so often occurs. At the outset we encountered considerable resistance to this concept, but once people saw that it was working well, we found the resistance disappeared very quickly.

Finally, in considering all of these options, we cannot ignore the cost to taxpayers as well as to litigants. Our focus should be on how we can obtain the advantages of reform while preserving some of the benefits and efficiencies associated with the existing structure. Generally, our Provincial Courts in Canada are very efficient. They process a huge number of cases with very few procedures. It is essential to consider what any move towards trial court amalgamation might mean in terms of adopting processes that slow things down and add considerably to costs. Let me conclude by quoting from the Nova Scotia Task Force report 1991: 'The unified Criminal Court is only worthwhile if it solves more or bigger problems than it creates and it does it better than any other alternative.'

## NOTES

1 Marian Tyson was president of ACCA in 2002 at the time of the Trial Courts of the Future Conference.
2 See chapter 8 below.
3 *Justice Administration Amendment (2002) Act,* royal assent 30 May 2002.
4 Presiding justices of the peace must be lawyers with five years' experience, while administrative JP's (whose duties are limited to quasi-judicial functions) do not require these qualifications.
5 See chapter 2 above.
6 See chapter 4 above.

# 7 Trial Court Unification in Nunavut

NORA SANDERS

*Nunavut, the recently created territory in the Eastern Arctic, is the only jurisdiction in Canada that has adopted a one-tier trial court. Nunavut's circumstances are, of course, highly distinctive: a small, predominantly Inuit population, spread thinly over a vast territory. As Nora Sanders, who was the territory's senior justice official when Nunavut was established in 1999, explains, giving full jurisdiction to Nunavut's tiny cadre of itinerant trial judges simply made good practical sense. In Nunavut's circumstances a two-tier trial court system would have seemed a ridiculous extravagance.*

*Nunavut's single trial court, the Nunavut Court of Justice, is a Superior Court to which the only Territorial Court judge in the Eastern Arctic has been appointed and to which two additional judges were added. Justices of the peace, who are locally resident and mostly Inuit, play an important role in Nunavut's one-tier system, not unlike that of lay JPs in the years immediately following Confederation. Provision has been made for judicial review of subordinate judicial officers and a system of appeals to a Nunavut Court of Appeal. This indicates that there are ways of dealing with the technical legal issues frequently raised in discussions of a one-tier system.*

*In her account of establishing Nunavut's justice system, Nora Sanders makes it clear that the one-tier trial court structure was not the most significant issue. Much more important were innovative ways of making the justice system responsive and accessible to the people of Nunavut. Nonetheless, her account shows how a single-tier system provides a convenient platform for managing this kind of change.*

As the deputy minister of justice for Nunavut I felt it was appropriate to begin my presentation with a few words in Inuktitut to help you understand the context of court reform in Nunavut. Those were my most careful and practised words of Inuktitut, and I think that they would be understandable to an Inuk whose first language was Inuktitut – but just barely. I am reminded of the term 'Diefenbaker French,' and I think you can understand that my Inuktitut is somewhere on that level. Indeed, that is the case with pretty well all of the *qallunaaq* or non-Inuit professionals who are working in Nunavut. It is the case with our judges and our lawyers, both Crown and defence: there is no one in that group that has a comfortable, functioning level of proficiency in Inuktitut. At the same time, we must recognize that Inuktitut is the language of the majority of people of Nunavut and that many Nunavummiut, who are the people who live in Nunavut, are not functionally comfortable in English.

Going through the experience of trying to speak in front of an esteemed group like this in a language that I am only slightly familiar with helps me understand the experience of many Inuit as they come before the courts in Nunavut. Of course, translation is provided whenever it is needed, but that is not the same as being able to understand directly what is said or being able to make yourself understood in your own words. Along with this language disparity, there are cultural gaps that are probably even more significant, although not as readily evident. These factors are much more significant in dispensing justice in the North, than determining the best legal structure for our courts.

Nunavut is the only jurisdiction in Canada with a single-level trial court, the Nunavut Court of Justice, that handles all kinds of criminal and civil cases. To those who are trained as lawyers, this is a very interesting development. There are a lot of questions to ask about how it works and whether it works. In legal terms the establishment of this single-level trial court was a major accomplishment. But to the average person in Nunavut, that is not the most significant thing about our court. The legal structure is something that is there and more or less left to the lawyers to work out.

To understand the Nunavut court, it is important to provide a little bit of the history and the setting. Nunavut became a territory officially on 1 April 1999.[1] Its creation by an act of Parliament was the result of the signing of a Land Claims Agreement between the Government of Canada and TFN, the Tungavik Federation of Nunavut, which was the organization representing the Inuit land claims beneficiaries. The government of Nunavut is a public government created as the result of a Land Claims Agreement and, as far as I know, that is something which is unique in the world. We are still learning just what that means in practice.

Between the time of the signing of the Land Claims Agreement and the birth of the new territory there were a few short and very busy years to set up the new government. Although, at the time, people often said that it would be great to start with a blank slate, that is not quite what we did. We had to have something, and often the 'something' ended up looking very much like things that we already had in the Territories or elsewhere in Canada. However, it did provide a rare opportunity to think about what structures we were going to have and what would best suit this new territory of Nunavut.

The Nunavut Implementation Commission was appointed and tasked with making the plans for all the things that needed to be done to set up the new territory. One of those things was the establishment of a court system for the new territory. The plans that the Nunavut Implementation Commission made had to be approved by three parties: the federal government, the government of the Northwest Territories, and NTI (which was what the Tungavut Federation of Nunavut had by then become) representing the Inuit land claims beneficiary group. At the time, I was the assistant deputy minister of justice in the Northwest Territories, and my initial involvement with all this was in that capacity. Partway through the process, about a year before the division of the Northwest Territories and the creation of Nunavut, I was appointed deputy minister of justice for Nunavut with the job of making sure that all of the things that we needed to have in the justice sector were in place in order to begin life as a new territory.

The decisions that were made at that time – and now I'm going to focus more specifically on the decision about courts – were made having in mind the unique character of the territory that was about to be created. Nunavut, by its very nature, presents tremendous challenges. I have touched on the language and the cultural issues. Geographically Nunavut is a huge area, about one-fifth the size of Canada but with only twenty-six communities and a population of about 27,000 people. There are no roads between any of the communities, so the main connection is by air. There are only two resident judges, both based in the capital, Iqaluit, with plans to add a third. Fly-in court circuits serve all the other communities. There are no specialized court facilities in any of the other communities. Courts are held in community halls, hamlet offices, or the school gymnasium. These premises lack any of the facilities such as interview rooms normally found in court buildings. Our geography can require the judges and the circuit court to travel distances equivalent to the distance from Edmonton to Montreal, and that is with weather, equipment, and other local conditions that can be quite challenging.

When plans were being made for the division of the Northwest Territories before the creation of Nunavut as a separate territory, there was concern about such a large territory being served by a small number of judges. At the time there was only one resident judge in what is now Nunavut, and the plan was to have a bench that would total three. Now, based on population, that might not sound too far off, but given the distances, the climate, the language and cultural gaps, it was clear that the courts in Nunavut would function in very challenging circumstances. Currently we have two full-time judges in the Nunavut Court of Justice, supplemented by deputy judges from other jurisdictions as the caseload requires – and the caseload is heavy. The judges of the Nunavut Court of Justice, although based in Iqaluit, spend many weeks of the year flying to other communities for circuit court. Generally, these are not just day trips. Often they are traveling all week, visiting several communities a great distance from home.

Operating a court on this basis may sound impossible to some. It pretty nearly is. I think what makes it possible is having exceptionally dedicated people serving as our judges and court staff, people who are willing to put up with the schedules and conditions that would probably not be considered acceptable anywhere else in Canada.

What would make it truly impossible would be having two levels of court flying around to all these communities at all this distance and having to explain to people in those small communities why this judge who comes so far and so seldom could not actually deal with their case, but someone else was going to have to come and deal with it. We think that would have made it impossible.

The decision to have a single-level trial court in Nunavut was made after consultation. This was in keeping with the spirit of the Nunavut Land Claims Agreement, which anticipates that major government decisions that have a social impact will be made after consultation with Inuit. In November 1997, there was a conference in Iqaluit organized by the Office of the Interim Commissioner for Nunavut that brought together about fifty people: judges, lawyers, justice officials, community people, court workers, Inuit JPs, many of them with experience with one aspect or another of the justice system.

The consultation conference was based on the theme 'Justice that Brings Peace.' I still like that name as I think it symbolizes the idealism of that time in our planning and perhaps some of the idealism that can continue in the ongoing work of building Nunavut. The outcome of the conference was a general consensus that we should be adopting a single-level trial court for Nunavut. The delegates concluded that court unification could meet many common interests such as simplicity, efficiency, and eliminating unnecessary levels of administration.

It was recognized that the single-level trial court was not, in itself, an Aboriginal justice initiative or a community justice initiative. It was just something we had to adopt to make the formal court system as simple and uncomplicated as possible. The decision was based much more on practical considerations than on philosophical debate. And perhaps it was easier in Nunavut because the general public there does not have a deep long-standing commitment or even understanding about the formal justice system as we know it in Canada. The system tends to be regarded as something that was brought in by outsiders, replacing the ways used traditionally for centuries to resolve disputes.

In the days before Nunavut was created, when the planning was taking place, I remember a time when a group of us were sitting around talking about the possibility of a unified court model. Someone asked what the community view was likely to be about this change, and another person in the room who had years of experience in the courts in the North explained it something like this: 'If you tried to explain to someone from the community the way the court is set up now, that we have a formal system that has two different kinds of judges that have more or less the same kind of training and experience, but we don't let some of them handle these kinds of cases and we don't let other ones handle these other kind of cases, the community member would likely turn to you and say that this seems crazy, of course we wouldn't want a system like that!'

Once the decision in principle was made to have a single-level trial court for Nunavut, there were of course the legal issues to be dealt with. Legal authority for a single-level trial court required careful study. It required consideration of many different situations that might arise and how they might be handled so as to ensure that Nunavummiut would continue to enjoy the same procedural rights as people elsewhere in Canada. That was an essential requirement. To deal with these issues we had an excellent working relationship with Justice Canada, the Interim Commissioner's Office, NTI, and the government of the Northwest Territories. Through numerous conference calls and faxes we consulted with various members of the bar and researchers from the federal Department of Justice who in turn consulted with judicial scholars across the country. Out of all this came Bill C-57 setting up the new court as well as amendments to existing legislation to eliminate the Territorial Courts Act for Nunavut and establish a new Judicature Act for Nunavut.[2]

All the legal things were done so that the Nunavut Court of Justice could come into being as a new court on April 1 1999. The judges are appointed by the federal government and have the status of Superior Court judges. That model was agreed to before the government of Nunavut had come into existence. The interim commissioner (responsible for administering Nunavut during the transitional period) gave up Nunavut's right to make judicial appointments. It is clearly easier to give up an appointing power before you have it than it is later. No formal protocol has been established yet for Nunavut participation in the federal appointment process. However, Nunavut officials have worked quite closely with federal officials on the first appointments.

The legal challenges to create the Nunavut Court of Justice did not happen in isolation. They were done in the context of a broader political and social transformation. Creation of this new and unique court was one of the things done, just one, to bring about a better set of institutions for the people of Nunavut, one that could be better understood and better respond to the needs of the public.

In fact, the single-level trial court model, which is of such interest to us as lawyers, is by no means the most significant court reform for the people of Nunavut. A number of other initiatives are much more visible and, in a practical way, touch people's lives much more closely than any change in court structure could.

One of these is increased training and responsibility for justices of the peace. Of course, that is not unique to Nunavut. But in Nunavut, where justices of the peace are not lawyers, it means we can have people exercising a judicial function who are using Inuktitut and are from that community. This gives the advantage of language as well as the advantage of not always having to wait for the court circuit to come from afar. That was a key consideration in designing the new court structure as one in which the JPs would be trained to take on a larger role.

Another important feature of the Nunavut Court of Justice is that the judges routinely have community members, usually elders, sitting with them as they hear cases. The elders advise and assist the judges and provide important community perspectives. Though such an arrangement is practised in a number of Provincial Courts, I think that it is the exception in Superior Court proceedings. The experience in Nunavut demonstrates that it is possible for Superior Court judges to use this kind of approach.

There has been a transformation in the court office in Iqaluit since 1998, and not just in the creation of the new court, the Nunavut Court of Justice. In legal and constitutional terms, the creation of the new court is an event of historic proportions. In practical terms, for anyone who walks into the court office today, the most noticeable change is the personnel who are working there. This was achieved through aggressive recruitment and individualized training programs. Now almost all of the court staff are Inuit, the workplace conversations take place in Inuktitut, and members of the public can be assisted in either Inuktitut or English. When the court party travels to communities, Inuit clerks who are able to speak to the people appearing in court in their own language go along. For most Nunavummiut, this change is more fundamental than the court structure.

Community justice committees exist in pretty well every community. There are variations from place to place in how the committees operate, and what kinds of things they take on, depending on the experience of the members, and the priorities they set. Cases are diverted to community justice committees, usually pre-charge, but sometimes post-charge. Committee members are encouraged to rely on Inuit Qaujimajatuqangit, their own cultural values, in working with the people who come before them.

A mediation project is under way called Inuusirmut Aqqusiuqtiit. It operates in the family law area as a pilot project. One of the realities with the circuit court system is that because of the size of the criminal workload, there is seldom as much time as there ideally should be to deal with family or civil cases. Many people in our communities are still largely unaware of their family law rights. Those who are aware may find it difficult to access counsel to assist them with those rights. Inuit in two communities are being trained as mediators, and they will work in conjunction with the Family Support Office in Iqaluit. Our vision is that through a family mediation process using local people operating in Inuktitut, real progress can be made in developing an alternative processes which could ultimately be expanded into other civil law areas.

Nunavut is unique in that we don't have enough lawyers. We don't have enough lawyers generally, and we especially don't have enough Inuit lawyers. In fact the only Inuit lawyer in Nunavut is our premier, also minister of justice, Paul Okalik, and he isn't available just now to take on cases.

The Akitsiraq Law School has been established at Nunavut Arctic College, in partnership with the University of Victoria Law School. It was made possible by a unique arrangement involving the governments of Canada and Nunavut, and Inuit organizations. The students started in September of 2001 and were scheduled to graduate with law degrees from the University of Victoria in 2005. We are very excited about Akitsiraq, and the difference that these students will make to the delivery of justice in Nunavut. We are hopeful that a future Nunavut chief justice and deputy minister of justice will come from this class.

I have been mentioning all these initiatives so that you will understand that the creation of the court was one of many reforms that accompanied the creation of Nunavut. The creation of the Nunavut Court of Justice did not occur in isolation, and the court does not function in isolation either.

I should note that the new court structure has not been the target of any legal challenges to date. The single-level trial court model has been in operation now for three years. There have been lots of little issues related to the administrative side of setting up a new office, where new staff are learning new tasks, and where the appointments to bring the bench to full strength have not yet been made, but the court structure itself has not been a problem. In fact, given the logistics of operating courts in Nunavut, it has most likely allowed some problems, such as unacceptable delays, to be avoided.

Before finishing, I would like to acknowledge the crucial contribution to the work of the new Nunavut court system of Justice Beverley Browne. As the only Territorial Court judge in what is now Nunavut to the present day, she has dedicated herself to empowering community justices of the peace, to working with community justice committees, and to establishing a richer dialogue with court officials, lawyers, the judiciary, and communities. She has been central to the very exciting initiatives that I have mentioned, including the law school. None of them would be where they are now without her participation.

Nunavut was also fortunate in its first court administrator, Marvin Bruce, an active member of ACTA who had worked in courts in NWT, Alberta, and Manitoba. Bruce could have retired, but he had the dream of a single-level trial court and the chance to actually be part of making it happen.

I have no doubt that the single-level trial court is the right model for Nunavut. That said, I realize that circumstances vary across the country and each jurisdiction will have to consider for itself whether it's the right thing for its circumstances. In doing this, it might help to pretend for a moment that you are free to simply plan the best trial court system, as we were, starting from scratch. Would you opt for one tier or two?

## NOTES

I would like to express my thanks to Susan Hardy, Legal Counsel, Nunavut Department of Justice, for her help in the development of this paper.

1 For an account of the establishment of Nunavut, see Jens Dahl, Jack Hicks, and Peter Jull, eds., *Nunavut: Inuit Regain Control of their Lands and Their Lives* (Copenhagen: International Working Group for Indigenous Affairs, 2000).
2 *An Act to Amend the Nunavut Act with Respect to the Nunavut Court of Justice and to Amend other Acts in Consequence*, S.C. 1999, c. 3, assented to 11 March 1999.

# 8  Reforming Alberta's Trial Courts

DAVID HANCOCK

*In his presentation to the Trial Courts of the Future Conference, David Hancock, who at the time was Alberta's minister of justice and attorney general, came out strongly in favour of a one-tier trial court system. 'In today's Canadian society,' he writes, 'a two-tier system of trial courts has lost its relevance.'*

*Two years earlier at an intergovernmental meeting of justice ministers, Hancock, as other provincial justice ministers had done before him, urged his colleagues to support a feasibility study of structural reform of the court system. Following an all-party summit on justice reform, Hancock began to push for Alberta to join those provinces that were unifying the adjudication of family law issues in their superior courts. Here he sets out his reasons for moving forward with a similar unification of criminal trial courts. He is convinced that such a restructuring will provide better service in all localities, more flexibility in the deployment of judicial resources and a stronger platform for innovation.*

*Accepting that the Supreme Court's decision in McEvoy is still good law, the only unification model Hancock could consider was to have the provincially appointed judges elevated to Alberta's superior court, the Court of Queen's Bench. He is willing to have Alberta's trial judges federally appointed providing the province is adequately involved in selecting the top candidates. Hancock notes that one advantage of having all the province's trial judges federally appointed and remunerated is that this would free up provincial funds for other needed reforms of the justice system.*

*Following the conference, David Hancock launched a consultation process in Alberta on a single trial court as 'a focus for reform and a catalyst for change.' The first phase of this consultation took the form of workshops throughout the province for stakeholder groups, including youth justice committees, victims organizations, business groups, Aboriginal communities, and the police. A report of this public consultation, released in November 2003 (http://www.justice.gov.ab.ca/publications/default.aspx?id=3379), concludes that 'while a STC [single trial court] may be beneficial, it is not an end in itself.' The second phase of the consultation involving the legal profession began in July 2003 with a paper prepared by Wayne Renke, a law professor at the University of Alberta, carefully setting out the pros and cons of the single court proposal (http://www.justice.gov.ab.ca/downloads/documentloader.aspx?id=44289).*

*Mr Hancock received the report of phase two of the consultation in June 2004. Soon after that, following a provincial election, Hancock moved from the Justice portfolio to Advanced Education. The phase two consultant reported general agreement among stakeholders that Alberta's court system is very good but that there is room for improvement. He also indicated differences as to the scope and pace of reform in relation to any restructuring of the courts. Currently the province is working on a 'family justice strategy' that aims at offering a common set of procedures to all family law applicants regardless of the court to which they apply.*

Let me begin by acknowledging that tradition is, and always will remain, an important part of the justice system. Change should not be pursued simply for change's sake. As we consider structural reform we are not looking to discard tradition, but rather considering ways to enhance our justice system to ensure that it meets the needs of the people it is intended to serve, the public.

In 1999 the Alberta government sought the advice and direction of the public on a wide range of justice issues during our government's first ever summit conference on justice. The public consultation process is one that has served our province well on a variety of topics, and the justice summit was no exception. One of the messages we heard time and time again was to simplify the justice system. Clearly, delegates felt that the complexity of the system created unnecessary delays, discouraged access, and in some cases resulted in citizens being denied justice. Another clear message was that victims needed to be more a part of the process; they needed to be taken into account, and their needs considered as important, perhaps, as those of the accused.

The Alberta Justice Department and I took those observations seriously, and since that time we have worked hard to improve access, streamline the process where possible, and make better use of available resources to make Alberta's justice system the best it can be. And I have to say that our courts at all three levels have been leaders, and sometimes co-conspirators, in that process.

Since the summit, Alberta Justice and the Alberta courts have taken several steps, particularly in the area of family law. For instance, we have made numerous resources available on line and in person at family law centres, which allow people to get information they need on the legal process, and in some cases allow them to do much of the work by themselves. Last year I also assigned a taskforce of members of the legislature and justice stakeholders to look at the concept of the unified family court and other provincial family matters for our jurisdiction. Again, the main intention of the review was to look at ways to streamline the process, improve access, and provide services in a way that minimizes the damage to individuals and, most importantly, to children.

The task force proposed that the unified court be established as the division of the Court of Queen's Bench. This was not a unanimous decision. I have been open to the opposing views and alternative models which will be considered before we make any final decisions. But the concerns that were expressed with that model, again, were relative to the question of access. The Provincial Court sits in more places, has a broader scope and simpler process than Queen's Bench. People are more comfortable with the Provincial Court process than they are with the rules in the Queen's Bench process.

The rationale of the task force in proposing the Queen's Bench division model, as I understand it from talking to members, was primarily the constitutional barriers that are discussed in the literature and that have been raised at this conference. There was also the question of federal control of the appointment of Queen's Bench under section 96 of the Constitution, and the ability of a court to deal with all aspects of family law in the same forum.

We have had a number of discussions with the federal government and the previous federal minister of justice about those constitutional barriers, and I am fairly convinced that it is important, as has been pointed out by others, that we can and should deal with those constitutional barriers by way of agreement. This will require a real commitment to cooperative federalism. Strange words, you might think, coming from an Albertan politician, but words that I can assure you, at least in the area of justice, have been our model.

There is no reason, for example, that the appointment process cannot be dealt with. We have already given up all or most of the 'grubbiness' of the appointment process that was talked about earlier. At the provincial level, there is, in fact, a process in place to appoint through merit, if that was not always the case (I believe we have had a fairly meritorious process throughout time). So it really should not be too difficult for us to come to some agreement with our federal counterparts that will provide for a joint short list, from which the federal government could make an appointment. There is no magic, as far as I am concerned, in who actually makes the appointment, as long as there is an agreement as to who is on the short list of outstanding candidates.

The example of the Unified Family Court task force emphasizes for me that we should not allow a tradition of resistance to change to hinder our ability to move forward. As someone who has been in the legal profession for more than two decades, I know that the legal profession, the judiciary, and other stakeholders do not always unanimously accept innovation and change. Peter Russell has observed that justice ministers are not likely to go forward with unification without considerable support from the bar and the bench. But I think it is also clear to most of us that change is going to happen. So really the question is, do we want to be part of planning our preferred future or not?

As administrators of justice, I believe we are obligated to be open to new ways to serve the public better, and that is precisely the reason why I have been a proponent of studying the unified criminal trial court concept. Perhaps we even have an obligation from the Alberta perspective. Alberta was the last, or one of the last, to get on board with the concept of a unified family court process. Perhaps we should be one of the first to get on board with the unified criminal trial court process. Perhaps we should be offering to lead in establishing a pilot project in that area.

The concept itself is not new. It has been kicked around since Martin Freidland's report in 1969. It has been recommended on at least one occasion (perhaps more often) by the Law Reform Commission of Canada.[1] In my opinion, for what it's worth, it is time that we came up with a definitive answer and got moving.

For that reason, at the fall 2000 meeting of the federal/provincial/territorial ministers responsible for justice, I put forward the idea, supported by my colleagues, of conducting a feasibility study on the structural reform of the judicial system. Alberta was pleased to lead the reclassification of offences section, and also to take a look at the single-level trial court model. Once the feasibility study is completed, the next step will be for my justice colleagues and I to look at the results, determine whether any further work needs to be done, and then a decision will have to be made to determine how next to proceed. Alberta Justice remains strongly supportive of the process in light of our goal of improving access to justice.

However, one of the real problems in doing this through a federal/provincial/territorial working group is that these processes, by their very nature, take forever. Indeed, this is sometimes the reason why issues are diverted to such a process. I do not believe that we can wait. In fact, I have already started on a process of bilateral discussion of the unified family court system with the federal government. I would like to talk with the federal government about doing a bilateral process on an integrated court process that will allow us to consider moving ahead with a pilot project.

Over the years, I believe that the jurisdictional distinction between superior and inferior courts has practically been eliminated. In today's Canadian society a two-tier system of trial courts has lost its relevance. In fact, access to justice can be impaired by the two-tiered system. The current system causes the perception that Superior Court judges are in some way better qualified to deal with legal issues than Provincial Court judges. This can sometimes cause the misperception that an accused is receiving some kind of second-class justice when the matter is decided in Provincial Court. It is important that an accused not only receive a fair trial, but also that there is no doubt in the accused's mind, and in the public's mind, that the trial process was fair.

However, it is not strictly an issue of perception. There are also many practical reasons to consider carefully a unified trial court model. It is believed that a single court could alleviate some of the systemic delays that result from two courts dealing with the same subject-matter. We have heard this not only from the accused, but also from victims and witnesses, who are affected by the delays.

One such delay is caused by 'judge shopping,' or the deliberate delay of proceedings by re-electing. Currently, an accused may go through docket court appearances, having a preliminary inquiry and setting a trial date in a Superior Court and then can re-elect for trial in Provincial Court. This can create delay in resolution of the case. The whole process has the effect of re-victimizing the victims, failing to deal with the fact that victims are a very, very important part of the system.

In Alberta, 18 per cent of the cases heard in the Court of Queen's Bench are re-elected to Provincial Court Criminal. That, in my view, is a significant number of cases each year that uses up a tremendous amount of court time, while delaying the proceedings.

Currently, Alberta maintains two separate administrative offices and staff to service the two-tiered court system. With a shift to a single court, significant administrative savings could be reinvested to address other pressure points in the justice system. These include the counselling process, pre-court mediation processes, community conferencing processes and other issues of that kind for which we never seem to have enough resources. Of course, that, in itself, is not a good reason to restructure the courts, because we could re-organize the administrative processes and still maintain the two-tiered level of courts and may well do so.

Another advantage of moving to a unified court system is the assignment of judges. This would be particularly important in smaller communities across the province, which may not have the regular attendance of a Superior Court judge. A unified trial court could provide better access and create a more understandable justice system.

But the model is not without its challenges. There are issues that will need to be addressed by the feasibility study and in any future studies being done. For instance, judges from the same court will be doing both preliminary hearings and trials arising from that inquiry, assuming, of course, that we retain preliminary hearings. Initial bail hearings and bail reviews of those decisions, summary conviction trials, and appeals from those trials, would all be handled in the same level of court. Extraordinary remedies will also involve one judge ruling on the conduct of another judge from the same court.

In all of these examples, the court will be both rendering and reviewing a decision which could potentially create the appearance of conflict, which does not happen in the existing system. But I believe these are challenges that can be overcome with appropriate study, an appropriate implementation plan, and cooperation across the country in developing practical solutions.

There are proponents and opponents of the unified trial court model who have taken strong positions on the issues under discussion. That being said, after thirty years of discussion I think it is time for those on both sides of the issue to resolve the differences in the interests of creating the best justice system we can.

The most important point to remember in my view is that this discussion is not inherently about the court, it is not about the judges, and it is not about the lawyers. This discussion is about the people we serve. This discussion must be about the community. Do we have the justice system we need to enhance the safety of our community, to protect the rights and liberties of citizens, to understand and involve the victims in the process and help the victims achieve closure, to provide for appropriate manners of resolving disputes, to deal with the root causes of crime so that we can improve the safety of our community by dealing with the problems rather than recycling the individuals?

These are the real issues. All of us in the system are secondary to the outcomes which we are trying to achieve. That is why I am a strong proponent of the current study and am eagerly awaiting its results. However, I am not prepared to wait before taking action. Justice ministers do not have that kind of luxury. Time is our enemy. Worthwhile initiatives evaporate because, in the political system, we change portfolios frequently. One of my goals as justice minister is to make ideas that have promise move forward as fast as possible during my term, and one of my goals is to move forward and make some headway with this idea of a unified trial court system, whose time, I believe, has come.

Canada's first and only single-level trial court in Nunavut shows that it can be done. The initiative evolved over several years and required significant federal and territorial legislative amendments. Nunavut has a relatively small population and only a handful of federally appointed judges; however the example is invaluable as we study the unified trial court model.

A similar unification of courts took place in California in 2000 (discussed by Clark Kelso in chapter 11). Although operating with a different constitutional framework, the unified trial court is providing greater cooperation and teamwork among the judiciary, other branches of government and the community, more uniformity and efficiency in the case processing and more timely disposition of cases, enhanced opportunities for innovation within court operations, and greater public access and increased focus on accountability and service. While I am not proposing it as part of an Alberta model, in California it was the judges who voted for the reformed system.

Tradition will always remain an important part of our justice system. However, we cannot allow it to stand in the way of improving services to the public. The public has high expectations of their justice system and of their government as administrators of justice. On a service delivery model it may be much more appropriate to organize our courts and court services on a horizontal rather than on a vertical or hierarchical basis. Perhaps we should be looking at organizing our courts more in terms of the different types of problems they deal with – for instance, a family court, a criminal court, and a commercial and personal injury court. Such a system would allow for a domestic violence court, a drug court, or perhaps a guns or weapons court, and a youth court. This approach would allow for much more diversity of treatment and approach.

A new system must not be set up in a hasty manner that might result in some of the smaller items being left to justices of the peace, in effect creating a new court under the unified court. Even now we have discovered that we need a judicial compensation commission for justices of the peace because they were handling so-called judicial functions. So we must make sure that in setting up a new model we do not try to download to JPs and end up with another level of court that we had not intended.

We need to recognize what is judicial and what is administrative, and determine what things can be taken out of the court process because they're truly administrative in nature, rather than requiring adjudication. Also, in a unified court we would have to make sure that appointments were to the court as a whole so that judges could move from one of the court's functions to another and enjoy a diversity of opportunities in terms of hearing cases and developing expertise.

One of the fundamental benefits of an integrated court, assuming again that we can deal with it on a cooperative federalism basis, is that resources could be freed up at the provincial level. With the federal government paying the salaries of all of the unified court's judiciary, the funds saved at the provincial level could go into some of truly valuable reforms to our court processes for which we now lack resources. These include encouraging more mediation and alternative dispute resolution and increasing counselling in the family law and other areas. The aim of strengthening counselling and these alternative processes is to keep out people who do not need to be in the courts. This will mean that even if the marriage is broken down – which so often involves children – ongoing relationships can be built on a more positive basis than is normally possible through the strictly adversarial process of the courts. Lots of work is happening on that through the collaborative law efforts and other efforts, but we as government, and as administrators of the court system, and you as the courts, need do more to encourage things to happen before they get to court.

The courts in Alberta and elsewhere are already doing a lot of this – for example, in terms of mediation processes in Family Court and judicial dispute resolution in Queen's Bench. But one of the real values that I would see in the reformed system is that it will allow us to maximize the value of the resources we have. We will be better able to deal with people who don't need to be in court in an alternative way, through diversion programs or others that I have mentioned, and leave the courts to do the adjudication in the areas where they are really necessary to settle disputed points of fact or law.

A unified criminal court is only one example of the ways that we can streamline our justice system. I believe it is the responsibility of our provincial, territorial, and federal governments to work together with the judiciary and the legal community, and with the public, to ensure that our system is efficient and provides Canadians with better access to justice. In the name of better access to justice, the unified criminal court is an option worthy of at least intense study, if not action. And Alberta is well positioned to take that action and to take it soon.

Since I was appointed almost three years ago I have been impressed with the willingness of Alberta courts at all levels not only to embrace but to lead change in areas where they believe it to be important. If we are prepared to completely change the way we resolve disputes, we must be prepared to change the structures with which to resolve those disputes.

I can't wait to get home, to get started on this. The real question in my mind is how can we organize the justice system, including the courts, to deal with the outcomes which we value as a community and as a society?

NOTE

1 Law Reform Commission of Canada, *Toward a Unified Criminal Court*, Working Paper 59 (Ottawa: Public Works and Government Services Canada, 1989).

# PART THREE

## Competing Visions

# 9 The House of Justice: A Single Trial Court

GERALD T.G. SENIUK AND JOHN BORROWS

*In this chapter Gerald Seniuk, chief judge of Saskatchewan's Provincial Court, combines with John Borrows, one of Canada's leading Aboriginal legal scholars, to present a vision of Canada's trial courts designed to capture the full potential of the original Confederation arrangements. Instead of the bifurcated system of Provincial and Superior Courts that has evolved since Confederation, they envisage an integrated community-based institution in which adjudicative and justice services of all kinds are provided by a single-status judiciary encompassing the relevant specializations.*

*The Seniuk-Borrows approach to trial court integration is not a matter of simply elevating the provincially appointed judiciary into the Superior Court. Their House of Justice model lays considerable emphasis on making non-adjudicative, therapeutic, alternative dispute resolution processes available through the same institutional setting that administers the formal trial process. It also draws upon Aboriginal traditions of restorative justice and the institution of peacemakers – a feature of great salience in the province whose population has the highest proportion of Aboriginal people.*

*Like all single trial court models, the House of Justice would make considerable use of justices of the peace. The JPs in this model, however, would not be a lower level judiciary but justice officers whose primary function would be to provide effective links between each House of Justice and the local community it serves.*

*To bring justice closer to the people the House of Justice would be considerably more decentralized than traditional Superior Courts. The need for consistency would be met by a somewhat expanded and centralized provincial Court of Appeal, although some of the judicial review functions traditionally performed by Superior Courts would be absorbed into the new integrated locally-based justice institutions.*

*With the momentum for trial court unification for the moment abated in Alberta, Saskatchewan may well become the next province to take up the cause. The holistic approach built on the promise of Canada's constitutional foundations and put forward here by the chief of its Provincial Court and a leading Aboriginal jurist provides a thoughtful and innovative model for moving in this direction.*

The purpose of this article is to outline for discussion purposes the concept of a House of Justice: a single one-stop Superior trial court with various 'rooms' with options where citizens can seek individual justice, dispute resolution, reconciliation and community healing in an efficient and accessible forum. Such a House of Justice would institutionally knit our country together by both implementing the vision of the judicature provisions at the time of Confederation[1] and strengthening the ability of the provinces and Aboriginal communities to pursue justice according to their communal values. This concept does not envision a merger of the Provincial Court into the existing Superior Court model with downloading to a 'lower' separate court. It contemplates the creation of a strong unified court with specialized divisions that regularly sit in many communities rather than being concentrated in a small number of court centres.

However, in addition to holding court in these communities, the concept of a House of Justice also envisions a system that would not be as insulated from the community or as separated from other non-judicial justice functions as has traditionally been the case. For example, we believe that the office of the justice of the peace within a House of Justice could perform many essential non-judicial functions of the court and provide an important institutional link with the community. To accomplish these purposes, it is vital that the function and office of the justice of the peace be closely associated with the judicial office of the court, so that both are fully integrated into the House of Justice. Such integration would help avoid the redevelopment of a separate lower-level court, and thereby prevent the recreation of the current two-tiered structure. In addition, by integrating the office of the justice of the peace with the court, the House of Justice could be institutionally linked to the community in a meaningful way without jeopardizing the independence of the judges of the court.

**The Concept**

In the House of Justice concept, in each province there would be one Court of Appeal whose judges are federally appointed. The Court of

Appeal would continue to perform some of the important review functions based on the traditional constitutional roles of the central courts of London, while some of the other of these roles would remain with the trial court.[2] Some of the functions of the old central courts of London are now performed by the various Courts of Appeal (which did not exist in 1701) and not by the superior trial courts. It is necessary that some of those types of functions – for example, bringing consistency to disparate trial court rulings and to the law – remain with a collegial body that is relatively centralized and not diluted numerically. At this level there is a concern about 'uploading' of the Superior Court's trial division's appellate jurisdiction and creating an unmanageable burden at the Court of Appeal. Although in many provinces there are relatively few summary appeals, it would be necessary for the Court of Appeal to have the necessary numerical strength or procedures to ensure that the caseload can be handled. But not all of these constitutional roles that historically are derived from the central courts of London need remain with a centralized, small Court of Appeal. Many other Superior Court roles would remain with the decentralized trial court in order to ensure accessibility to the communities where the court would function.

To ensure accessibility, there should be one trial court. The goal of removing jurisdictional barriers by merging courts is not new, including the desire to create a single trial court. We experienced the beginning of that process thirty-five years ago, when the County and District Courts merged into the existing Superior Courts in each province. However, at the same time there was a downloading to the then Magistrates' Courts. As Carl Baar has documented, this began the process that eventually transformed 'local magistrate's courts, once the dispersed third level of trial courts often staffed by lay judges, into province-wide systems of trial courts with increasingly significant statutory jurisdiction.'[3] The jurisdiction of the Provincial Court steadily increased to the point where it has 'more extensive jurisdiction than any court of limited jurisdiction in the United States, the United Kingdom or Australia [and] handles an increasingly higher proportion of serious criminal matters.'[4] The result of creating such a significant second trial court has been the development of strain within the existing two-tiered court structure that is difficult to address. As J.S. Ziegel pointed out, the cause of this continuing stress is 'the constitutional anomaly of provincially appointed judges carrying the bulk of the burden of enforcing federally enacted criminal laws while having to settle for provincially created and administered compensation packages.'[5]

In our opinion, the concept of The House of Justice would do away with this 'merger/downloading' cycle and create a single trial court in each province to replace the current fragmented court system.[6] The legislative template for such a court exists in Nunavut. There is some suggestion that a model that might work in a large territory with a small, dispersed population such as Nunavut is not applicable to other Canadian jurisdictions. However, the legislative template is a foundation to build upon. Other large urbanized jurisdictions, such as California, have unified structures. Judges in the single trial court would be federally appointed so that we would truly have a national court of the kind Russell argues was envisioned in the Constitution and which the present bifurcated system is not.[7] But this would not rule out provincial or Aboriginal input. For example creation of a Provincial Court such as the Cour du Québec and the appointment of judges to it has been an important feature of province-building. Although the unified court would be seen as a national court, it would be necessary to keep the provincial involvement in the appointment process as a result of this history. In this way, a joint appointment or a commission process would strengthen the national and provincial identity of the judicature, and the court structure would become an important weld of the Canadian confederation. Many have pointed out how this could be done in cooperation with the provinces[8] or, where self-government applies, the Aboriginal community.[9]

There would be specialized divisions within the generalist single trial court. Examples of traditional specialties include criminal, civil, and family. Examples of new specialties may include Aboriginal, treaty, or constitutional divisions. Although judges would generally remain in their specialized division, the chief justice would have the authority, with perhaps some limitation of transfer into some specialized courts, to reassign judges in the interests of the administration of justice or the court.

Merger of fragmented court offices under one court structure would provide rural areas with a fuller range of more easily accessible court administrative services. One enduring aspect of the merger of the County and District Courts with the Superior Courts was to decentralize the Superior Court in some jurisdictions, and to provide more communities with local access to the Superior Court judge where before there had been a resident District Court judge. The more accessible reach of the Provincial Court administration would now provide more communities direct access to Superior Court services.

If political will and judicial cooperation exist, then such a House of Justice is achievable within the existing constitutional framework. We are not suggesting that there are not many complexities and considerations that would have to be addressed. However, if there were a will and a cooperative spirit, these legal, technical, and practical issues could be resolved. This article is broad and conceptual, but others have explored some of these more concrete concerns. It is especially instructive to see the experience in other jurisdictions that are embracing unification, such as California, or seriously exploring the option, such as the United Kingdom. The enduring flexibility of the Canadian justice system is evident in such Provincial Court innovations as the Cree Court Party in Saskatchewan and the Tsuu T'ina First Nations Peacemaker Court in Alberta.

But political will and a flexible constitution have not been sufficient in the recent past to bring about such unification. Strong political will existed as recently as 1990, as Carl Baar has recorded: 'After June 1990 ... provincial attorneys general endorsed in principle complete unification of the trial courts ... Complete unification ... eliminating the two levels of trial courts and with them the distinction between federally-appointed and provincially-appointed judges.' [10] But the elimination of the fragmented trial court system did not happen because, as Baar recounted in his article above, it was opposed by section 96 judges and the Canadian Bar Association. It may be that the political will to overcome the fragmentation of our trial courts and make the move to unification will come only when there is wider appreciation of the full potential of the House of Justice concept.

**The Concept's Full Potential**

A House of Justice would provide more than just accessible courts with full jurisdiction. In addition, citizens would find within the court structure other justice-related resources. These would include mediation/alternate dispute resolution, witness and victim services, public legal education resources, restorative justice, diversion processes and innovative court processes, such as the domestic violence courts and other new specialized problem-solving courts or culturally/linguistically based courts such as the Provincial Court's Cree Court. The integration of these services into an all-purpose House of Justice would not require the re-creation of these programs, merely their coordination within one body. Such a development would render court procedures and outcomes more transparent and comprehensible to the average citizen. It would further enhance access to justice by placing these services on a firmer institutional footing. These services would gain greater legal credibility under judicial oversight and would enjoy enhanced efficiencies by reducing duplication and increasing productivity through their closer ties to the panoply of justice delivery services. They would also benefit from an increase in citizens' general knowledge of the services. The analogy would be to someone going to a large urban hospital for medical aid, where the profession puts the patient in touch with the appropriate specialty treatment. The creation of a House of Justice would rationalize and demystify the courts by establishing a one-stop location where citizens attend and choose from or are streamed within the panoply of services. In short, users would find the court structure to be a more accessible, responsive, and helpful place.

To facilitate the objective of enhancing accessibility, communities would be linked to the court structure through their community justice committees and the court's office of the justice of the peace. At the same time, to ensure the integrity of the judicial office, judges of the court would be of equal status and would exclusively do the work of the court. Judicial functions must be clearly demarcated so that judicial impartiality and independence are fully protected by judges exercising sole control over 'those matters which bear directly and immediately on the exercise of the judicial function.'[11]

Other legal officers, such as justices of the peace, would be lay officials and not members of the bar. One of the reasons for suggesting only lay justices of the peace is the desire to avoid downloading and recreation of the current two-tiered structure. They would generally be resident in their community, but closely integrated with the court structure. Within this framework there would be a variety of JP levels and functions. Many of these functions would assist courts with their workload, and could include dealing with appropriate summary offence matters and community bylaws. But only judges should perform adjudication or make orders that affect the liberty of a subject or result in a criminal record. Some of the functions performed by the resident justice of the peace would begin the development of more community-based justice systems in Aboriginal communities. But since the office would be fully integrated with the court, the community-based link would be part of and consistent with the standards of the single trial court. In such cases, the justice of the peace appointment may require federal input.

A key role for some of these House of Justice JPs would be as chair of their community's justice committee. This would ensure that local justice issues received appropriate attention from knowledgeable persons skilled in community dispute resolution. They would facilitate restorative initiatives, supervise diversion programs, and develop appropriate local mechanisms for dialogue about community and court concerns. Since communities would generate their own ideas as they address these issues, it is not possible to specify how these court–community linkages would develop. Synergistically working together as one House of Justice, these resources would enhance citizen and community participation in the pursuit of justice and link the court to justice's communal roots. Existing examples reveal the effectiveness and creativity that can develop when the justice system becomes responsive to community concerns.

Such justices of the peace/peacemakers are not meant to be adjudicators in the conventional sense, but instead would focus on restorative methods and seek new modes of dispute resolution and problem-solving. At the same time they would use their jurisdictional powers to assist community members as they navigate through the conventional justice system. What they clearly should not be is a forum of downloaded functions that should be done by judges. At present the Provincial Court of Saskatchewan has embarked on a study and discussion process to explore the various options for such a justice of the peace reform.

The Yukon and the Northwest Territories have a long history of integrating resident justices of the peace with the workings of the court. In Saskatchewan the Cree Court, presided over by the Honourable Judge Gerald Morin of the Provincial Court of Saskatchewan, began its first sittings in October 2001. The court sits in Cree-speaking communities, and persons appearing before the court can conduct their matters in the Cree language. The judge, legal aid lawyer, prosecutor, clerk, probation officer, and Native court worker all speak Cree. Proceedings can be translated for those who are non-Cree speaking. The process is analogous to providing French-language trials in Saskatchewan. The court can also conduct its affairs in English. In Alberta, the Honourable Judge L.S. Mandamin of the Alberta Provincial Court presides over the Tsuu T'ina First Nations Peacemaker Court on the Tsuu T'ina Nation on the outskirts of southwest Calgary. The court, which began in October 2000, is integrated with the Provincial Court, and also with the community and its justice traditions. Judges Morin and Mandamin are both highly qualified First Nations members of the bar fully qualified

Figure 1. The House of Justice

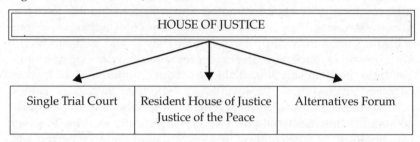

for the bench, who have demonstrated an ability to bridge the cultural divide between the Euro-Canadian legal system and the First Nations community. The court clerks are recruited from the community. The Tsuu Sina/Stoney Corrections Society provides the court worker and probation services. In addition, two peacemakers who are elders also sit in court as community witnesses to the proceedings. The peacemaker coordinator calls on peacemakers who are from the community and who hold the trust and respect of the community.

All of the resources discussed above currently exist, but are fragmented and scattered within our communities, serving sometimes to frustrate and confuse rather than to help and to heal. Figure 1 shows how the single trial court, the resident JP, and Alternatives Forum constitute three pillars in the House of Justice. Bringing them together requires political will and judicial cooperation. Although consolidation of initiatives such as those outlined above is a means of improving the administration of justice, one would also expect efficiencies and cost savings to result. Thus, each addition to the court structure may result in reduced, not added, cost.

**Realizing the Potential of Confederation**

At many levels, it should be unnecessary to argue for a single trial court. The onus is more properly upon those who would seek to restrain reform by maintaining the status quo with its bifurcated system. This is because the current approach is largely incompatible with the system of federalism adopted by Canada's founders.[12] As Peter Russell has pointed out, the Canadian constitution, unlike most other federal systems, was premised on the vision of an integrated judicial system whose main institutions were courts created and administered by the provinces presided over by federally appointed judges.[13] This was done in order to knit the country together through the harmonization of legal practice and principles at all levels.[14] Peter Russell has elaborated on this unique characteristic.

> Comparatively speaking, the Canadian judicial system ranks as one of the most integrated, or least federalized. The judicial provisions of the Canadian Constitution lean strongly in the direction of the judicial system of a unitary state … The only judicial arrangements specifically provided for in the Constitution are the very essence of an integrated federal provincial system: federally appointed judges of provincial superior and intermediate courts. No other federation has this element of judicial integration.[15]

But, as Russell points out, unfortunately there has been a tragic incremental move away from an integrated system to a bifurcated system. As he observed:

> The tragedy is that the politicians who have operated the system have had neither the will nor the vision to work together to enable Canadians to realize the full benefits of this system … There has been no coherent or intelligent plan guiding the evolution of this trial court system.[16]

An integrated judicial system is an important mechanism in shoring up national standards in a federal system.[17] It also strengthens the country by protecting provincial and local political units and enabling them to function within a context of the broader political community.[18] Russell questions the constitutionality of the status quo because it fails to live up to its potential. He notes that continuing such a dualistic system has 'very bad practical implications for litigants and tax-payers [and] is a barrier to the efficient deployment of physical and human resources and to the coherent management of the trial court system.'[19] If this were changed through a new appointment process it would

> make it possible for Canadians to have disputes about their legal rights and duties – disputes which they do not perceive as falling into purely federal or provincial categories – adjudicated at conveniently located centres by judges who, while they may be specialists in some particular area of law, are all highly skilled professionals and not segregated into groups of 'superior' federal appointees and 'inferior' provincial appointees.[20]

Thus the creation of a single trial court would comply with the likely intent behind Canadian federalism to have a national judiciary as intended. Referring to the writings of W.R. Lederman and P.W. Hogg, Russell argued that a nominating commission with members from both levels of government, from both opposition and government benches, and with lay members and members of the bar, would 'produce a much more pluralistic basis for judicial recruitment and a check on unjustifiable patronage appointments.' If the judges were chosen from such a commission process, then Russell states that regardless of whether the federal or provincial governments made the appointment, 'This judiciary, a truly national judiciary, would be one which both levels of government could confidently entrust with the application of their laws and one which would command the respect of the citizenry which both levels of government serve.' We agree, and suggest that this concept could be extended to appointments involving First Nations.

## Including First Nations in the Confederation Scheme

The federal-provincial constitutional integration outlined above conceptually could be extended to indigenous communities as their constitutional situation becomes more clarified. The Cree Court Party in Saskatchewan, the Tsuu T'ina First Nations Peacemaker Court in Alberta, and the various innovations in the Yukon and Northwest Territories utilizing the justice of the peace office to provide integration indicate something less than a separate justice system might satisfy aboriginal self-government initiatives.[21] Allan Cairns,[22] for example, contrasts the *Report of the Royal Commission on Aboriginal Peoples* (RCAP), which is based on 'arguments that stress self-government and minimize citizenship connection with the majority society,' and the position of the Federation of Saskatchewan Indian Nations (FSIN). Cairns implies that the FSIN position 'argues a counter-position to the RCAP *Report* ... Its focus is the common future of all the people in Saskatchewan. Explicit, enhanced positive participation in normal provincial politics is a goal. There is no suggestion of a two-row wampum of exclusive separate paths, which we believe is a too-narrow reading of the agreement.[23] The goal of Aboriginal peoples is 'nothing less than to re-invent Saskatchewan.' Cairns points out that the then chief of the FSIN, Blaine C. Favel, refers to the 'common futures' of Aboriginal and non-Aboriginal peoples. As Cairns summarizes the position: the FSIN report is not advocating assimilation, or rejecting self-government, or sacrificing 'Indianness' on the altar of moderniza-tion. The explicit, guiding premise is that only by becoming fully involved in the Saskatchewan community will Aboriginal peoples become part of the province-wide 'we' community and thus have the moral levers to engage the majority as fellow citizens in tackling pov-erty and social malaise. The premise is that a common citizenship is the source of empathy.

As important as it is to address properly the possible constitutional deficiencies of the bifurcated system, we believe that a discussion of an integrated vision of the court system should not be limited to a discus-sion of unification of the federally and provincially appointed courts. If we instead conceptualize a House of Justice, there would be room to consider the integration of other constitutionally recognized communi-ties that extend beyond the federal/provincial/territorial restrictions. For example, we believe that the treaty nations of Saskatchewan could participate in a unified court structure that would be an all-purpose House of Justice within the province. Within such a unified structure indigenous peoples could exercise their own inherent powers of adju-dication within their communities, and could draw on existing resources through such an institution. They could apply indigenous and non-indigenous law in an inter-societal context, drawing upon the best of both legal worlds as they strive to create conditions facilitative of peace and order. In an urban setting this would be a welcome devel-opment because it would provide indigenous people with a forum that is more attentive to their concerns, as the House of Justice could have many different options available within it to pursue the resolution of disputes. There could be functions for peacekeepers, elders, mediation, adjudication, and justices of the peace.

In a reserve setting, a House of Justice, as part of a unified court structure, could solely apply the laws of the treaty nation of which it was a part. Such courts could function akin to tribal courts in the United States, except that the Houses of Justice proposed here would take their fiscal resources from the state and be part of a larger juridical structure. This could overcome a huge problem tribal courts in the United States face, in that they perpetually lack finances and respect from other levels of courts throughout the country. It would also ensure that these institutions functioned with the necessary indepen-dence from band chiefs and councils. If a House of Justice Tribal Court Division was part of a larger unified court structure in the province that amalgamated Provincial and Superior courts, diversified its functions, and was attentive to indigenous justice issues, this could go some distance toward implementing the peace and order promises under the treaties.[24] In connection with concerns that tribal courts could be overwhelmed by non-indigenous law, there could be ways devised to shield some of the decisions in these Houses of Justice from culturally inappropriate judicial review, where people are still protected in their due process rights. There could be an appeal structure within such a House of Justice that tests decisions of tribal judges before a body of their peers, before review travels on up the line. Having tribal courts in Saskatchewan that function in furtherance of the treaty relationship would be a very significant development. The fact that they would flow from the treaties, and draw their sources from indigenous and non-indigenous legal principles, could be a source of great strength to these institutions.

But the value of the House of Justice in integrating community values is not limited to First Nations.[25] It applies to all communities. The reason such a House of Justice should be able to respond to any community's justice concerns is because it would be linked to the community. If the community's desire for security and fairness is the wellspring of justice, then the court must be rooted in the community or it will wither. And without healthy courts, communities cannot achieve justice. This proposed model aims at more closely integrating the court and the community with each other and better coordinating their joint efforts. A key to such a link is the resident justice of the peace.

Justice is holistic, and fragmentation at any level is contrary to the public interest and to the best administration of justice. We should not attempt to unify at the trial court level while further fragmenting and downloading at the local level. We should think of different levels of justice of the peace offices that would perform diverse functions. However, all of the offices of the justice of the peace should be integrated within a single trial court as an integral part of the House of Justice. Through one level of the justice of the peace office, we should proactively explore our court/community relationships. Through the office of the justice of the peace, the House of Justice can remain rooted in the community and keep the court linked to the community while at the same time maintaining the necessary distance required for impartial and independent tribunals. Such projects should not require any new funding or legislation, but they would require that we work together differently so as to reflect the holistic and shared nature of justice.

   The analogy between 'health' and 'justice' can provide a framework
for discussion purposes. Community experiences of insecurity or
unfairness may be viewed as symptoms of social ills in need of diagno-
sis and treatment. Disharmony and discord may be indicators of
shared sicknesses requiring remedy and rehabilitation. What if we
thought of courts as the hospitals of a justice system whose goal was to
restore security and fairness in the community? What if we thought of
them as being analogous to healing lodges, whose objective is to re-
establish peace and order with all our relations? Instead of searching
through a fragmented system, people could enter through one door
and find a variety of rooms and specialized services. Instead of stumbling from one institution to the next, people could confidently
approach a single body for a range of processes that lead to healing.
Such a court system of the future would be integrated, accessible, flexible, and efficient. It would be characterized by principles of peace,
friendship, and respect, consistent with a treaty relationship and in
accordance with the highest principles underlying the rule of law.[26] A
court is not only a building, but should also be a system of people
working together in an integrated and helpful fashion. In such a system, there is no buck-passing. It is a one-stop place of assistance, refer-
ral, and coordination.
   The link between the court and the community should pivot around
a justice of the peace, or peacemaker who is resident in the community.
This person should either head or be part of a community justice committee, and should also have close working relationships with the local
police and other local justice leaders. Simultaneously, the JP should be
in close association with the judge presiding in that area. There should
be a variety of levels of justices of the peace: some that are limited to
administrative powers and may work under the direction of a judge,
and others who perform judge-like functions and who may work inde-
pendently under the assignment of the judge. But primarily these
should be 'good news' JPs, ones who perform a role like the peacemaker and can coordinate diversion pre- or post-charge. The same
administrative office would support the judge and the JP. Here is how
Judge Mandamin describes the initiative at Tsuu T'ina in Alberta:

   The Tsuu T'ina First Nations Peacemaker Court is a Provincial Court
   located on the Tsuu T'ina Nation on the outskirts of southwest Calgary,
   which handles regular Provincial Court matters as well as Tsuu T'ina
   bylaw charges. The peacemaker coordinator sits in court as a party and

may address the Court when peacemaking is considered. Diversions to peacemaking may be initiated by Tsuu T'ina police, the Crown prosecutor, the peacemaker coordinator, the judge or community corrections workers. The individuals who chose peacemaking have their proceeding adjourned while they are in the peacemaking process. The peacemaker coordinator initiates the peacemaking process. He assesses each case to determine if peacemaking would be suitable. If it is, he accepts the matter into peacemaking and assigns a peacemaker or peace-makers to each case. The peacemakers are Tsuu T'ina members who hold the trust of the community. The Tsuu T'ina invited every household in the community to name those from their families and from the community generally who would be fair in peacemaking. From those nominated, approximately fifty individuals were identified. The first third of that group were given an orientation and training course in peacemaking ... The successful peace-keeping outcomes may involve withdrawal of charges by the Crown or incorporation of the peacekeeping healing plan into sentencing.[27]

This can be especially helpful in isolated communities whose residents typically travel long distances to the regular court locations. Provincial Court judges who work with these communities intuitively understand the utility of having the functions of a justice of the peace integrated with the court and, in our experience, many judges are willing to work to develop such an integrated concept. The following is from a judge with the Provincial Court in Saskatchewan and is typical of the judicial response to this concept:

> I could not agree more about the need to involve J.P.'s to provide the link between the court and the community. Especially in areas like ours where many of the people we deal with are located significant distances from where they live, this link could provide such communities with an opportunity to be closer to the court and justice system and a greater chance that they could feel involved in the system and develop some sense of ownership of it.[28]

Communities also recognize the utility of having this connection to the court. A reserve in Saskatchewan brought the following example to our attention. The court party, which for occupational health reasons is not required to travel when the winter temperatures dip below -30 degrees Celsius, did not travel to its scheduled circuit point. However, many of the reserve residents travelled over icy, hilly back roads, where lives had been lost in the past, to get to court. As the chair of the reserve's justice committee pointed out, all that hardship could have been avoided had they a resident justice of the peace that was integrated with the court.

It was in that very First Nation's community, Pelican Lake, that the first new room in the House of Justice model opened in April 2005 with Her Worship Harriet Thomas, a resident Cree-speaking justice of the peace, presiding. That particular room in the Provincial Court of Saskatchewan's House of Justice is called the Pelican Lake Community Holistic Court. It is integrated with the North Battleford Provincial Court office, part of the circuit range of the Honourable V. Meekma of the Provincial Court and administratively linked to the Provincial Court office managed by Janice Schmidt, court manager for the North Battleford Provincial Court office. It is important to mention the individuals involved because these new rooms in the House of Justice require such a personal commitment that it could not be established without the individual cooperation of others working in the justice system. The coordinating role of the local police, in this case the RCMP at Spiritwood, is pivotal. But no one was more pivotal than Terrance Lewis, the justice coordinator for the Agency Chiefs' Tribal Council, who worked for over five years to institute this kind of innovation.

A second House of Justice room is being prepared at the Dene community of Dillon and Buffalo River and others are in line. The Saskatchewan Department of Justice is completing a formal evaluation before other communities are involved.

## Conclusion

This proposal aims at integrating or coordinating all aspects of the justice system's resources and responses. Because the court is a place of transparency, accountability, and public record, the court should be involved from the start to the finish to ensure justice is done, in process and substance. The court is not only the accessible and coordinated entry to services and resources, it is also the window through which the general community can observe the results achieved by these services and resources. It is here that the justice system is transparent and accountable. This should be the place of record for pre-charge diversion and post-sentence treatment where the community can see what was expected of the offender and what was achieved in the end. This place, the House of Justice, is where the parties in conflict, the community, the court, and the resource-providers are held accountable to each other and to the public. While many of the reforms we have discussed can be done and are being done on an ad hoc and partial basis within the existing court system, it is our strong conviction that so long as that system and its fragmentation of judicial resources continues, Canadians will not enjoy the full potential of our constitutional foundations or the full benefits of holistic justice.

## NOTES

1 See Peter H. Russell, *The Judiciary in Canada: The Third Branch of Government* (Toronto: McGraw-Hill, 1987) for a discussion of the judicature provisions of the British North America Act.

2 See W.R. Lederman, 'The Independence of the Judiciary' (1956) 34 *Canadian Bar Review* 1167–68, who located the definition of a Canadian superior court from within the history of the central courts of London.

3 See C. Baar, *One Trial Court: Possibilities and Limitations* (Ottawa: Canadian Judicial Council, 1991), 5.

4 See C. Baar, 'Judicial Independence and Judicial Administration: The Case of Provincial Court Judges,' (1998) 9 *Constitutional Forum* 120.

5 J.S. Ziegel, 'The Supreme Court Radicalizes Judicial Compensation' (1998) 9 *Constitutional Forum* 40.

6 See Gerald Seniuk and Noel Lyon, 'The Supreme Court of Canada and the Provincial Court in Canada' (2000) 79 *Canadian Bar Review* 80–97 on the bifurcation between the federally appointed courts and the provincially appointed courts, as well as the danger of further fragmentation with the developing justice of the peace courts.

7 Peter Russell, 'Evolution of Canada's Trial Court System From Confederation to Today' (paper presented at the Trial Courts of the Future Symposium, Saskatoon, 15–17 May 2002).

8 See the Law Reform Commission of Canada, *Toward a Unified Criminal Court, Working Paper No. 59* (Ottawa: Public Works and Government Services Canada, 1989), 35–8, for a discussion about the constitutional issues surrounding the appointment process. But see Peter Russell's paper at the Symposium in support of William Lederman's appointment process, and the national judiciary it would foster.

9 As treaty federalism and the justice concepts in self-government are developing, it is not possible to say how these specific appointments would fit into the one-court structure. But the structure would allow for specialization, and these appointments may reflect this. See Sakej Henderson, 'Empowering Treaty Federalism' (1997) 35 *University of Alberta Law Review;*

James (Sakej) Youngblood Henderson, 'Implementing Treaty Order' in R. Gosse, J. Henderson, and R. Carter, eds., *Continuing Poundmaker and Riel's Quest* (Saskatoon: Purich Publishing, 1994).

10 Baar, *One Trial Court*, 12.

11 See Chief Justice Lamer's discussion *In Reference re Independence and Impartiality of Judges of the Provincial Court of Prince Edward Island*, [1997] 3 S.C.R. 3 at para. 258, 118 C.C.C. (3d) 193, 150 D.L.R. (4th) 577. Chief Justice Lamer reiterated and further developed those matters over which courts have administrative independence, as identified previously in *R. v. Valente*, [1985] 2 S.C.R. 673, 23 C.C.C. (3d) 193, 49 C.R. (3d) 97. Examples of these matters include 'the assignment of judges, sittings of the court and court lists, the allocation of courtrooms, and the direction of administrative staff in carrying out these functions.'

12 Peter Hogg 'Federalism and the Jurisdiction of Canadian Courts' (1981) 30 *University of New Brunswick Law Journal* 9.

13 Russell, *The Judiciary in Canada*, 4th ed. 49–50.

14 Peter Hogg, *Constitutional Law of Canada* (Toronto: Carswell, 2000), 175.

15 Russell, *The Judiciary in Canada*, 49–53.

16 Russell, 'Evolution of Canada's Trial Court System,' 1–2.

17 *R. v. Thomas Fuller Construction Co. (1958) Ltd.*, [1980] 1 S.C.R. 695, 106 D.L.R. (3d) 193, 12 C.P.C. 248; *Canada (Attorney General) v. Law Society of British Columbia*, [1982] 2 S.C.R. 307 at 327, 137 D.L.R. (3d) 1, [1982] 5 W.W.R. 289; *Ontario (Attorney General) v. Pembina Exploration Canada Ltd.*, [1989] 1 S.C.R. 206 at 215 and 225–6, 57 D.L.R. (4th) 710, 33 O.A.C. 321 *sub nom. Siddall (William) & Sons Fisheries v. Pembina Exploration Canada Ltd.; Hunt v. T & N plc*, [1993] 4 S.C.R. 289, 109 D.L.R. (4th) 16, [1994] 1 W.W.R. 129.

18 *Morguard Investments Ltd. v. De Savoye*, [1990] 3 S.C.R. 1077, at 1099, 76 D.L.R. (4th) 256, [1991] 2 W.W.R. 217.

19 Russell, 'Evolution of Canada's Trial Coourt System.'

20 Russell, *The Judiciary in Canada*, 251.

21 See John Borrows, 'Landed Citizenship: Narratives of Aboriginal Political Participation' in Will Kynticka, ed., *Citizenship in Diverse Societies* (Oxford: Oxford University Press, 2000).

22 Alan C. Cairns, *Citizens Plus: Aboriginal Peoples and the Canadian State* (Vancouver: UBC Press, 2000), 208–9.

23 See John Borrows, *Recovering Canada: The Resurgence of Indigenous Law* (Toronto: University of Toronto Press, 2002), 148–50.

24 The peace and order clauses in the Saskatchewan treaties read as follows: 'The undersigned chiefs, on their behalf and on behalf of all other Indians inhabiting the tract within ceded do hereby solemnly promise and engage

to strictly observe this treaty and also to conduct and behave themselves as good and loyal subjects of Her Majesty The Queen. They promise and engage that *they will in all respects obey and abide by the law; that they will maintain peace and order between each other, and also between themselves and other tribes of Indians or whites,* now inhabiting or hereafter to inhabit any part of the said tract, or that they will not molest a person or property of any inhabitants of such ceded tract or the property of Her Majesty The Queen, or interfere with or trouble any person passing or travelling through the said tract or any part thereof, and *that they will aid and assist the officers of Her Majesty in bringing to justice and punishment any Aboriginal offending against the stipulations of this treaty or infringe the laws in force in the country so ceded.*' For further commentary on Saskatchewan treaties, see Harold Cardinal and Walter Hildebrandt, *Treaty Elders of Saskatchewan: Our Dream Is that Our Peoples Will One Day Be Clearly Recognized as Nations* (Calgary: University of Calgary Press, 2000); Arthur Ray, J.R. Miller, and Frank Tough, *Bounty and Benevolence: A History of Saskatchewan Treaties* (Montreal: McGill-Queen's University Press, 2000); and David Arnot, 'Treaties as a Bridge to the Future,' (2001) 50 *University of New Brunswick Law Journal* 59.

25 Though there are constitutional considerations that suggest that, at a minimum, Aboriginal peoples' community values should be integrated with the administration of justice.

26 For a discussion of these principles, see John Borrows 'Wampum at Niagara: First Nations Self-Government and the Royal Proclamation,' in Michael Asch, ed., *Aboriginal and Treaty Rights in Canada: Essays in Law, Equality and Respect for Difference* (Vancouver: UBC Press, 1997), 155.

27 This information is taken from Judge Mandamin's paper, 'Tsuu T'ina Court and Peacemaking Initiative,' which was prepared for the Alberta Provincial Judges Education Seminar, Red Deer, Alberta, 17 May 2001.

28 The Honourable Judge Earl Kalenith, Provincial Court of Saskatchewan, Meadow Lake, in personal correspondence with the authors in discussion the development of the concept and the article.

# 10  Report of the Ontario Superior Court of Justice

*The toughest critics of the one-tier court system have been the Superior Court judiciary. This chapter presents a critical analysis of one-tier proposals prepared by a group of judges from Ontario's Superior Court. It is reproduced here, in a slightly edited form, with the kind permission of that court's Chief Justice, the Honourable Heather Smith.*

*A speech given in January 2000 at the annual Opening of Courts in Toronto by James Flaherty, then Ontario's attorney general and justice minister in the Harris Conservative government, occasioned the judges' report. A unified criminal court was one of the structural reforms Mr Flaherty suggested as a possible means of improving the efficiency and reducing the complexities of the criminal justice system. The judges begin their report by noting that a unified criminal court was not among the 115 recommendations of the Criminal Justice Review that had been produced just three years earlier by a committee representative of all levels of the judiciary, government and the bar. Ontario's Superior Court judges are convinced that the reforms needed to improve the criminal justice system do not require any restructuring of the trial court system.*

*The Ontario judges' report gives us a detailed account of the work of Ontario's Superior Court in the criminal law field. It is evident from this account that statistics showing that a very small percentage of criminal cases are disposed of in Superior Courts can be misleading. In 1998, though only 3 per cent of criminal charges were disposed of in Ontario's Superior Court, at any given time 37 to 38 per cent of the Superior Court's resources are assigned to criminal justice work. The criminal trials that are conducted in the Superior Court tend to be much longer and more complex than the standard fare of Ontario's Provincial Court, the Ontario Court of Justice. Also, various kinds of appellate work are prominent in the criminal justice matters dealt with by the Superior Court. The Superior Court, as the judges remark, functions in effect as an intermediate court of appeal in Ontario.*

*In comparing Ontario's trial court system with Quebec's, it is important to bear in mind that Ontario's Superior Court, unlike Quebec's, continues to try non-jury cases for indictable offences where the accused elects trial in the Superior Court. If the Quebec model were adopted in Ontario it would mean transferring 48 per cent of the Superior Court's criminal trials to the Provincial Court. The judges doubt that Ontario's Provincial Court is prepared for such a sudden increase in its criminal trial caseload.*

*Ontario's Superior Court judges believe there is merit in continuing with a hierarchical two-tier system in which the Superior Court specializes in long, difficult trials and appellate work, while the Provincial Court handles the bulk of criminal trial work. However, they suggest that a 'cooperatively administered' two-level system could effectively manage the province's criminal trial resources and recommend that administrative unification of the criminal courts begin at least in some regions of the province.*

At the Opening of Courts in January of 1997, Chief Justice Patrick LeSage of the Ontario Court, General Division, noted: 'We are not disposing of cases quickly enough ... Trials are taking much too long. We must find some way to make trials more efficient.'

In October of 1997, the Criminal Justice Review was established to study the operation of the criminal justice system in Ontario and recommend measures to combat delay and inefficiency. The review was a combined initiative of the judiciary (Chief Justice LeSage and Chief Judge Linden), the attorney general (the Honourable Charles Harnick), and the Ontario Criminal Lawyers' Association. The committee's terms of reference were as follows:

The focus of the committee's recommendations will be on the practical solutions to increase the efficiency of the criminal courts, further reduce delay in bringing matters to trial and shorten trials. Short and long-term solutions will be considered, including the following key areas of the criminal justice system:
pre-trial and release proceedings;
remand and set date process;
disclosure and pre-trial resolutions; and
trial procedure.

The co-chairs were the Honourable Mr Justice Hugh Locke of the General Division, the Honourable Senior Judge John Evans of the Provincial Division, and Murray Segal, assistant deputy attorney general, Criminal Law Division. The committee included members of the judiciary from the Court of Appeal, General and Provincial Divisions, crown attorneys, defence counsel, Legal Aid, the Department of Justice, and representatives of Court Operations.

Over a period of seventeen months the full committee met eighteen times. As well, there were numerous subcommittee meetings. The committee did not restrict itself to the members' ideas on improving efficiency. Before making any recommendations it 'invited interested members of the public, criminal justice stakeholders, and the judiciary to share their thoughts and ideas on how the criminal justice system could be improved.' Sixty-five submissions were received.

After lengthy deliberation and consultation, the committee made 115 recommendations to improve the efficiency of Ontario's courts, thereby providing a thoughtful and detailed analysis of the criminal justice system.[1] The recommendations, if followed, would reduce delay and improve court efficiency. As yet, however, the majority of the recommendations have not been implemented. Those few which have are yet to be evaluated.

At the Opening of Courts in January of 2000, the attorney general, the Honourable James Flaherty, said this about criminal justice in Ontario:

The justice system of tomorrow will be a service enterprise focused on meeting the needs of the public and moreover, a system that underpins our quality of life, which is part of the broader picture of the quality of life in the Province of Ontario ... nothing could be more abhorrent than the ultimate failure of the justice system, the loss of cases because of delay.

As you know, we are taking action in two stages to prevent the Askov crisis from ever happening again. First of all, the successful backlog blitz in the Province's six busiest court locations, and the Criminal Justice Review, whose recommendations are now being implemented.

A third stage, I would suggest, should be an examination of key structural changes to the criminal justice system. We should think seriously, I suggest, about such options as: abolishing preliminary inquiries, which often force victims to testify twice, and which have been eclipsed by case law that now requires full disclosure to the defence; establishing a unified criminal court to eliminate the complexities, expenses and delay of moving cases back and forth between two different levels of trial court; and as an interim measure, having all non-jury criminal trials held in the Ontario Court of Justice (the Quebec model).

The Criminal Justice Review report gives the government a comprehensive plan for obtaining its objectives without restructuring the criminal justice system. It is a full, thorough review based on broad input. Delivered about eleven months before the attorney general's comments at the Opening of Court, it was considered for less than a year. No mention of a unified criminal court appears in the report, nor was one recommended to the committee. The adoption of the 'Quebec model' was not discussed. We find it surprising that the same government, with a different attorney general, without notice or consultation, now maintains there is too much delay, too much duplication, and that consideration should be given to a unified criminal court with the Quebec model in the interim.

Nevertheless, the attorney general has asked for 'suggestions for enhancing the quality of service provided by the criminal justice system.' The following is our response.

However, we must make one thing clear. In most proposals for court restructuring or procedural change, a detailed outline of the proposals is presented for examination and consultation. To date, the government has not provided such information. Of necessity, this is a preliminary response to the attorney general's comments. If, and when, the government provides additional information, we will respond appropriately.

## The Current Court Structure

The current criminal justice system in Ontario provides for two trial courts. Looking at their respective jurisdiction is a logical starting point for an examination of the present system, but does not present a complete picture of the roles of the Provincial Court and Superior Court. (While the Provincial Court in Ontario is named the Ontario Court of Justice, we will refer to the court throughout the report as the Provincial Court, which is consistent with the interpretation section of the Criminal Code, section 2, and avoids confusion.) In addition to jurisdiction, we must examine the kind and number of cases, the time needed for completion, and the style and approach of the two courts.

*Jurisdiction*

While the courts share common jurisdiction for most indictable offences in non-jury trials, there are areas that, in practice, are distinct to each court; this is so despite the Superior Court being a court of inherent jurisdiction.

Judges of the Provincial Court preside at:

- some bail hearings (except s. 469 offences) although most are conducted by justices of the peace
- bail reviews from Youth Court where the original hearing was conducted by a justice of the peace (s. 8, *Young Offenders Act*)
- all summary conviction offence trials
- all trials for hybrid offences where the Crown elects to proceed summarily
- all trials of absolute jurisdiction offences (s. 553, Criminal Code)
- all Crown election offences where the Crown elects to proceed by indictment and the accused elects to be tried in the Provincial Court
- all indictable offences where the accused elects trial in the Provincial Court except those offences in the exclusive jurisdiction of the Superior Court (murders, accessory after the fact to murder, attempted murder, conspiracy to commit murder, bribery by the holder of a judicial office and a series of rarely used offences (s. 469, Criminal Code)
- preliminary inquiries on indictable offences in the exclusive jurisdiction of the Superior Court
- preliminary inquiries on other indictable offences where the accused elects to be tried in the Superior Court
- preliminary inquires on hybrid offences where the Crown elects to proceed by indictment and the accused elects to be tried in the Superior Court
- preliminary inquiries in Youth Court cases to be tried in Superior Court (s. 19, *Young Offenders Act*)
- *in facie* contempt of court (s. 484, Criminal Code)
- appeals under the *Provincial Offences Act*
- references by firearms acquisition certificate applicants who were refused a certificate (s. 106 (15), Criminal Code)
- appeals from refusals to issue and revocations of certificates and permits for firearms (s. 112, Criminal Code)

Judges of the Superior Court exercise exclusive jurisdiction in the following areas:

- all jury trials
- all trials of offences within the exclusive jurisdiction of the Superior Court (s. 469, Criminal Code)
- non-jury trials on indictable offences where the accused has elected trial in the Superior Court
- murder trials under the *Young Offenders Act* where the trial is deemed or ordered to be held in the Superior Court (s. 19, *Young Offenders Act*)
- appeals from summary conviction cases tried in the Provincial Court, including the *Young Offenders Act*
- prerogative writs under Part XXVI of the Criminal Code, including *certiorari, mandamus, habeas corpus*, and prohibition
- contempt of court, *in facie*, in relation to the Superior Court and *ex facie*, for both courts (s. 9 and 10(2), Criminal Code)
- abuse of process motions respecting some matters tried in the Provincial Court[2]
- original bail applications for section 469 offences (s. 515(1) and 522, Criminal Code)
- bail reviews by the accused or Crown (s. 520 and 521, Criminal Code)
- review of detained accused's trials which have been delayed (s. 525, Criminal Code)
- bail estreat and forfeiture (Part XXV, Criminal Code)
- review of detention of witnesses (s. 707(1), Criminal Code)
- the release of a person in custody into the custody of a peace officer for the purpose of assisting a peace officer acting in the execution of his or her duties (s. 527(7), Criminal Code)
- originating notices of motion for declaratory relief under the Charter with respect to the constitutional validity of statutory provisions
- supervisory review, in appropriate cases, of the disclosure process
- issuance of wiretap authorizations (s. 185 and 188, Criminal Code)
- issuance of proceeds of crime orders and special warrants regarding enterprise crime offences (Part XII.2, Criminal Code) These are complex and lengthy applications and frequently involve areas of law with which a generalist court is conversant such as restraint orders, control and management of seized assets, forfeiture and voidable transfers. The proceeds of crime regime requires an

understanding of civil and real property law in order to properly interpret the Criminal Code provisions.

- special jurisdiction respecting search and seizure such as solicitor/client privilege hearings (s. 488.1, Criminal Code), items seized pursuant to conventional warrant authority (s. 490 (3)(8)(9)(9.1)(10)(17), Criminal Code) and forfeiture of offence-related property (s. 490.2(5), Criminal Code)
- issuance of process and compulsion of persons not in the province (s. 527(1)(2), 699(2)(b) and 703, Criminal Code)
- orders for the release of blood samples for testing (s. 258(4), Criminal Code)
- non-broadcast orders respecting the identity of a victim or a witness where there is no presiding justice at the time (s. 486(4.4), Criminal Code)
- post-sentence reviews of parole eligibility in murder cases (s. 745.6 and 745.6(1), Criminal Code)
- applications to eliminate or reduce the term of long term supervision orders (s. 753.2(3), Criminal Code)
- applications by the Crown to prevent disclosure of information on the grounds of specific public interest (s. 37, *Canada Evidence Act*)
- appeals from decisions of the Provincial Court regarding the confirmation or not of the chief firearms officer, registrar, or provincial minister (s. 77(1)(2), *Firearms Act*).

## The Kind and Number of Cases

Traditionally, the Provincial Court disposes of the majority of criminal charges laid in Ontario. In 1979 the Provincial Court disposed of more than 95 per cent of criminal matters.[3] In 1998 the figure was 97 per cent.[4] With increased hybridization, more charges are disposed of in the Provincial Court. Crown attorneys elect summary procedure in most cases where the option exists. At the same time, the number of indictments filed and tried in the Superior Court has diminished.[5]

This has led some to conclude there has been a *de facto* transfer of criminal law jurisdiction from the Superior Court resulting in a single criminal court for Ontario, the Provincial Court, leaving the Superior Court to deal primarily with matters of property and civil rights. It has also been concluded that three-quarters of what was previously a significant and difficult Superior Court caseload of criminal matters has been transferred to the Provincial Court. These conclusions fail to take into consideration the differences between *charges* and *trials*, and the nature of criminal litigation in the Provincial and Superior Courts.

In spite of the increased jurisdiction the daily average sitting time of the Provincial Court has not increased significantly over the past few years (1994–95, 4.1 hours and 1997–98, 4.3 hours).[6] This apparently anomalous result is understandable when we examine other changes to court procedure and court statistics.

The Martin Committee recommendations and the investment strategy revolutionized criminal procedure in Ontario.[7] Not long ago, trial dates were set and witnesses subpoenaed for trial before disclosure was obtained. Counsel usually discussed a resolution on the morning of trial, a morning with heavy trial court dockets. Often the Crown counsel who reviewed the file immediately before trial was the first Crown to do so.

The emphasis is now on charge-screening by Crown attorneys before the first court appearance, disclosure before trial dates are set, and pre-trial conference or resolution meetings before dates are set. Crown counsel screen out charges in which there is no prospect of conviction, or amend the charges laid by police. Alternative measures and diversion programs insure that many charges never proceed to a plea or trial.

Crown counsel now give their 'best settlement offer' at the outset, which means fewer cases proceed to a preliminary inquiry or trial. The investment strategy set the objective of resolving 72 per cent of charges before trial dates were set, and having only 9 per cent of charges proceed to trial. In 1993, for example, about 60 per cent of charges were disposed of before trial and about 10.7 per cent of charges proceeded to trial. While not every jurisdiction achieves the objectives, the new strategies are working well.

*The Time Needed for Completion*

Focusing on the number of charges does not reflect the judicial activity and time required to dispose of a case. The time required for a withdrawal, diversion, or guilty plea is substantially less than if the matter proceeds to trial or preliminary inquiry. An analysis which treats all charges the same fails to account for this significant fact. For example, a 'murder' and 'accommodation fraud' are both charges. To treat them the same for statistical purposes illustrates the problem of relying on the number of charges to determine a court's workload.

While subject to some of the noted frailties, a more meaningful analysis examines *cases* since one incident can result in multiple *charges*. The Ministry of the Attorney General's *Court Statistics Annual Report, Fiscal Year 1998/1999* provides the number of charges and indictments in the Superior Court, but does not include the number of informations for the Provincial Court. Since there are roughly three Criminal Code charges per indictment, the number of charges disposed of in the Provincial Court significantly inflates the number of cases.

We must examine what is needed to complete a particular case or charge. In the United States this is referred to as the 'case weight.' Without a similar analysis available, to compare 500,000 *charges* laid in the Provincial Court with 4,189 indictments added or 4,586 indictments completed, in the Superior Court, both distorts and misleads.

In spite of the difficulties inherent in charge analysis, hybridization has resulted in more charges being disposed of in the Provincial Court. However, to conclude the Superior Court has effectively gone out of the criminal law business ignores three factors: the frailties inherent in relying upon statistics using charges; the difference between Superior Court trial statistics and reality; and, the Superior Court's exclusive criminal law jurisdiction in non-trial matters.

The overall percentage of judicial resources assigned for criminal work in the Superior Court is roughly 37 to 38 per cent at any given time.[8] Criminal trials are considerably longer now than in the pre-Charter era. What was a one-to-two-week trial in 1980 is now likely to be a one-to-two-month trial.

Fifty-two per cent of the trials conducted in the Superior Court between 1996 and 1999 were jury trials, which in themselves are longer than non-jury trials, particularly with increased challenges for cause.[9] The average length of jury trials has dramatically increased, with many trials lasting several months. For example, a special assignment court in Toronto in 1999–2000 listed seven cases, all scheduled for from three to eight weeks, while a previous list included one estimated for four to six months and a second for three months.

While the Provincial Court targets trials on 9 per cent of charges, the percentage of cases which proceed to a contested trial in the Superior Court is significantly higher. Examining withdrawn indictments, guilty pleas, trials held, and bench warrants issued, between 1997 and 1999, 36 per cent of indictments proceeded to trial. Because of the relatively new procedures designed to resolve cases at the earliest opportunity, Superior Court cases are more likely to proceed to trial than before. When one adds to this workload over a thousand bail reviews and initial bail applications, over a thousand summary conviction appeals and the other areas of exclusive jurisdiction listed above, an accurate picture of the Superior Court's involvement in criminal law emerges. While the Provincial Court carries a heavy workload in criminal law, so does the Superior Court.

*Style and Approaches of the Courts*

The above analysis helps to illustrate the fundamental difference between the two courts. In general, the Provincial Court works on hourly and daily schedules with the vast majority of their cases being resolved without trial; those proceeding to trial or preliminary inquiry, are scheduled primarily for a number of hours, less frequently a number of days and, on occasion, for weeks. Where insufficient time has been allotted for the trial or preliminary inquiry the continuation date is often several weeks or months later. In the Superior Court, trials are occasionally scheduled for months, usually for weeks and, on occasion, for days.

The cases tried in the Superior Court are determined in three ways. First, Parliament has determined that some indictable offences are so serious they must be tried in the Superior Court. Second, Parliament has determined that most indictable offences can be tried in the Superior Court, on election by the accused. Third, in hybrid offences, Crown counsel can choose to proceed by indictment.

The *Report of the Ontario Courts Inquiry,* (the Zuber Report) concluded the Provincial Court was geared to handle a very high volume of cases with maximum dispatch and minimum cost. The Superior Court, on the other hand, has fewer but longer cases, normally requiring written judgments, rulings, and jury charges in criminal matters.

All judges in criminal cases in Ontario contribute to the administration of justice and provide the public with a high quality of justice. They are competent and dedicated. While sharing jurisdiction on most indictable offences, the judges of the two divisions preside over cases that differ in style, volume, and type. The public is well served by the complementary two-tiered structure, each with its own strengths, and each presided over by men and women of high quality who, for their own individual reasons, sought appointment to the particular court on which they serve.

## Court Restructuring and the Administration of Justice

While courts should be efficient and avoid unnecessary delay, the measure of any court must be the quality of justice it dispenses. In the post-*Askov* era,[10] one of the regrettable by-products of that crisis is a preoccupation with quantity over quality in the justice system's most visible component, criminal law. To regard the justice system as a 'service enterprise' risks undermining the quality of justice. In the effort to provide an efficient and timely procedure, the quality of justice and fairness must not be sacrificed on the altar of expediency. As Professor A.W. Mewett wrote in 1990, 'efficiency is no doubt a very desirable thing, but justice is even more desirable. The starting point for any reform, whether of the court system or anything else, cannot and must not be allowed to be efficiency for the sake of efficiency. The goal of reform must be the furtherance of justice.'[11] Any proposal for court restructuring or procedural change must start with an analysis of the problem to be solved. Is it real or perceived? Is it advanced by informed or uninformed observers? Is the statistical data sufficiently reliable and detailed to reach an informed conclusion?

If a problem has been identified, it is essential to determine the nature and extent of the problem. Is it systemic, requiring fundamental restructuring or procedural changes? Is it a local problem found in one centre or region, or is it case-specific? A case-specific problem may be an aberration, not something mandating structural or procedural changes to the entire court system. Once a valid concern has been identified, any solution must guarantee an equivalent or better quality of justice.

In his speech, the attorney general noted the O.J. Simpson trial took 474 days from arrest through trial, while in Ontario 'we all know of murder cases pending for three, four, five or even six years after the arrest.' This reference to murder trials requires an examination of the reasons for the delay, as well as the pre-trial delay time for other murders cases. Is the problem systemic, regional, local or case-specific? In the absence of a systemic problem there is no need for structural or procedural changes province-wide. If there is a problem in Toronto, there is no need for a provincial solution. Neither local problems nor aberrations should provide impetus for major restructuring.

Given the time available to prepare this initial report, a detailed analysis of every murder trial in Ontario was not feasible. However, we did examine 76 murder trials occurring since 1995 which revealed the following times from first appearance in the Court of Justice to verdict: under 12 months, 8.3 per cent, 12–18 months, 25 per cent; 18–24 months 28.9 per cent; 24–30 months, 14.5 per cent; 30–36 months, 9.2 per cent; 36–42 months, 2.6 per cent and over 42 months, 7.9 per cent. These cases indicate 89.4 per cent of murder trials are completed under the time frame the attorney general indicated as causing concern.

It should also be remembered that the Supreme Court of Canada has indicated as a guideline that delay in the range of 14–18 months after the intake period to the start of trial does not violate section 11(b) of the Charter.[12] The intake period for murder cases is generally longer than the norm because of the volume of disclosure including reports from the Centre for Forensic Sciences. In addition, longer and more complex cases have been acknowledged to take longer to get to trial and not breach section 11(b).[13]

No doubt some trials are delayed for lengthy periods. However, the reasons for the delays must be examined. Once it is determined why a particular case was delayed, an informed decision can be made regarding what, if any, changes are required to remedy the problem. Examining a small percentage of cases should not be the basis for structural change.

## Delay

As a result of the combined efforts of the judiciary, Crown attorneys, defence counsel, and court administrators, pre-trial delay has been significantly reduced across Ontario since the decision in *Askov*. Although the attorney general spoke of the bench and bar tending to focus on the specific case before them and losing sight of the larger picture, his comment fails to recognize the countless hours members of the administration of justice have spent on committees such as the Martin Committee, Criminal Justice Review and local bench and bar groups, all with a view to improving the administration of justice in Ontario. We agree there are still areas of concern. The public has a right to be concerned about cases not getting to trial for several years. However, the starting point for any analysis is the reasons for the delay.

The attorney general mentioned the 'complexities, expense and delay of moving cases back and forth between two levels of court.' We disagree with the assertion there are complexities in court structure.

The court levels are straightforward. The multiple classification of offences in the Criminal Code may be complex but that does not relate to the levels of courts. The reference to the expense and delay caused by cases moving back and forth is troubling if one believes many cases are committed for trial in the Superior Court and then returned to the Provincial Court. The number of cases in which that occurs is about 1 per cent.[14] Most are remanded back for a plea of guilty which completes the case more quickly than a trial in the Superior Court. There is no realistic basis of concern for cases going back and forth.

There can be delay between the committal for trial and the commencement of proceedings in the Superior Court. That time has been reduced in many jurisdictions in which the Provincial Court trial office has Superior Court pre-trial dates available, so that the accused is remanded directly to the mandatory pre-trial instead of a monthly or biweekly assignment court and then to the pre-trial. The quality of justice in Ontario is high. The delays which occur are caused by the number and complexity of cases as well as human failings of counsel, judges, witnesses and accused. Most of the delay cannot fairly be attributed to a system which functions remarkably well for anything as personal and important as the criminal justice system. When the following summary of the primary reasons for delay is examined, it is clear structural change will not solve the problems.

## The Unified Family Court

It may be suggested that a unified criminal court is the next logical step after the creation of the Unified Family Court. That suggestion fails to consider the rationale for establishing the Unified Family Court and the lessons to be learned from that court.

There is no single solution for every perceived problem in the judicial system. One must first determine whether there is a problem, and if so, determine if it is case-specific, localized or systemic. The rationale for the creation of the Unified Family Court is found in the following conclusion of the Zuber Report:

> [The] jurisdiction in family law matters is spread among all three levels of courts. In general terms, the Provincial Court (Family Division) is empowered to deal with custody of children, support of children and spouses, crown wardship and the enforcement of support orders of other

courts. The District Court has jurisdiction over custody, support of children and spouses and the division of family property. District Court judges acting as local judges of the High Court, and the judges of the High Court have jurisdiction over custody, support, the division of property and divorce.

The deficiencies in this jurisdictional mosaic are obvious. Parties to a family dispute are sometimes involved in more than one court at the same time because each spouse may commence proceedings in a different court. Further, there are those who commence proceedings in the Provincial Court and find that only a partial resolution of their problems is possible and that they are obliged to go to a second court to resolve the property and divorce issues that remain outstanding. The Provincial Court (family Divisions) finds that there are difficulties in enforcing the support orders of the District Court and High Court. In those cases where circumstances have changed, the Provincial Court is powerless to vary the order. Parties are obliged to go to the court that made the order to address the issue of variation and then return to the Provincial Court to deal with the issue.[15]

While the remarks refer to the former three-level court structure which existed at the time Unified Family Courts emerged, they reflect family law problems before and after merger. Those problems do not exist in criminal law. Although both criminal trial courts share some jurisdiction, there are no parallel proceedings occurring, as was the situation in family law. In addition, the current two-level criminal trial court structure was intentionally established by federal legislation as opposed to being the by-product of the distribution of legislative authority in the *Constitution Act.*

A second important distinction is found in the approach of the Unified Family Court: the provision of a wide range of legal and social strategies for the resolution of disputes, through conciliation and counselling. Mediation, in the view of many, is the cornerstone of the court. In criminal law there is mediation for minor offences in the Provincial Court, in some locations. For serious criminal offences this fundamental approach of the Unified Family Court is not appropriate.

The Unified Family Court was first established in Hamilton as a pilot project in 1977. In 2000 the provincial government committed to expand the court province-wide. However, over two decades after the pilot project started, only 40 per cent of Ontarians have access to the court.

The continued expansion of the Unified Family Court will continue to create administrative issues that will challenge and engage the time and attention of the Superior Court for years to come. To add the unification of the criminal courts would result in administrative problems that could threaten the integrity of the entire court system of the province.

There is a lesson to be learned from the Unified Family Court in relation to the proposed unified criminal court. It involves the emergence of subordinate judicial officers. As will be seen below in dealing with unified criminal courts, this is a hallmark of court unification and runs contrary to one of the objectives of unification, removing the hierarchy in courts. Increasing use of dispute resolution officers in some jurisdictions results in some judicial functions being delegated to non-judicial officers. While the Unified Family Court may efficiently deal with the problems specific to family law, the problems, real and perceived, in the criminal justice system are not the same.

## A Unified Criminal Court

Since we have received no details of the proposed unified criminal court, our analysis will focus on the concept of criminal court unification and the positions presented in earlier proposals.

A threshold question: What court structure is envisaged for such a court? Is it to be a separate court with one level or class of specialist judges doing only criminal cases? Is it to be a division of a single trial court with generalist judges who would rotate through the various areas of law-specific divisions? Our research reveals no jurisdiction in North America which has the former style of court. Earlier proposals suggested the latter approach, a single trial court with generalist judges. Lacking any indication of the type of court proposed, we will examine both options.

### Background

The concept of a unified criminal court was first discussed by Roscoe Pound in 1906.[16] To date, several American states have adopted variations on the proposal.[17] In Canada, the Zuber Report rejected structural court divisions along functional lines, noting, 'It is not apparent that this plan contains any substantial benefit to the public in terms of accessibility or efficiency ... the radical changes involved in the three unified court proposal fall outside the ambit of realistic expectation of success.'[18]

The Law Reform Commission recommended a unified criminal court in 1989, citing difficulties of complexity, confusion, inefficiency, and inequality.[19] The commission's paper was one of a series of suggestions for completely revamping the criminal law and courts in Canada. It is difficult to divorce the unified criminal court proposal from their other suggestions in substantive and procedural criminal law. Yet no paper was ever produced on appellate court restructuring, a key component of any change.

In 1989 Ontario Attorney General Ian Scott introduced a proposal for structural change which included, as part of Phase II, a unified criminal court. Following a change in government in September of 1990, this was never implemented. A number of legal organizations have also examined the establishment of a unified criminal court over the years. The proposals were analysed and it is instructive to recall the conclusions reached and positions taken previously.

In 1990 the Joint Committee on Court Reform, composed of the Advocates' Society, the Canadian Bar Association of Ontario, and the Criminal Lawyers' Association concluded: 'In the interest of the public in maintaining the quality of our justice system, we urge the Attorney General of Ontario to abandon all plans to implement Phase II for criminal law. We urge him to improve the quality of justice by providing adequate funding, adequate facilities and improved administration.'[20] The report was also endorsed by the Criminal Lawyers' Committee of the Sudbury District Law Association, the Hamilton Criminal Lawyers' Association, the Defence Counsel Association of Ottawa, the executive of the London Criminal Lawyers' Association, and the Windsor Criminal Lawyers' Association.

In 1990 the Provincial attorneys general unanimously proposed a unified criminal court, while the Judicial Council rejected the concept in 1991. The Judicial Council had commissioned a study by Professor Carl Baar, *One Trial Court: Possibilities and Limitations*, prior to taking their position in opposition. The Canadian Bar Association's 1991 Task Force Report on Court Reform in Canada rejected the concept of a unified criminal court. The report of the Manitoba Aboriginal Justice Inquiry recommended a unified criminal court in 1991.[21] In 1994 the New Brunswick Department of Justice proposed New Brunswick as a site of a pilot project for a unified criminal court.[22] The court was never established.

*Identifying the Problems*

No structural change should be undertaken until there is an analysis of the problems and a determination made that the proposed solution is not only responsive to the problem but, of greater importance, will ensure the same or better quality of justice.

*Administration*

When examining the concerns with the current justice system, a clear distinction must be drawn between inefficiencies in administration, and inefficient court structure. The unification of courts as an administrative organization and the unification of the judiciary are very different proposals aimed at different perceived problems. Many of the concerns raised about inefficiency relate to administration, not court structure. As the Canadian Bar Association Task Force Report concluded: 'The experience of the Crown Court in England suggests that a single administration can successfully manage a court composed of three different levels of judges. We think it wrong to say that a unified court structure is a necessary condition for unified administration and management.'

From an examination of the American state courts the same report reached the following tentative conclusion: 'Structural unification on its own is not likely to bring about the sorts of improved performance which are the stated goal of unification. Improved trial court performance depends more upon effective management than it does on court structure.'[23]

The Joint Committee on Court Reform Report concluded: 'Court structure ought not to be sacrificed on the altar of administrative efficiency where there are equally effective ways of promoting administrative efficiency in the overall criminal justice system.'[24]

A single administration for the criminal courts should be studied to determine if a more efficient justice system would follow. In our view, a cooperatively administered two-level trial court could solve any problem of staff duplication.

On his return from a visit to Nunavut, the attorney general commented that he was impressed with a system where the public can go to the front counter of the courthouse and do everything from filing a small claims court case, to appealing a conviction, to inquiring about legal aid. The one-stop-shopping approach can only be achieved in consolidated courthouses where the single-counter vision is a reality without structural change. In the vast majority of the province (including Toronto with nine separate buildings and roughly 30 per cent of the charges), multiple facilities make the one-stop shopping concept unattainable without an enormous capital outlay by the provincial government.

## Complexity

It has been suggested the current criminal court structure is complex. While there are areas of criminal procedure that may be regarded as complex, such as the classification of offences, we do not agree that the court structure in Ontario is complex. Whether a system is complex or confusing must be seen through the eyes of people who have taken some time to familiarize themselves with the subject. There is no evidence the public or the bar are confused about court structure. As the Canadian Bar Association Task Force concluded, 'The problem is more the product of the law of criminal procedure than of court structure.'[25]

## Delay

A unified criminal court alone will not reduce the time from arrest to disposition in any meaningful way. There will remain the intake procedure, pre-trial conferences, early resolutions, trials or preliminary inquiries. The 1991 Canadian Bar Association research suggested that the existing system can manage delay, when given sufficient resources and soundly managed. To suggest a new court structure would reduce delay is an unfounded and misleading assertion.

## Costs

The attorney general proposes the salaries of all unified criminal court judges be paid by the federal government, with the province to pay operating expenses and the cost of 3,500 court staff. The operating and staff expenses are currently paid by the provincial government. The only saving to the public would be in administrative consolidation which does not require structural unification.

As regards judicial salaries, the net effect of the proposal is to shift the salaries of all judges of the Provincial Court to the federal government.

The salaries and benefits paid to the judges of the Provincial Court in Ontario alone would cost the federal government an additional $50 million annually. Since there is a salary differential between the two courts, the cost of judicial salaries would increase. Since the public pays the salaries, it will now have to pay for a more expensive justice system. Therefore there is no cost saving to the public from court unification. If the preliminary inquiry remains, there is no saving to the litigants from unification.

*Precedents*

While the concept of a unified criminal court has been debated for close to a century, very few jurisdictions have adopted one. There is no jurisdiction in North America which has a separate criminal court with specialized judges. Several American states have a unified generalist trial court. However, most have an intermediate court of appeal, a structure not accepted in Canada. In addition, the Americans have a parallel federal court structure with criminal law jurisdiction covering each state.

While not determinative, the experience in other jurisdictions, particularly the United Kingdom, with a justice system similar to ours, should inform the current debate. As the Joint Committee on Court Reform concluded, 'The criminal justice system could be done irreparable harm by creating an untested vision in a jurisdiction as large as Ontario.'[26] We would add to that conclusion, in a jurisdiction as large and diverse as Ontario.

*The Effects of a Unified Criminal Court*

An examination of the following factors leads us to conclude a unified criminal court will create insurmountable problems. It would not solve problems but create new ones.

COURT SIZE
There are 288 judges in the Superior Court and 255 in the Provincial Court. If a unified criminal court is to be a division of a single trial court with generalist judges, the trial court would have 543 judges. If the current 278 justices of the peace were included, the total would be 821 judicial officers. Managing a court of either size would be an administrative nightmare. Five hundred and forty-three judges would

be larger than the world's largest unified court, while 821 judicial officers would be twice the size of that court.[27] It is difficult to imagine such
a court being efficient. The members of a court of either size would feel
it difficult to act as part of a cohesive judicial body, rather than just
individuals in a huge bureaucracy.

One of the hallmarks of a generalist court is the ability to rotate
judges amongst the areas of law-specific divisions. With a huge court,
that objective would be difficult, if not impossible. If the aim of restructuring is to better serve the public, the proposal fails.

CIRCUITING

If the proposal is to have a separate court of specialized judges, the
proposal will result in a less efficient system and reduce service to
Ontarians. Under the present system, Superior Court judges circuit for
several weeks each year both inside and outside their own region,
although less frequently for Toronto-based judges. Circuiting judges sit
in smaller communities where there is insufficient demand for full-
time courts. While sitting in these centres, judges hear motions in family and civil law, criminal summary conviction appeals, and pre-trial
conferences. During jury sittings the judge will hear both criminal and
civil cases. One judge can, and does, handle those functions daily or
during a jury sitting. The smaller communities are well served.

Under the proposed unification, one judge would not be able to deal
with all areas of law. Two or more judges would have to serve the community, likely on different days, to do part of the current list. The
advantages of a generalist judge in these circumstances is obvious. It is
difficult to see how unification would be more efficient or serve the
public better.

HIERARCHY

In past debates on unification, much was said and written about court
hierarchy. At the outset it is important to distinguish between two very
different concepts, hierarchy, and status. Hierarchy relates to the levels
of courts and is used in this paper only because of repeated references
in earlier discussions. Status involves the alleged perception of an inferior quality of judge and justice in a lower court. As regards hierarchy,
it not only provides significant benefits to the public and the administration of justice, but unified courts do not remove it.

The Superior Court performs an important and essential supervisory function in relation to the Provincial Court. In dealing with bail
reviews, summary conviction appeals, and extraordinary remedies,

the Superior Court provides a more efficient and less expensive method of dealing with appeals and reviews than proceedings in the Court of Appeal. Ontarians are better served having local recourse to these appeals and reviews by a single judge than having to proceed before three judges located a significant distance from the original proceedings. The perception of impartiality is enhanced when an appeal or review is conducted by a judge of a different court. In addition, any proposal for appeals to judges of the same court will erode the principle of *stare decisis*. The effect will be less efficiency and, in some instances, confusion with conflicting decisions given by appellate judges of the same court.

In addition, there is a need for institutional distance between the appeal level and trial courts to ensure the independence and integrity of the appeal court. This principle has been acknowledged by the Ministry of the Attorney General in the *Architectural Design for Court Houses*:

> The independence of the courts should be reflected in the planning of the building where possible. Justices of the Superior Court of Justice are required to review their Ontario Court of Justice counterpart's decisions through appeals and other 'supervisory' activities. Therefore this functional requirement for separate identities must be observed when planning their respective judicial offices.[28]

In relation to trials, traditionally the judicial system has provided a different level of court based upon the nature of the crime itself, not the procedure by which it is tried. This should be maintained. Where a serious crime is tried by the same judge in the same court system as a minor charge, the public may perceive all crime to be the same degree of seriousness.

Court unification does not eliminate hierarchy. Unification establishes a new hierarchy where cases are downloaded to subordinate judicial officers or separate groups of judges. In the United States, the federal court is a highly unified court structure but the pressure of workload, combined with concern for expense and accessibility, led to the development of a large 'subordinate judiciary' within a unified system. In Illinois, a large single trial court with generalist judges, there are 'associate judges' for minor offences.[29] In Ontario, this phenomenon has already occurred with justices of the peace now conducting virtually all bail hearings as well as intake and assignment courts.

The phenomenon was recognized in 1987 in the *Report of the Ontario Courts Inquiry*:

The division of the courts by class of cases would mix the short and simple cases with the long and complicated. Inevitably, these specialist courts
would have to establish a division to handle short, high-volume cases and
a separate division for slow-moving, more complex cases and jury trials.
Thus, in fairly short order, the basic three courts would multiply by the
creation of internal divisions and soon the three would become six and
the resulting system could be more complex than the system now.[30]

The Canadian Bar Association Task Force, after examining the
American federal court system, noted that their investigation suggested at least two things: 'First, there will always be a need arising
from practical considerations and fiscal restrictions to have some form
of lower court. Second, and following on the first, it will not be possible to eliminate judicial hierarchy as there is a systemic need for subordinate judicial officers.'
A second form of hierarchy is the practical result of unification. The
Canadian Bar Association report, after examining the American State
trial court experiences drew the following tentative conclusion:

> Unification rarely does away with hierarchy. It simply takes away some
> forms of hierarchy and substitutes others ... Even in systems in which
> most judges have authority to preside in all courts, hierarchy is preserved
> by the authority of administrative judges to assign the more demanding
> or less interesting work to the judges under his or her direction. The elim-
> ination of hierarchy within the judiciary is unlikely to be achieved
> through unification.[31]

The existence of an actual hierarchy was implicitly recognized in the
proposal of former Attorney General Scott: 'Judges may certainly continue to perform different functions but within a single court ... The
new court structure must ensure that judges of the highest quality are
available to hear all criminal matters and that *the most difficult and important cases are directed to the best qualified judges'* (emphasis added).[32] A
hierarchy imposed by an administrative judge may very well be more
difficult for some members of the judiciary to accept than one created
by legislation.

## SUMMARY CONVICTION APPEALS
The appellate jurisdiction exercised by the Superior Court is, in some
measure, a court of last resort for the majority of the criminal cases
tried in the province. Pursuant to section 829 of the Criminal Code the

Superior Court stands as the appeal court for all offences tried by summary conviction. Any further appeal is by leave of the Court of Appeal on a question of law alone.

There are five possible methods of hearing summary conviction appeals in a unified criminal court: by a single judge of the unified criminal court; by three judges of the unified criminal court; by three judges of an intermediate court of appeal; by a single judge of the Court of Appeal; and by three judges of the Court of Appeal. All methods are fundamentally flawed.

As regards members of the same court hearing criminal appeals, while not perhaps meeting the test of reasonable apprehension of bias, it is surely unacceptable to the public to have members of the same court sitting on criminal appeals of other members of the court. What is acceptable in civil matters (the Divisional Court) should not be extended to criminal matters where the liberty of the subject is involved. This model would surely diminish respect for the administration of justice and lead to confusion. It is a model which has been generally avoided, with very limited exceptions, in criminal law.

In addition, there are obvious delay and expense issues associated with members of the same court sitting on appeal of one another, particularly where three judges hear the appeals. In effect, another court is created within the unified criminal court, leading to stratification in any event. Having three members of the unified criminal court hear appeals would also increase the costs to litigants required to file three copies, at least, of all material, as well as increased travel costs and reduced convenience, since the parties would have to travel to central locations where the appeals would be held. This is independent of the cost of scheduling three judges to sit on these appeals.

Various reports of members of the Ontario Court of Appeal, including Justices MacKinnon and Brooke, have called for the creation of an intermediate Court of Appeal.[33] There is no recent activity on this front; the Court of Appeal has significantly reduced its backlog. The creation of an intermediate court of appeal, is, in effect, the creation of another level of court beyond the unified criminal court and accordingly fails to reduce the hierarchical chain. The Superior Court is effectively an intermediate court of appeal and is increasingly recognized as such.

Uploading the appellate caseload from the Superior Court to the Court of Appeal would soon paralyse that court and increase its backlog. Even from a jurisdiction as small in terms of population as Nunavut, the increased workload of its Court of Appeal has been significant and unexpected. Uploading the current appeals to the Court of Appeal would also detract from the jurisprudential leadership of that court. A larger Court of Appeal would diminish the consistency and predictability of the court. Having one member of the Court of Appeal hear the first-level appeal with a final appeal to the Court of Appeal raises the same problems as discussed above regarding public confidence and perception.

Any proposal for summary conviction appeals to be heard outside the location of the offence ignores the important role geography plays in sentencing, and the response to local problems. The Superior Court, acting as a summary conviction appeal court and sitting in every county or district is, more so than the Ontario Court of Appeal, knowledgeable about local conditions and problems.

The objectives of efficiency and easier access to justice will not be met by any of these proposals, indeed they will be hindered by them. Any suggestion that three judges do what one judge does now is the antithesis of efficiency.

BAIL ISSUES

The Superior Court exercises exclusive jurisdiction respecting initial bail applications for Criminal Code section 469 offences (primarily murder, accessory after the fact to murder, and conspiracy to commit murder), significant bail review jurisdiction under sections 520 and 521 of the Criminal Code and section 8(6) of the *Young Offenders Act* and a supervisory function to review the pace of litigation in the Provincial Court under section 525 of the Criminal Code. The comments above about conferring a review power on members of the same court are equally applicable to these areas, as are the comments about conferring this jurisdiction on the Court of Appeal. Of particular note is the anomaly that would result if one judge of a court were to review the pace of litigation of the same court.

EXTRAORDINARY REMEDIES

Currently, the Superior Court exercises the important and historical supervisory function respecting prerogative writs. The remedies of *certiorari, mandamus,* prohibition, and *habeas corpus* have existed for hundreds of years. The review of committals to trial, of warrants, of the legality of detention of the citizen, and the exercise of other supervisory controls are all required in any orderly and efficient administration of criminal justice.

The extraordinary remedies, in particular *certiorari*, are considered to be discretionary remedies and as such the Superior Court is, as a general rule, the court of last resort respecting the review of decisions within the scope of the prerogative writs. As such, the prerogative writ jurisdiction has long stood as a significant area of expertise within the Superior Court. The above comments about members of the same court exercising appellate review and uploading to the Court of Appeal are applicable to extraordinary remedies.

If prerogative remedies are to be available for all trial court judges (as in Nunavut), extraordinary delays with particularly injurious effects on jury trials would occur. The result would be delay, added cost, inconvenience to the jurors, and potentially mistrials if the jury could not be reassembled.

THE JUDICIARY

While the focus of the attorney general's proposal is service to the public and court efficiency, the position of the judiciary cannot be ignored. In the current system the public benefits from a highly qualified and dedicated judiciary in both trial courts. All sitting judges, after at least ten years at the bar, chose to end their practice and seek appointment to a specific court. Such a decision is not made in haste. It is highly individual, arrived at with considerable reflection. The current proposals undermine the choices made.

CURRENT APPOINTMENTS

There are two options for appointments to the unified criminal court. First, the current Provincial Court judges would all be appointed to either a separate unified criminal court with specialist judges or to the unified criminal court division of a single trial court with generalist judges. In this scenario, the balance of the judges required for either style unified criminal court would be drawn from the current Superior Court. Second, as occurred with the Unified Family Court, the members of the Provincial Court who sought appointment to the unified criminal court would apply to the federal government for a new appointment.

Either approach results in manifest unfairness to judges. If the first approach is adopted and all current Provincial Court judges become unified criminal court judges, current judges of the Superior Court who left practice and sought appointment to a generalist court which would permit them to do criminal work would be excluded from criminal litigation permanently (if the unified criminal court is a specialist judge court) or for large periods of time (if the unified criminal court is a division of a single trial court). The second approach would leave some judges of the Provincial Court without a court and some members of the Superior Court excluded from criminal litigation when they sought appointment to a court which permitted them to hear criminal cases.

FUTURE APPOINTMENTS

The public is best served when candidates of the highest quality are appointed judges. Currently applications are received from specialist and general practitioners. On the approach advanced by the former attorney general, Ian Scott, these benefits of the current approach would be placed in jeopardy, thereby risking a reduction in the quality of justice instead of increasing it.

The Scott proposal was based on specialization: 'Judges would be assigned to divisions which reflect their area of expertise. The structure encourages the best qualified candidates to seek appointment and ensures difficult and important cases are assigned to experienced and expert judges.'[34]

In the area of criminal law, those with expertise would be Crown attorneys, defence counsel, and some law professors. Similar restrictions would apply in family and civil law. While it was suggested this would attract the best-qualified candidates, it would also eliminate general practitioners or solicitors, many of whom have become exceptional jurists in criminal and other areas of the law. Since those who practice in smaller communities are predominantly general practitioners of necessity, appointing experts would not only eliminate general practitioners from applying but exclude almost all lawyers who practice in small communities. For potential applicants who prefer a variety of judicial duties, either style of unified criminal court would deter their application. We agree with the 1991 Joint Committee on Court Reform conclusion that it is not clear a more specialized court would attract the best-qualified applicants.[35]

It would be a curious result if only specialists in criminal, family, and civil litigation were to be appointed to specialized trial courts or divisions of a single trial court, when all judges of the Court of Appeal and the Supreme Court of Canada hear cases in all areas of law.

FACILITIES

With the exception of the consolidated courthouses found in less than twenty-five locations, Ontarians are generally served by smaller facilities for the separate courts. In Toronto, where roughly 30 per cent of the criminal charges are laid, there are nine separate buildings, of which only two are equipped for jury trials. Most of the criminal courts in the province at present cannot accommodate jury trials. Accordingly, the public will not have more access to justice in jury trials in a unified criminal court.

If a unified criminal court were to be implemented, a likely result would be judges moving from one court facility to another away from their offices, libraries, and support staff. Instead of increased efficiency there would be inefficiency.

Absent a massive capital expenditure to build consolidated courthouses, the current facilities could not cope with structural unification. In Toronto, a committee is looking at alternatives for the various downtown court buildings and has concluded a courthouse for both divisions would require eighty-eight courtrooms, the largest in Canada and one of the largest in the world. There has been no commitment to date from the provincial government to fund such a project.

CONSTITUTIONAL CONSIDERATIONS

The earlier studies to which we have referred all raised the issue of constitutional concerns with unification. The 1982 New Brunswick attempt to establish a unified court was found to be constitutionally flawed by the Supreme Court of Canada.[36] While beyond the scope of this report, it is important to consider the earlier reports and the issues raised.

THE QUEBEC MODEL

Quebec has two levels of criminal trial courts, the Quebec Court and the Superior Court of Quebec. The Quebec Provincial Court is the Quebec Court, which has exclusive jurisdiction to try all non-jury trials, including indictable offences. Preliminary inquiries are held in the Quebec Court. If a jury trial is elected, the case proceeds in the Superior Court. If a non-jury trial is elected, a judge of the Quebec Court (different from the preliminary inquiry judge in the absence of consent) hears the trial.

With preliminary inquiries, there is no reduction in the time required to complete an indictable trial as the two procedures remain. There are cases where the accused will elect a jury trial and after appearing in the Superior Court will re-elect, with the consent of the Crown, for a non-jury trial in the Quebec Court. This 'back and forth' shifting of cases ought to be avoided. In the Ontario Superior Court, this sort of re-election occurs frequently, and is done in the same court, before the trial judge and takes only minutes to accomplish. In his address at the opening of courts the attorney general noted, 'nothing could be more abhorrent than the ultimate failure of the justice system, the loss of cases because of delay.'

In our view, imposing the Quebec model as an interim or permanent solution in Ontario will hasten the 'ultimate failure' of the justice system for countless cases. Assuming all current Superior Court non-jury trials would remain non-jury cases under the Quebec model, the result would be the transfer of 48 per cent of the criminal law trials from the Superior Court to the Provincial Court. It would threaten the creation of another *Askov* problem.

The most glaring impediment to improving efficiency with the Quebec model is inadequate judicial resources. There is no evidence to suggest the judges of the Provincial Court are not working to their capacity. From recent published reports they are maintaining the status quo in terms of delay in some areas, while in others they are falling behind. The administrative judge of the East Mall Court in Toronto noted his court was 'at the edge' and 'falling behind every month.'[37] Newmarket, an area targeted in the blitz to remove backlogs, has seen the time to trial increase in recent months.

It may be argued that judges of the Provincial Court now hear the preliminary inquiries so that there would be no meaningful increase in their workload. This argument is fundamentally flawed. First, while counsel will elicit evidence at a preliminary inquiry on Charter issues in order to explore the feasibility of trial arguments and/or prepare an evidentiary foundation for a pre-trial motion, there is a significant difference between hearing some evidence on the issue and the full Charter application. At trial the Crown will often lead further evidence on the Charter issue. In addition, at trial full argument is presented on the Charter issues and a judgment, often reserved, is required. Any suggestion the time requirements are the same or similar is misleading.

However, preliminary inquiries can save time at trial. Often the Charter issue is not pursued and on other occasions the application record consists of the preliminary inquiry evidence. Having said that, as a general rule the time required for trials is considerably longer than for preliminary inquiries. Often at preliminary inquiries the Crown will call one witness, such as the complainant, in a sexual assault case. The hearing may take two hours or half a day. At trial, the case proceeds with Charter, *Seaboyer*, and *O'Connor* applications. The half-day preliminary inquiry becomes a ten-day trial.

A second problem is scheduling in a court structured for trials the duration of which is measured in hours or half-days instead of weeks. Working on calendars created for hours and days is not compatible with longer trials. If the case is not completed in the allotted time (a frequent occurrence) the result will be a lengthy adjournment to continue the trial, an unsatisfactory result. Perhaps in larger centres with more judges, having one or two judges engaged in multiple-week trials would not create total chaos. Several judges engaged in long trials would. In smaller jurisdictions the court could not function with one or two courtrooms and heavy dockets if one or two judges were engaged in longer proceedings.

Finally, the current facilities will not accommodate an increased number of trials. The courthouses where the Provincial Court currently presides are generally being used to their capacity. Any increase would have to go to other courthouses, in some instances in other jurisdictions, which would impair the public's access to justice in their home jurisdiction.

Unless the provincial government is prepared to appoint many more judges and build new court facilities, the Quebec model will result in more delay, not less.

NUNAVUT

In April 1999 the Nunavut Court was created to serve twenty-six communities, with a total population of 30,000 people. The largest centre is Iqaluit with a population of 5,000. Some of the communities are as small as 200 to 300. The land mass is overwhelming, with Iqaluit north of Ottawa and Kuglugtug, the most westerly community, west of Edmonton.

Nunavut has a single trial court for all areas of law with generalist judges. It does not have a unified criminal court. At the present time, there are two full-time and twenty deputy judges who travel to the communities. Significantly, the appeals, bail reviews, and prerogative writs are heard in the Nunavut Court of Appeal by a single judge, not a judge of the Nunavut Court. Indictable appeals and summary conviction appeals, with leave, are heard by three or more Court of Appeal judges. As indicated earlier, the uploading cases to the Court of Appeal has resulted in an unexpected increase in that court's workload.

Whether a single trial court will work in Nunavut will be ascertained only after several years, experience. Nunavut is not Ontario, nor is it a city or region of Ontario. The issues and challenges which arise in that territory are unique to the region. Given the size of the territory, the population, the types of cases, and unique issues in Nunavut, neither the court structure nor procedures from that territory can be transferred to Ontario.

PILOT PROJECTS

Earlier proposals and studies have suggested a pilot project for a unified criminal court and/or the Quebec model. As for the Quebec model, the dangers of implementing that structure in any form are expressed earlier. As for the unified criminal court, any pilot project in one region or location in Ontario would inevitably invite Charter scrutiny under sections 7 and 15 which would have the potential to undermine the entire project.

There is a more fundamental concern for pilot projects involving altered court structures. While statistics can be collected, they can be distorted and manipulated. What cannot be measured statistically is the quality of justice. We have grave concerns that any pilot project would be evaluated on the basis of statistics alone, without consideration for the quality of justice.

## Recommendations

We believe the court system can become more efficient and the public better served without jeopardizing the quality of justice in Ontario. Implementing the following recommendations will achieve the goals sought by the attorney general.

### Judicial Appointments

The federal and provincial governments should be encouraged to make timely appointments when vacancies occur. While both have procedures in place, the current pace of appointments is unacceptable and does not serve the public. It is inconsistent to champion the elimination of delay while delaying the appointment of judges.

### Administrative Unification

Many of the concerns advanced as justification for structural unification relate to administration. Consolidation of the administration of the two trial courts might be explored in some regions where it would be operationally efficient to do so. When the Integrated Justice initiative is fully implemented this objective will be facilitated. In addition, that program should be able to provide more accurate information on the court system than is currently available.

The Criminal Justice Review Committee recommended the establishment of a provincial criminal justice coordinating committee composed of representatives of the key participants in the criminal justice system. Each court location would also set up a local committee. The committee's report was released in February 1999. While some steps have been taken to establish the committees, they have yet to meet. This initiative will be an important component of a more efficient justice system. The pace of implementation must be accelerated.

These committees will be able to identify local and provincial problems and recommend solutions. The local component is particularly important in a jurisdiction the size of Ontario. A problem in Toronto does not automatically require changes in Thunder Bay.

## Conclusion

The citizens of Ontario benefit from the high quality of criminal justice currently administered in the two trial courts. Quality should not be jeopardized by attempts to improve efficiency through proposals aimed at solving problems which, on analysis, are unrelated to court structure. In the tradition of the bench and bar in criminal matters, cooperative solutions can be found to improve efficiency while maintaining quality. Solutions such as a unified criminal court, the Quebec model or the elimination of the preliminary inquiry do not address the real problems, but instead create a substantial risk of inefficiency and the impairment of the excellent quality of the criminal justice system in Ontario.

NOTES

This paper is based on a report prepared by a committee of the Ontario Superior Court Judges' Association, whose members were Justice Douglas Cunningham, Justice Michael Dambrot, Justice Bruce Durno (chair), Justice Stephen Glithero, Justice Casey Hill, Justice Barry Matheson, Justice Colin McKinnon, Justice Douglas Rutherford, and Justice Bonnie Wein. It was subsequently adopted by the then Chief Justice of the Court, Patrick LeSage, on behalf of the Superior Court of Justice. I am grateful to Chief Justice Heather Smith for permitting its inclusion in this book.

1 See Criminal Justice Review Committee, *Report of the Criminal Justice Review Committee* (Toronto: The Committee, 1999).
2 *Re: Riley and the Queen* (1991), 60 C.C.C. (2d) 193 (Ont. C.A.).
3 Proposal prepared by the Canadian Association of Provincial Court Judges, 26 November 1979.
4 *Fourth Triennial Report of the Provincial Judges' Remuneration Commission*, (Toronto: The Commission, 1998), 26.
5 Comments at the Opening of Courts, 2000, by the Honourable Chief Justice Patrick LeSage.
6 Provincial Judges' Remuneration Commission *Minority Report Fourth Triennial Report of the Provincial Judges' Remuneration Commission* (Toronto: The Commission, 1999), 14.
7 G. Arthur Martin (chair), *Change, Screening, Disclosure, and Resolution Discussions* (Toronto: Ministry of the Attorney General, 1993). The Ontario government's response to the Martin report, of ten referred to as the Criminal Investment Strategy, can be found at http://www.attorneygeneral.jus.gov.on.ca/english/about/pubs/ejr/firstreport/court.
8 Survey of Regional Senior Justices, 12 May 2000.
9 *Superior Court of Justice Statistics, 1969–1999*, prepared for the Office of the Chief Justice by CISS, from the Program Development Branch, Ministry of the Attorney General.
10 *R v. Askov*, [1990] 2 S.C.R. 1199 is the case in which the Supreme Court ruled that a delay of six to eight months between committal and trial might be deemed a violation of the Charter right to trial within a reasonable time. It resulted in the dropping of thousands of criminal charges.
11 A.W. Mewett 'Editorial,' (1990) 32 *Criminal Law Quarterly* 4.
12 *Regina v. Askov* (1990), 59 C.C.C. (3d) 449 (S.C.C.); *Regina v. Morin* (1992), 71 C.C.C. (3d) 1 (S.C.C.).
13 *Regina v. Faulds, Regina v. Tyler* (1996), 111 C.C.C. (3d) 39 (Ont. C.A.).
14 Superior Court of Justice Indictment Caseflow proposed by Information Planning and Court Statistics. Note: this figure is inflated by a one-month figure of thirty-seven indictments. For twenty-five of the thirty-six months analysed no re-election occurred.
15 Honourable T.G. Zuber, *Report of the Ontario Courts Inquiry* (Toronto: Ontario Ministry of the Attorney General, 1987), 95.
16 Roscoe Pound 'The Causes of Popular Dissatisfaction with the Administration of Justice' reprinted in (1962) 46 *Journal of American Judicature* Society 55.
17 *Want's Federal–State Court Directory* (New York: WANT Publishing Co., 2000).
18 Zuber Report, 79–80.

19 Law Reform Commission of Canada, *Towards a Unified Criminal Court*: *Working Paper 59* (Ottawa: Public Works and Government Services Canada, 1989).

20 Ontario Bar Association, Joint Committee on Court Reform, 'Submission to the Attorney General of Ontario re: Unified Criminal Court' (Toronto: The Association, 1990).

21 Aboriginal Justice Inquiry, *Report of the Aboriginal Justice Inquiry of Manitoba* (Winnipeg: The Inquiry, 1991), ch. 8.

22 Proposal for Joint Initiatives by the Governments of Canada and New Brunswick, 21 March 1994.

23 Canadian Bar Association, *Canadian Bar Association Task Force Report: on Court Reform in Canada* (Ottawa: The Association, 1991), 107, 97.

24 Joint Committee on Court Reform, 18.

25 Task Force Report, p. 103.

26 Joint Committee on Court Reform, 17.

27 Circuit Court of Cook County, *An Informational Guide, State of Illinois*. The court of four hundred judges serving a population of 5.1 million is described as the world's largest unified court system.

28 Ministry of the Attorney General, *Province of Ontario Architectural Design Standards for Court Houses*, (Toronto: Queen's Printer, 1999), B-2.

29 *Want's Directory*, 169.

30 Zuber Report, 79.

31 Task Force Report, 95, 97.

32 Ministry of the Attorney General, *Discussion Paper*, (Toronto: Queen's Printer, 1989).

33 Mr Justice MacKinnon prepared an initial paper which was expanded upon by Mr Justice Brooke.

34 Ministry of the Attorney General, Court Reform – Phase II (Toronto: Queen's Printer, 1989), 3.

35 Joint Committee on Court Reform, 16.

36 *McEvoy v. Attorney General (New Brunswick)*, [1983] 1 S.C.R. 704.

37 *Globe and Mail*, 23 March 2000.

# PART FOUR

## Comparative Perspectives

# 11 Organizational Change in California's Court System: Unification of the Trial Courts

J. CLARK KELSO

*The cradle of the single trial court movement is the United States, where Roscoe Pound set out the advantages of trial court unification in his famous 1906 address to the American Bar Association. The movement always pertained to state courts systems which function beside a separate system of federal courts that is much more extensive than Canada's purely federal courts. For instance, suits between citizens of different states are tried in Federal District Courts whereas in Canada they are tried in provincial Superior Courts. So even though many states have moved towards unification of their trial courts, the United States maintains a dual system of courts.*

*In this essay Clark Kelso, a leading scholar and practitioner of trial court unification, sets out the rationale for trial court unification and the steps taken to achieve it in the most populous state in the American union, California. Although important differences of legal and institutional context must be borne in mind in considering foreign models and experience, there are aspects of the unification process in California that may be instructive to Canadian reformers. One is that progress towards unification was gradual and evolutionary, beginning with the integration of administrative services. Another is that the process, particularly in its final stages, was judge-led.*

*Clark Kelso's description of the California system bears out Carl Baar's point that all of the American states that have moved towards unification of their trial services rely on subordinate judicial officers to carry out a wide range of functions in the justice system. This is consistent with Canadian unification models that have been put forward. There is also a good deal of specialization among the judiciary of the California court. In assessing the benefits of unification, Kelso emphasizes how it has served as an effective platform for major changes needed to meet new challenges to the justice system.*

In the United States, the decade of the 1990s has been a Golden Age of Judicial Administration. We have seen courts around the country leading change efforts that reach to the very core and foundation of the judicial branch and the judicial function.

We have quite a few national organizations to thank for inspiring many of these developments. Just a few that come to mind are the National Center for State Courts, the State Justice Institute, the Conference of Chief Justices, the Conference of State Court Administrators, and the National Association of Court Managers. These organizations provided a lot of the intellectual energy to the change efforts and created a forum and venue for court leaders to consider more systematically than before where the courts should be moving.

We started the 1990s with 'Futures Commissions' in several states around the country.[1] Those commissions helped re-focus court leaders on the importance of thinking in general terms about the future, about how the future may affect the courts, and about how courts can respond and influence that future. Today, courts around the country are engaged in more detailed strategic planning processes that move courts a big step closer to being directly involved in planning their own future.

The California state court system participated fully in this process of self-reflection and renewal. Under the leadership of former Chief Justice Malcolm M. Lucas and Administrative Director Bill Vickrey, California's judicial family produced a futures report, *Justice in the Balance – 2020*, that laid out a bold agenda for court reform.[2] Slowly but steadily, the recommendations from that report are being implemented under the strong leadership of current Chief Justice Ronald M. George and Bill Vickrey.

This article focuses on one of the foundational changes recommended by the *2020 Vision* report: unification of California's several local trial courts into a single trial court of general jurisdiction.[3]

## Change in the Information Age

The Information Age began fifty years ago with the invention of the transistor. We all know what the Information Age has meant in terms of the pace and quality of change and the democratization of information and power. Government agencies and the military were the primary beneficiaries early on, since computers were beyond the financial means of most people and organizations. The most visible use of technology over these years was NASA's space program. The first thirty years or so of the Information Age saw only a few improvements in consumer goods as manufacturers figured out how to use the new electronics.

The big change came around the beginning of the 1980s with the invention of the personal computer and the development of techniques of mass production for silicon chips. That is when we began to see the Information Age expand its influence to all aspects of our daily lives.

The pace of change at this point is truly extraordinary. According to Moore's Law, computing power increases by a factor of ten every eighteen months while cost is cut in half over the same period of time. Sceptics worry that Moore's Law will soon reach its limit, but so far, the sceptics have been proven wrong. Developments within the nanotechnology and quantum-computing industries suggest that Moore's Law is going to remain valid for years to come.

As prices have dropped, instruments of mass media have blossomed with the proliferation of cable and satellite technologies. Cellular telephone systems have given us unprecedented mobility. The convergence of voice, video and data is upon us. And the internet, even though it lives up to only about half of the hype, has transformed and will continue to transform our daily activities. Global broadband is our future.

Consumers now expect solutions to problems to be delivered faster and cheaper than ever before. We are a 24/7 society that demands services anywhere, anytime.

## Change and the Courts

How have courts accommodated our rapidly changing society – a society that has an entirely new way of communicating and of processing information? At a very basic level, computers are making their way into court executive offices and into the courtroom, although compared to other government agencies, courts have been a little slower to adapt to the new technologies.

But that's not the real story. The problem for the courts is that the Information Age has fundamentally changed people's expectations. It has changed what we expect from manufacturers, from schools, from banks, from builders, and from government. When expectations change so fundamentally, an organization is presented with a choice: it can either change to keep up with the new expectations, or stay put and, over time, become increasingly obsolete and irrelevant. People will find alternatives. Courts do *not* have an ironclad monopoly on all dispute resolution.

Change does not come easily to any organization. Organizational scholars have focused upon the magnitude of a proposed change as one of the critical determinants of the possibility of its success. The continuum of change ranges from (on the low end of the scale) incremental, first-order change to (on the high end of the scale) strategic, second-order change. Incremental change refers to relatively small, routine changes that do not fundamentally disrupt continuity within the organization.[4] Strategic change refers to 'non-routine, non-incremental, and discontinuous change which alters the overall orientation of the organization and/or components of the organization.'[5] Second-order changes are never simple to design and implement successfully and can take much longer to accomplish than expected. Resistance to second-order changes will, as a general rule, be higher than resistance to only incremental change.

Research on the topic of organizational archetypes helps explain why second-order changes are so difficult to achieve. An archetype consists of the beliefs and values represented as interpretive schemes through the 'composition of structures and systems' of an organization.[6] A second-order change involves an archetype change, which means changing the most basic assumptions and parameters of an organization. It involves a change in the organization's culture, and employees immersed in one culture will naturally be reluctant to embrace change that requires a partial rejection of long-held organizational culture and norms.

Recent doctoral research suggests that organizations which are dominated by rule-mediated communication and processes will be particularly resistant to substantial organizational change. In particular, this research suggests that the more an organization communicates and acts on the basis of specific rules that are grounded in well established standards and principles (i.e., the more the organizational archetype is rule-based), the more likely it is that the organization will be characterized by a strong preference for conformity to the status quo.[7] This research also found that, because of the legal training of judges and the structure of the judicial system, both of which emphasize rule-based reasoning and action, there is an overwhelming preference in court organizations for conformity to the status quo.

### An Example of Successful Change in the Courts:
### Trial Court Unification in California

Organizational change in the courts is not for the faint of heart. Proponents of change in the judicial system must possess an almost inexhaustible reservoir of energy, enthusiasm, and patience. There is a lot of resistance to overcome.

We examine in this article the unification of trial courts in California. In 1998 the California constitution was amended to permit superior and municipal courts within a county to unify into a single superior court upon a majority vote of both benches.[8] As of today, the courts in all fifty-eight of California's counties have unified their trial courts. It has been a very long journey.

*Historical Background: Principles of Reorganization*

The modern organization of the courts has been studied by some of the leading legal figures of the century. Roscoe Pound, long-time dean of the Harvard Law School, made court reorganization one of the centrepieces of his distinguished career, beginning with his famous 1906 address to the American Bar Association and culminating in the publication of his influential book on the subject.[9] Chief Justice Arthur T. Vanderbilt, of the Supreme Court of New Jersey, was another early leader in the reorganization movement.[10] His works, along with the efforts particularly of Chief Judge John J. Parker of the United States Court of Appeals for the Fourth Circuit, led to the 1937 adoption of standards of judicial administration by the Judicial Administration Division of the American Bar Association.

Roscoe Pound identified four general principles to guide court reorganization efforts: unification, flexibility, conservation of judicial power, and responsibility. He explained these principles as follows:

> Unification is called for in order to concentrate the machinery of justice upon its tasks, flexibility in order to enable it to meet speedily and efficiently the continually varying demands made upon it, responsibility in order that some one may always be held and clearly stand out as the official to be held if the judicial organization is not functioning the most efficiently that the law and the nature of its tasks permit. Conservation of judicial power is a *sine qua non* of efficiency under the circumstances of the time.[11]

Pound's principles remain the guiding beacon of reorganization efforts. The 1990 Standards of Judicial Administration promulgated by the Judicial Administration Division of the American Bar Association provides in its very first section as follows, essentially reaffirming Pound's observations:

> The organization of a court system should serve the courts' basic task of determining cases justly, promptly, effectively, and efficiently. To this end, the organizational structure should promote judicial accountability, authority over all judicial operations, clear delineation between judicial and non-judicial responsibilities, and common management systems so that the delivery of services may be administered uniformly throughout the jurisdiction.[12]

*Trial Court Structure in California*

Following the prevailing practice of the times, the 1849 California Constitution created and authorized a multiplicity of trial courts:

- district courts
- county courts
- probate courts
- justice of the peace courts
- other inferior courts as the legislature may establish
- courts of session
- municipal courts
- tribunals for conciliation.[13]

The constitutional convention of 1878 saw the first proposal to unify all trial level courts into a single trial court. That proposal was rejected, however, in favour of a more modest consolidation of county and district courts into superior courts.[14] The 1879 Constitution retained justice courts and provided for the legislative establishment of other inferior courts.

The other inferior courts were not long in coming. Small claims courts were established in 1921. Justice courts were divided into Class A and Class B courts. Municipal courts were similarly divided into two branches. Local government created police and city courts. By 1949 there were 767 court systems with jurisdiction inferior to the superior court and eight different types of inferior courts.

This patchwork of courts with overlapping jurisdictions and limited coordination was replaced in 1950 when the voters approved a constitutional amendment, Proposition 3, which had been recommended by the California Judicial Council, the policy-making body for California's courts. The 1950 amendment, which provided the basis for California's trial court system until the 1990s, authorized only superior, municipal, and justice courts. Each county had a superior court. Municipal courts were created in districts with a population of more than 40,000, and justice courts were created in districts with a population of 40,000 or less.

The 1950 reorganization eliminated the power vested in the cities and counties to create new types of inferior courts, and the legislature was given the responsibility to prescribe the jurisdiction of municipal and justice courts. The legislature was also given the responsibility to prescribe the number, qualifications, and compensation of judges, officers, and employees of the municipal court. With respect to justice courts, the legislature had only to 'provide' for the number, qualifications, and compensation of judges, officers, and employees, and the legislature delegated that task to the counties.

The implementing legislation provided, among other things, that municipal courts had jurisdiction of misdemeanours and civil cases in which the amount in controversy was $3,000 or less. Justice courts had jurisdiction over criminal cases involving failure to provide for a minor child and civil cases involving $500 or less.

Passage of the implementing legislation was secured only by compromising with local government on a number of issues. Among the most significant compromises:

1   Retention of part-time judicial position and lay judges in rural areas;
2   County boards of supervisors were given discretion to set the number and boundaries of the lower court districts within the county, subject only to constitutional requirements regarding the size of the district and a requirement that no district boundary could divide a city (a requirement ultimately amended to exclude San Diego County);
3   Creation of a legislatively-based revenue distribution system which gave cities a substantial share of court revenue; and
4   County governments, which accepted the burden of court financing, were given the authority for judicial districting decisions,

retained local control over justice court staffing, and shared in a portion of court revenue.

There has been a steady reduction in the total number of municipal and justice court districts in California from the high point of 767 in 1948. The 1950 amendment reduced the number to 400, and consolidations (often because of increasing population within a district) reduced the number to 143 in 1992.

Along with a reduction in the number of lower trial courts, there has been a rationalization of their jurisdiction, and the practical distinctions between municipal and justice courts all but vanished in the 1970s. In *Gordon v. Justice Court*,[15] the court held that due process requires a justice court judge to be an attorney (rather than a lay person) in criminal cases where the defendant faces the possibility of a jail sentence. As a result of this holding, the legislature enacted provisions that eliminated lay judges from the justice courts and in 1976 eliminated the differences in jurisdiction exercised by justice and municipal courts.[16] The state also began participating in payment of compensation for justice court judges, and justice court judges' salaries were equalized with municipal court judge salaries. With these changes, the reasons for maintaining separate justice and municipal courts entirely disappeared.

## Early Unification Proposals

After the 1950 constitutional amendment, interest in trial court unification subsided and did not revive until the 1970s, when Assemblyman James A. Hayes, introduced legislation to create a unified trial level court. As a result of this renewed interest, in April of 1970 the Judicial Council commissioned Booz, Allen & Hamilton, a nationally recognized management consulting firm, to study the feasibility of creating a unified trial court. The study concluded that '[a] single-level trial court with one type of judge is ultimately the most desirable form of trial court organization.' The study proposed a three-stage process for achieving total unification:

1. Enact statutory and rule changes to consolidate municipal and justice courts into one inferior court, and create a unified administrative structure for the superior and inferior courts;

2. Enact constitutional, legislative and rule changes to unify superior and inferior courts with provision, as necessary, for two levels of judges within that court; and
3. Enact legislative and rule changes to create a single trial-level court with one type of judge. [17]

In the years following this report, court unification amendments were regularly proposed in the legislature, but none was enacted. The only proposal to make it out of the legislature, Proposition 10, which authorized counties to unify superior, municipal and justice courts, failed at the polls in 1981.

Recognizing in 1971 that there would be resistance to court unification, the Booz, Allen & Hamilton study also recommended a number of interim alternatives to unification that did not require legislative action or constitutional amendments. These alternatives focused largely upon administrative coordination:

1. Unifying only the administrative functions of the lower and Superior Court levels through the use of a centralized judicial management structure.
2. Unifying some or all of the activities and resources which support the judicial services of these courts, such as bailiffing, common jury pools, court reporters, court clerks, data processing systems, financial management, secretarial and other support functions.
3. Unifying the types of judges and subordinate judicial officers who render judicial services as well as their jurisdictional levels, in terms of types of cases.
4. Combination of two or more of the three unification approaches outlined above.[18]

These interim measures proved more successful. The legislature authorized multi-district bailiff services provided by the county sheriff or by a marshal with county-wide jurisdiction. Municipal court reporters, deputy clerks and deputy marshals were permitted to serve in superior courts. Municipal court jurors were drawn from panels selected and qualified by the superior court jury commissioner. Official reporters of the superior court were assigned to act pro tempore as official reporters of the municipal or justice courts.

In 1980 the Judicial Council released its *Final Report of the Court Administration Consolidation Project*. Building upon the 1970s legislative

226   J. Clark Kelso

successes, the final report recommended 'that each court administrator
be urged to examine the operations of his court together with those of
adjacent court districts in light of the information contained in the
report to determine whether or not there is an opportunity to reduce
costs and improve services by means of the consolidation of one or
more administrative services.'[19]

## The Final Push towards Unification

Unification discussions resurfaced in 1992 because of a serious backlog
problem in our superior courts, particularly in civil cases where litigants in many counties had trouble getting to a courtroom for four or
five years, even though the parties were ready for trial. When analysts
examined the workload in the courts, they discovered that municipal
court judges had some additional time on their hands. At the same
time, superior court judges were swamped. The solution was obvious:
we needed to figure out a way of applying municipal court resources
to superior court cases.

Unification was the most obvious solution, but it was also a solution
that had proven itself to be controversial within the courts. A more
modest, incremental approach was the right strategy to achieve change
in the courts.

Coordination, the sharing of resources between courts, was the first
step. Coordination did not firmly take hold until 1992 after the California legislature, acting on recommendations from the state bar, mandated increasing levels of coordination in the Trial Court Realignment
and Efficiency Act of 1991.[20] This legislation made the courts themselves responsible for designing and implementing their own coordination activities in a way that would best achieve the desired efficiencies.
The desired efficiencies were the reduction or elimination of duplication of administrative activities and personnel between the superior
and municipal courts. Toward that end, the act required submission of
coordination plans from all courts within the state to the Judicial Council by 1 March 1992, for its review and approval no later than 1 July
1992. The act contained an illustrative list of coordination activities:

(1) The use of blanket cross-assignments allowing judges to hear civil,
criminal, or other types of cases within the jurisdiction of another court.
(2) The coordinated or joint use of subordinate judicial officers to hear or
try matters.

(3) The coordinated, joint use, sharing or merger of court support staff among trial courts within a county or across counties. In a county with a population of less than 100,000 the coordination plan need not involve merger of superior and justice court staffs if the court can reasonably demonstrate that the maintenance of separate administrative staffs would be more cost effective and provide better service.

(4) The assignment of civil, criminal, or other types of cases for hearing or trial, regardless of jurisdictional boundaries, to any available judicial officer.

(5) The assignment of any type of case to a judge for all purposes commencing with the filing of the case and regardless of jurisdictional boundaries.

(6) The establishment of separate calendars or divisions to hear a particular type of case.

(7) In rural counties, the use of all court facilities for hearings and trials of all types of cases and to accept for filing documents in any case before any court in the county participating in the coordination plan.

(8) The coordinated or joint use of alternative dispute resolution programs such as arbitration.

(9) The unification of the trial courts within a county to the maximum extent permitted by the Constitution.[21]

All trial level courts submitted coordination plans, and significant aspects of trial court administrative and judicial functions were effectively consolidated as a result of these plans. For example, as of the end of 1992, 93 per cent of the trial courts reported cross-assignment of judges as necessary to handle the work flow, 89 per cent coordinated the use of support staff; 80 per cent coordinated case calendars; and 78 per cent shared common jury pools.

Unification was not inevitable; there was still significant resistance. Trial court unification finally happened only because the courts themselves were willing to lead the campaign. Not all courts, of course, but there was sustained leadership from the California Judicial Council, Chief Justice Ronald M. George, and Administrative Director Bill Vickrey, among many others. The California Constitution gives the chief justice the power to assign a judge to a higher court. He also has the power to assign a judge from a higher court to a lower court, but only with the consent of that judge. The chief justice, exercising his personal charm, was able, in a number of counties, to get agreements with the entire superior court bench and the entire municipal court bench for routine cross-assignment of all judges. This was the virtual equivalent of unification.

Absent judicial leadership, unification would not have happened. In fact, all of the earlier efforts to unify in California failed precisely because of court opposition or neutrality (and when it comes to change efforts, neutrality is often as difficult to overcome as outright opposition). Trial courts simply did not want to change. It was safer to keep things the way they were. The California Constitution had created superior court judges and municipal court judges, and they were intended to be kept separate and apart. How could they possibly be mixed together? It simply was unthinkable.

The unthinkable became reality only as a result of a lengthy dialogue among courts and court leaders that stretched over most of the 1990s. For example, the Judicial Council's 1992 annual report describes the communication activities associated with trial court coordination. Anticipating the need for promoting discussions between trial courts about basic values and norms, the statewide Administrative Office of the Courts organized two all-day workshops to give pointers on coordination to court officials. Representatives of 135 trial courts – 67 per cent of the states' 201 trial courts – attended and program materials were made available to courts not represented at the workshops. Four other regional coordination workshops were held throughout the state on coordination plan development and the AOC planned further sessions about coordination at its annual Court Management Conference in 1992.[22]

In addition to these organized meetings, the AOC developed a newsletter to keep courts informed about statewide coordination progress and innovations. This steady stream of communications over many years slowly broke down organizational resistance.

In many counties, coordination was limited to specific agreements to share certain resources, such as court reporters, court interpreters, jury pool lists, accounting systems, and case management systems. In a few counties, the judges of the superior and municipal courts established a higher degree of trust and had such congruent visions for the trial courts that the judges voted to share power by creating a single presiding judge and single court executive officer for both courts. In terms of the ultimate goal of unification, these courts had established a new type of organizational relationship, and a new term was even used to describe this level of coordination to reflect the new organizational relationships: 'consolidation.'

Substantial resistance to coordination from many trial courts began to develop when some proponents of unification began to describe *consolidation* as the *equivalent* of *unification* and at the same time to argue that any court that had not fully *consolidated* had not fulfilled the coordination mandate. The resistance was most obvious when a proposal to change the Standards of Judicial Administration regarding coordination was distributed in 1993 for comment. The proposal specifically identified 'unification' as the goal of the coordination program. The proposal was sent out to over two thousand persons, including all presiding judges and court administrators in California. The greatest number of negative comments to the report related to the stated goal of trial court coordination as being 'the unification of the trial courts within a county to the maximum extent permitted by the Constitution.' The courts were ready for coordination, and even consolidation in some counties, but not for unification.

In light of the negative comments, the Judicial Council decided not to adopt the proposed amendment to the Standards of Judicial Administration. Instead, the Judicial Council convened a broadly representative Select Coordination Implementation Committee to seek consensus on coordination issues, and to provide additional guidance to the council for its meeting in January 1995. The select committee concluded that after years of debate, a consensus had emerged regarding appropriate methods of coordination to maximize the utilization of judicial and other court resources to promote increased efficiency in court operations and service to the public. Without using the word 'unification,' the committee recommended the adoption by the Judicial Council of rules of court that required all trial courts to enter into power-sharing arrangements, which would necessarily require the courts to agree on fundamental aspects of court administration.

The select committee's recommendations, which were adopted by the Judicial Council in 1995, required creation in each county of a coordination planning and governance committee, coordination of judicial and administrative resources within the county, submission of an integrated budget for all trial courts within the county, and election of a single presiding judge and court executive officer for the county.

The committee's recommendations had the consequence of creating new communication pathways between the superior and municipal courts where the dialogue would, of necessity, begin by establishing a working consensus on organizational norms, culture, and governance. Within the context of this organizational framework, the trial courts could then turn to the specifics of coordinating particular resources within the courts.

Another way in which we made the transition to unification more palatable was that when we amended the constitution to permit unification, we did it on a county option basis, so that a county would unify its trial courts only if a majority of the judges in the municipal court and a majority of the judges on the superior court voted to unify.[23] This provided the superior court judges, who normally would be opposed to unification, an opting out process, and this opt-out process significantly reduced opposition to the constitutional amendment. This was a very successful tactic. Organized opposition from courts mostly vanished, the constitutional amendment was approved, and within two months of the constitutional amendment passing, forty-nine of our fifty-eight counties had voted to unify. In fact, a number of counties which voted for unification raced to the chief justice to have their vote certified so that they would be recognized as the first county to have unified.

The immediate and rapid embrace of unification around the state was a marked departure from where trial courts stood only four or five years earlier. The rapid change in viewpoint is explainable by the Judicial Council's success in facilitating and requiring discussions in every county between the superior and municipal courts as part of coordination efforts. By requiring that the courts communicate with each other about basic court norms, culture and group rules, the Judicial Council set the stage for quick agreement on unification once that option was approved by the voters.

Ultimately, the courts in all counties voted to unify. Was this unification all done voluntarily? Well, mostly. Once fifty-five of fifty-eight counties were unified, the Judicial Council did have to apply some pressure, mostly through budget control, to move the last three counties towards unification. The good news is that even the courts which were most resistant to unification, within a month or two of unifying, dropped their resistance. Nearly all of the negative talk and all of the animosity disappeared very quickly. Once the decision had been made, everybody reassessed their roles in the organization and began the process of collaboration.

## Was It Worth the Trip?

Critics can still be heard arguing that unification was entirely unnecessary, that the system could have continued to function perfectly well without the change, that promoting all of those municipal court judges has diluted the quality of the superior court bench, and that the people are not as well served with a unified court as they were with a separate municipal court focused on their needs in smaller cases. It seems to me these critics raise a critical question. What is so wrong with being a 'protector of the status quo'? If it worked for my grandparents, it should work for me. If it ain't broke, don't fix it.

There is, I think, a compelling answer to this question. In the context of a changing environment, clinging stubbornly to the status quo can result in organizational decline and death. We've seen this happen to the courts before, and it is still happening today. One of the lessons from the trial court unification debate was that long-range planning by the courts actually can result in major transformations. Along the way, courts in California have discovered that they possess truly enormous resources which, when coordinated thoughtfully, can be brought to bear to address major criminal justice problems in society.

For example, over the course of the last decade, California's courts have been thrown a series of big challenges by the state's voter initiative process: three strikes; the juvenile justice initiative; and most recently the drug courts initiative. These were huge changes in judicial administration, yet California's courts handled them with seemingly little difficulty, in very large part because our courts have become accustomed to managing and leading large change efforts.

Unification doesn't mean that we have a uniform, one judge fits all, scenario. We still have, within the courts, specialization. We have drug courts that handle particular types of felony crimes, integrated family courts, and complex litigation courts that handle complex civil litigation. We are maintaining distinctions that are appropriate to the type of case, the size and the complexity of the case, as well as the subject matter. A major difference, however, is that these distinctions are dealt with by rule of court; the court may now decide how to assign cases as well as decide what types of divisions the court needs. I think that's a much better way for the courts to manage their own affairs.

## Conclusion

I think we are now seeing the emergence in California of a much stronger and more clearly defined Judicial Branch which is capable of addressing in a more comprehensive way the justice needs of our diverse society. Fifty years ago, we spoke of a Judicial Branch, but all we really had was a collection of courtrooms with judges. Today, the Judicial Branch in California is much more than that, encompassing a statewide network of judges, lawyers, court clerks, and analysts, providing much more in the way of services than just a courtroom with a judge or jury. And California's Judicial Branch has adopted a 'can do' service attitude to provide full and open access to justice for all.

In the United States, we are at a fork in the road as we enter the twenty-first century. In one direction lies the tried and true, the road to status quo. It is, ultimately, a road that leads nowhere. In the other direction is a road that leads into largely uncharted territory. That is where I think courts and court leaders need to go. We need to confront the changing environmental condition we face with new solutions and new approaches. As Oliver Wendell Holmes advised, we must immerse ourselves in the controversies of our time at peril of being judged not to have lived. I cast my vote for courts as agent of change.

## NOTES

1 The National Center for State Courts maintains a list of reports from the many futures commissions on its website available at http://www.ncsconline.org/WC/Publications/KIS_CtFutStateLnksPub.pdf.
2 Commission on the Future of the California Courts, *Justice in the Balance – 2020* (San Francisco: The Commission, 1993).
3 'Recommendation 2.1. The courts must become a true, integrated 'system,' coordinated, connected, efficient, and affordable, yet respectful of local differences in judicial and social culture. Strategy: 2.1.a. As a first step toward greater integration and efficiency, the trial courts should be unified.' Ibid., 40.
4 A.M. Pettigrew, 'Context and Action in the Transformation of the Firm,' (1987) 24 *Journal of Management Studies* 271.
5 N.M. Tichy, *Managing Strategic Change: Technical, Political and Cultural Dynamics* (New York: John Wiley and Sons, 1983), 17.
6 C.R. Hinings and R. Greenwood, *The Dynamics of Strategic Change*, (New York: Blackwell, 1988), 26.
7 Kari C. Kelso (2000) 'Conformity and Variation Within the Legal System: An Organizational Communication Analysis' (Ph.D. dissertation, University of Texas at Austin, 2000).
8 Cal. Const., Art. VI, Section 5(e) (added 2 June 1998).

9 R. Pound (1906) 'The Causes of Popular Dissatisfaction with the Administration of Justice,' reprinted in (1962) 46 *Journal of American Judicature Society* 55; and *Organization of Courts* (Boston: Little, Brown, 1940).

10 A.T. Vanderbilt, *Minimum Standards of Judicial Administration* (New York: Law Center of New York University for the National Conference of Judicial Councils, 1949).

11 Pound, *Organization of Courts*, 275–6.

12 ABA Standards of Judicial Administration, Section 1.00.

13 California Constitution of 1849, Art. VI, Section 1.

14 California Constitution of 1879, Art. VI, Section 1.

15 12 Cal. 3d 323 (1974).

16 1974 Cal. Stats. ch. 1493; 1976 Stat. ch. 1288.

17 Booz, Allen & Hamilton, *California Unified Trial Court Feasibility Study* (1971), v, 68–73.

18 Ibid., 49–50.

19 California Judicial Council, *Final Report of the Court Administration Consolidation Project* (San Francisco: Judicial Council of California, 1980), 31.

20 1991 Cal. Stat. ch. 90.

21 Gov't Code § 68112(b).

22 California Judicial Council, *Annual Report* (San Francisco: The Council, 1992), 8.

23 Cal. Const., Art. VI, Section 5(e).

# 12  Trial Court Integration in England

I.R. SCOTT

*Ian Scott is a leading authority on the English courts and one of the leading international scholars on court systems. His chapter addresses fundamental theoretical questions about the relationship between court structures and cases, and between court hierarchies and judicial qualifications.*

*In his account of the England's trial court system we can see some of the roots of the original Canadian court system: centrally based Superior Court judges for major civil cases and criminal jury trials, with County Courts providing a locally based service for the adjudication of smaller civil suits and a community-based, mostly lay magistracy for the trial of summary criminal offences. Scott shows us how the original rationale for a two-tiered system of trial court has become increasingly indefensible as the pyramid of cases no longer matches the hierarchy of courts. This has provoked major reviews of the England's court structure by Lord Woolf on the civil side and by Sir Robin Auld on the criminal side.*

*While court unification was a serious option in both the Woolf and Auld inquiries, neither led to a restructuring of the two-tier system. Instead there has been a movement to amalgamate the administrative services of the courts. Administrative integration may for now be the limit of trial court reform in England, at least in relation to the trial courts with criminal jurisdiction. The institutional structures of England's two-tier system are deeply embedded – even a centralized system of court administration raises serious constitutional concerns.*

*Scott suggests that England's multi-tiered judiciary of High Court judges ('officers'), circuit and district judges ('other ranks'), and magistrates ('volunteers' or 'reservists') might well survive within a unified court. However, changes now under way in the English system of recruiting and appointing judges may cast a very different light on judicial organization and court structure.*

In this chapter I will examine trial court unification or integration from an English perspective. I am sure you all know that, in England and Wales (hereinafter 'England'), we do not have unified trial courts but we have a two-tiered trial court system, both on the civil and criminal sides. I have not tried to stick to the word 'unification' because it is not a word that has been used consistently in England in this context. Often the words 'amalgamation,' 'merger' and 'integration' have been preferred.

In what follows, after some preliminary observations, I deal first with the civil side and then with the criminal. There is much more to say about the civil side. The English civil courts have been the object of consistent official scrutiny for a continuous period of twenty years and, as a result, many changes have been made to the jurisdictions and procedures of these courts. By comparison, since 1971 the criminal courts and their procedures remained in a fairly stable state until 1999 when a detailed inquiry was launched. The consequences of that inquiry, including its impact on the issue of trial court integration, were still being worked out when this paper was written.

I should point out at the outset that I make no mention of the family law jurisdiction of the English civil courts. From time to time it has been urged that a single family court should be established in England. However, that has not come to pass and the family law jurisdiction is split between, not two, but three levels of court (the High Court, the county courts, and the magistrates' courts) in a manner which I would find very difficult to explain coherently in a short compass. If I did manage to do so I doubt whether you would believe me (foreign observers invariably find the arrangements bizarre).

**The Case Pyramid and Procedural Compaction**

Which came first, courts or cases? It is an intriguing question. Did courts set themselves up in the adjudication business and say, in effect, 'Here we are, bring us your cases'? Or were courts set up in response to a perceived need for adjudication services? If the former is the correct answer we are talking about a supply-driven phenomenon. If the latter is correct we are talking about a demand-driven phenomenon. There is of course a threshold question which I have glossed over; and that is, what do courts do? That question is masked by my use of the phrases 'adjudication business' and 'adjudication services.'

The preferred answer to the question I have posed is that courts are set up to meet a demand, but we should not forget that there have been times in English legal history when courts have competed for business, and the signs of that are still evident today in our jurisdictional and procedural arrangements.

Whether we are talking about criminal trial courts or civil trial courts it is helpful to begin with the concept of the 'case pyramid'. Imagine a pyramid with two axes, one representing the height of the pyramid (the $y$ axis), and the other the width of the bases (the $x$ axis). The $y$ axis measures (for want of a better word) 'seriousness' (serious–trivial); and the $x$ axis measures volume (high volume–low volume). The pyramid represents the social phenomenon that trivial cases arise in much higher volume than serious cases.

How should the court system respond to this phenomenon? What judicial organization would be best fitted to deal with it? How is the case pyramid to be mapped on to judicial organization? It seems obvious that a multiple response, distinguishing (at least) serious (low-volume) cases and trivial (high-volume) cases, is required. ('Trivial' is not the best word but it is convenient; by using it I do not mean to suggest that some cases are unworthy of judicial attention.)

The most serious cases (which arise in low volume) should get a response that is the best that a court system could be expected to provide; the best judges, the best procedures, and so on. This 'best' response is the paradigm and is bound to be expensive to provide and expensive to operate; therefore we would expect it to be a rationed resource with restricted access. For convenience, we could call this best response 'formal justice.'

The trivial cases (which arise in high, sometimes very high, volume) do not deserve the best response, because a lesser response is quite capable of being a satisfactory response and, in any event, the expense involved in providing and operating the best response cannot be justified in trivial cases. The less-than-best response is distinguished by features that are in derogation of the paradigm. For convenience, we could call this less-than-best response 'summary justice.'

The logic of the multiple response leads to the phenomenon of 'horizontal forum fragmentation,' a force that operates against the unification of courts. Thus, in England, on the civil side we have two levels of court, the High Court dealing with the more serious civil claims, and the county courts dealing with the less serious claims. And on the criminal side we again have two levels of court, the Crown Court dealing with the more serious cases and the magistrates' courts, dealing with the less serious criminal prosecutions. The High Court and the Crown Court are both superior courts. The county courts and the magistrates' courts are inferior courts.

Behind the phenomenon of horizontal forum fragmentation is the assumption that multiple response means multiple courts. It is assumed that one court could not provide both formal justice and summary justice. In this respect it seems to have been assumed that courts should specialize. The bases for this assumption are many and subtle and have complicated explanations, many of which are connected with 'geography of justice' issues.

In what I have said above, I have assumed that judicial organization will stratify the pyramid into two segments. But why stop at two? Why not three or four? Why not have three or four levels of trial court rather than just two? The practical answer to this would seem to be that, although it is difficult, it is not impossible to classify the bulk of cases arising according to whether they should be in the top or the bottom segment of the pyramid, and to do so in a fairly logical way; however, further stratification becomes tricky. There have been times in English legal history when there have been more than two levels of trial court.

If for purposes of judicial organization, the case pyramid is divided into two levels, necessarily, there will be a middle range of cases that do not obviously fall on one side or the other. Thus, in England cases in the case pyramid are divided into three segments; first those to be dealt with at the higher level of trial court, secondly, those to be dealt with at the lower level of trial court, and thirdly, those that may be dealt with at either level, depending on certain circumstances.

In England, this three-fold division is most simply illustrated on the criminal side where the division is between (1) purely indictable offences (triable in the Crown Court), (2) purely summary offences (triable in magistrates' courts), and (3) 'either way' offences (triable in either court).[1] In ordinary civil matters the position is not quite so simple, and in family law matters it is quite complicated, but in both these jurisdictions the basic idea of a three-fold split, distinguishing the respective exclusive jurisdictions of the two levels of court and the jurisdiction which they share (concurrent jurisdiction), still holds good.

I explained above that the judicial organization response to the case pyramid phenomenon is horizontal forum fragmentation with the upper level of trial court offering formal justice and the lower level summary justice. I suggested that formal justice is the paradigm. The

English have always been very proud of the formal justice provided by their higher trial courts and have tended to look down on the standards of the courts occupying similar positions in foreign jurisdictions.[2]

Every jurisdiction in its own way will have its own view on what formal justice entails and will have a judicial organization and procedural regime to realize it. And each jurisdiction should also have a clear view as to what summary justice entails, although often this is not so. In English law there was a time when this was indeed the case. On the civil side, procedures of the county courts (offering summary justice) were very much different to the procedures of the High Court (offering formal justice). And the same could be said on the criminal side of the procedures of the magistrates' courts when contrasted with the higher trial courts. However, throughout the twentieth century one saw at work the phenomenon of 'procedural compaction,' with the procedures designed for the administration of summary justice at the lower levels of court being amended time and again for the purpose of bringing them into line with the procedures designed for the administration of formal justice at the higher levels. In its late stages of development, the phenomenon of procedural compaction manifests itself in the enactment of uniform procedural codes.

In English law, procedural compaction has been most in evidence on the civil side. Features of the county court rules that were obviously designed for the purpose of providing summary justice (e.g., rules limiting discovery and denying pleadings) were steadily whittled away. On the criminal side, the most significant difference between the procedures of the magistrates' courts and the higher criminal courts has been that in the higher courts cases have been tried by a judge sitting with a jury, whereas in magistrates' courts cases have been tried by a (professional) district judge or a bench of lay justices of the peace sitting without a jury. That distinction has been maintained to the present day, and to that extent procedural compaction has been resisted. However, signs of procedural compaction are apparent elsewhere, most notably in the way in which higher court rules as to the pre-trial disclosure of evidence were imposed on the lower courts in the 1980s.

For obvious reasons, procedural compaction means imposing formal justice rules on courts established for the purpose of providing summary justice. The effect of procedural compaction is to emasculate summary justice mechanisms. In England, on both the civil side and on the criminal side, the progress of procedural compaction went step by step with the increase of the jurisdiction of the lower courts. As the higher courts struggled to deal with their caseloads, successive governments were attracted by the quick-fix solution of devolving more and more cases on to the lower courts by the devices of increasing significantly the jurisdiction shared by both levels of court (i.e., the concurrent jurisdiction) and moving cases of certain types from the concurrent jurisdiction to the exclusive jurisdiction of the lower court. As a result, the mapping of judicial organization onto the case pyramid became increasingly skewed and no longer reflected a logically defensible distinction between serious and trivial cases and the distinction between formal justice and summary justice became blurred. The lower courts ceased to be predominantly summary justice courts. The jurisdiction of the magistrates' courts was increased very significantly in 1974. The jurisdiction of the county courts did not experience a comparable quantum leap until 1990.

But the quick-fix solution to higher court congestion has not been the only driver of procedural compaction. In the last part of the twentieth century it became increasingly clear that the whole idea of summary justice was under challenge. The developing awareness of 'procedural justice' and 'process values' and of the concept of 'fair trial' led to summary justice being branded as second class justice. It was argued that, on the civil side, summary justice was appropriate for only the most trivial of claims. And on the criminal side, it was argued that summary justice was not appropriate whenever the liberty of the defendant was at stake.

When procedural compaction reaches an advanced stage, whether or not a uniform procedural code has emerged, it is bound to be argued that horizontal forum fragmentation is no longer necessary or justifiable and that the upper and lower levels of trial court should be consolidated in a unified trial court. Trial court unification is a matter much discussed in Canada, the United States of America, and Australia, and in those jurisdictions plenty of examples of unification can be found.

### Civil Trial Courts – The High Court and the County Courts: Integration without Amalgamation

As explained above, in England, on the civil side there is a two-tier trial court structure consisting of, at the upper level, a superior court, the High Court, and at the lower level a network of inferior courts, the county courts. The High Court is based in London but sits also in the major provincial cities. The county courts sit in many cities and towns throughout England.

The High Court, together with the Crown Court and the Court of Appeal, constitute the Supreme Court of England and Wales.[3] These courts are superior courts and courts of record. As the relevant legislation says, the Court of Appeal 'consists of' ex-officio judges (including the Lord Chancellor, the Lord Chief Justice and the Master of the Rolls) and a number of ordinary judges (styled 'Lords Justices of Appeal'),[4] and the High Court 'consists of' certain holders of high judicial office (including the Lord Chancellor and the Lord Chief Justice) and a number of puisne judges (styled 'Justices of the High Court').[5] There is only one Court of Appeal, one High Court, and one Crown Court. The jurisdiction of these courts is not limited territorially. This singularity and the lack of limits on jurisdiction are hallmarks of superior courts.

It is important to notice that the Court of Appeal and the High Court 'consist of' judges because this makes clear in each instance that the judges are the court and the court is the judges. In legal terms and in organizational terms, the court is a combination of judges, nothing more and nothing less. This also is a feature of superior courts. But it is a feature lacking in the third constituent part of the Supreme Court of England and Wales, the Crown Court.

The county courts are inferior courts created by statute. They are courts of record. It is a feature of inferior courts that their jurisdiction is limited territorially. Thus, there is no single County Court but many separate county courts. The county courts do not 'consist of' judges. However, every judge of the Court of Appeal, every judge of the High Court, and every circuit judge shall, by virtue of his or her office, be capable of sitting (as assigned by the Lord Chancellor) as a judge for any county court for the purpose of exercising the jurisdiction and functions of a county court.

From time to time, the question whether the two levels of court should be merged has been canvassed. The High Court came into being in 1873 as a result of recommendations made in 1869 by the Judicature Commissioners to the effect that all of the many superior courts (including the principal equity and common law courts) should be consolidated into one single superior court. In their second report, in 1872, the Judicature Commissioners proceeded to recommend, by a majority, that the County Courts 'should be annexed to and form constituent parts or branches of the proposed High Court of Justice,' their objectives being to eliminate divisions of jurisdiction and conflicting rules, to reduce expense and delay, and to make the services of the High Court more readily available in the main provincial cities. This last-mentioned recommendation for which, during the nineteenth century, businessmen persistently lobbied and which the London-based English bar consistently opposed, was not implemented.

A hundred years later, in the 1960s the Royal Commission on Assizes and Quarter Sessions (the Beeching Commission) returned to the merger issue but felt unable to pursue the matter, principally because merger would involve 'a partial or total assimilation of the Rules of the Supreme Court and the County Court Rules' and this would have involved the commission 'in a study for which we are ill-qualified as a body and which would have seriously delayed our report.'[6]

In 1985, the Lord Chancellor, Lord Hailsham, set up the Civil Justice Review Body (CJRB) and in a consultation paper issued by that body views were canvassed on the question whether the High Court and the county courts should be amalgamated.[7] In its final report the CJRB said that the leading argument for a unified civil trial court was that it would enable judge power to be allocated to cases on an ideally flexible basis. The report explained:

> In a single court with two tiers of judges it would be possible to identify three bands of work, defined in terms of comparative importance, complexity and substance. The top band would go direct to upper tier judges and the bottom band to the lower tier, while a broad middle band would be eligible for trial by either. This band would reflect the overlapping competence of the two tiers of judges rather than assuming a clear dividing line between them, and would enable middle band case allocation to be made by reference to the availability of judicial resources rather than being dominated by rigid financial limits. Specialist cases requiring to be dealt with by High Court judges alone could be sent direct to that tier.[8]

The opening up of the unified trial court issue created a lively debate. The arguments put pro and con were fairly predictable. A foreign observer might have noted that the issue of court funding did not arise in the debate. This is because both levels of civil court were (and are) funded by central government; consequently, it could not be contended that merger would lead to increased funding for the courts overall. In the event, the CJRB concluded that the High Court and the county courts should remain separate and took the line that the

benefits of a unified system could be obtained without complete amalgamation through the implementation of a policy of 'integration without amalgamation.' The Review said that the principal objective of its
recommendations was to ensure that the business of the civil courts
should be allocated to the various tiers of judiciary in such a way as to
ensure 'that it is handled at the lowest level appropriate to each case.'[9]
It explained that the securing of this objective has several beneficial
effects. It ensures that 'the skills of higher level judges can be concentrated on the cases for which they are required most,' and that delays
are reduced 'at the top of the system without risking the dilution of
judicial quality at that level.' Moreover, it prevents ordinary level cases
from 'creeping inappropriately to the top of the system' and generating costs which are quite disproportionate to their substance, importance and complexity.

The relationship between the High Court and the county courts,
and in particular the issue of amalgamation, was more vigorously
debated than any other matter raised by the Review. The CJRB listed its
reasons for rejecting amalgamation.[10] Amongst them are reasons connected with the special constitutional position of the High Court
judges, and therefore, of the High Court itself. The High Court judges
are 'Her Majesty's Judges.' They exercise powers derived not exclusively or even primarily from statute but from the Royal Prerogative
and are buttressed by the common law. The law relating to the circumstances in which they may be removed from office gives them greater
protection than that enjoyed be lesser judges. Under the British constitution, the doctrine of the separation of powers is not entrenched, but
as a practical matter the separation of the judiciary from the legislature
and the executive is maintained ultimately by the independence of the
High Court judges. The High Court is the corporate expression of Her
Majesty's judges collectively. The individual independence of the
judges translates into the corporate independence of the Court (an
independence not enjoyed by the county courts, which are inferior
courts and creatures of statute). The High Court judges, and therefore
the High Court, have certain exclusive powers of high constitutional
significance, including powers of judicial review derived from the
power to issue prerogative writs and orders and powers under the
European Convention on Human Rights as incorporated in English law
by the Human Rights Act of 1998. Good governance, if nothing else,
requires that the High Court should remain independent and that nothing should be done to undermine the perception of the populace that it

is independent. Merger of the High Court with a network of inferior courts, it was argued, would ipso facto undermine that perception.

The question whether the High Court and the county courts should be merged surfaced again in the course of the inquiry into civil court procedures undertaken by Lord Woolf between 1994 and 1996. The matter was touched upon in the interim report of that inquiry[11] but was not pursued. In that report Lord Woolf appeared to accept that the need to preserve the special status of the High Court judges, and the need to preserve the integrity of the many special jurisdictions exercised by the High Court (including judicial review and work falling within the jurisdiction of the Commercial Court), made amalgamation unwise.

Lord Woolf's comments are worth noting because they brought out one matter relevant to the amalgamation issue that had not been articulated before, but which undoubtedly had played a part in maintaining the 'integration without amalgamation' policy over the years. That matter was the issue of rights of audience in the various levels of court. The English legal profession is a divided profession. It is argued, not only by barristers, but also by many judges and by some solicitors, that advocacy in the higher courts should be done by members of an independent bar. From the beginning both barristers and solicitors have had rights of audience in the county courts. However, until quite recently the rights of audience of solicitors in the High Court were very limited and, even now, solicitors do not have trial rights of audience unless they have obtained special qualifications. Inevitably, the possibility of the merger of the two levels of court is seen as a threat to the independent bar.

The detailed recommendations made by the CJRB for implementing the 'integration without amalgamation' policy were largely accepted and put in place by primary legislation[12] and by very substantial amendments to the Supreme Court Rules (which then governed High Court civil procedure) and to the County Court Rules. The mechanisms put in place in 1991 to implement the 'integration without amalgamation' policy recommended by the CJRB proved quite successful. They provided solid foundations for the next wave of civil justice reforms implemented in 1999 on the basis of Lord Woolf's reports. To a foreign observer, the mechanisms may look overly complicated. That may be so. Nevertheless, they work.

It is convenient for me to explain at this point that the relationship between the High Court and the county courts (or at least some of them) is a little more sophisticated than I have so far described.

Within the High Court, there is a considerable amount of judicial specialization. Upon appointment, a High Court judge is assigned to one of the three formal divisions of the court (the Chancery Division, the Queen's Bench Division, and the Family Division). Further (and confusingly), there are structures described as 'courts' within two of the divisions (and some of them have been given statutory recognition). Thus, within the Chancery Division there is a Patents Court and a Companies Court. And within the Queen's Bench Division there is an Admiralty Court and a Commercial Court. Recently, within the High Court an Administrative Court has been created (replacing the old Crown Office List). Further, work referred by the High Court to official referees (who are nominated circuit judges dealing with cases requiring the protracted examination of documents) is now dealt with by the Technology and Construction Court.

Sittings of the Queen's Bench Division and of the Family Division are routinely held out of London at the major provincial cities (arrangements for sittings of the Chancery Division may also be made). Sometimes, the jurisdiction of these divisions is discharged by circuit judges sitting temporarily as deputy High Court judges. Inevitably, it has been argued that the services of the specialist courts within the High Court should also be made available out of London. To a limited extent, attempts have been made to respond to this argument. Thus, for example, at some regional court centres circuit judges have been appointed to discharge the jurisdiction of the Technology and Construction Court.

Sittings of the Commercial Court are not held in the regions, much to the disappointment of lawyers practising in the major provincial cities. However, at certain county courts Mercantile Courts, where specially nominated circuit judges sit permanently, have been established. These courts do not have the full Commercial Court jurisdiction, but have a jurisdiction that exceeds that of the ordinary county courts and which approximates the Commercial Court jurisdiction. The model for the Mercantile Courts was the London County Court Business List, an arrangement put in place in London for the purpose of helping the Commercial Court to deal with its caseload. The creation of the Mercantile Courts can be seen as a further illustration of the working out of the 'integration without amalgamation' policy.

For the sake of completeness, it should be mentioned that in London there is, in addition to the Patents Court of the High Court, a Patents County Court in which a nominated circuit judge sits. This is a special arrangement, designed to provide a judicial service which is quicker and cheaper than that provided by the Patents Court for certain kinds of patents work, and which may be used by litigants in person and patent agents.

Earlier I explained that, over the years, the effect of what I termed procedural compaction has been to emasculate summary justice mechanisms. In England and elsewhere, to an extent this trend has been resisted by the development of special mechanisms for dealing with small claims. In England, in response to calls for the creation of a small claims tribunal quite separate from the court system, a procedure designed to provide an accessible, quick, cheap and informal means of deciding disputed civil claims involving small sums of money was grafted onto the arbitration jurisdiction of the county courts. The procedure was introduced by the Administration of Justice Act of 1973. Initially the procedure was limited to claims under £75 (Can $170), and could be invoked only if the parties agreed. Subsequently the limit was increased to £1,000 (Can $2,240), the range of cases falling within the jurisdiction was widened, and reference to the procedure was made automatic and mandatory (unless the court ordered otherwise). Under the Civil Procedure Rules for the allocation of cases to case management tracks introduced as part of the Access to Justice reforms, claims of not more than £5,000 (Can $7,700) (a very sizeable increase on the previous financial limit) will be allocated to the small claims track and dealt with in the county courts. Cases on this track are handled in accordance with the informal and restricted procedures set out in Part 26 of the Civil Procedure Rules.

The county court small claims track provides a good illustration of the fight-back against procedural compaction. It could be said that the small claims procedure is 'the new summary justice.' But the matter does not end there. It could also be said that the fast-track procedure too, at least when contrasted with multi-track procedure, may justifiably be described as 'summary justice.'

The High Court and the network of county courts, although in legal and constitutional terms quite distinct, are jointly administered. It might be said that the two-tier trial court arrangement would not have survived had the position been different, with the two levels of court being administered by different agencies (as it was on the criminal side until recently). On the other hand it might be commented, surely if one agency is administering both levels of court, it would be in the interests of the agency to see the several courts amalgamated? Why would such an agency support the 'integration without amalgamation' policy? The point justifies a digression and provides a useful bridge between what I have said above about the civil courts and what propose to say below about the criminal courts.

In 1971, as a result of the implementation of most of the recommendations made in the Report of the Royal Commission on Assizes and Quarter Sessions 1966–69 (the Beeching Commission), arrangements for the administration of the English courts above the level of magistrates' courts were substantially reformed. The report proposed an 'executive-based,' as distinct from a 'judiciary-based,' court administration system. The Lord Chancellor, in his capacity as a member of the government and head of a central government department, was given statutory power to 'appoint such officers and other staff for the Supreme Court ... and county courts as appear to him necessary' for setting up a unified administrative court service, and generally for carrying out the administrative work of those courts. No attempt was made to distinguish clearly between judicial administration functions that should remain under the control of the judiciary and those that could properly be irrevocably delegated to civil service administrators. However, it was asserted in the report that the recommendations made were 'consistent with preservation of all existing safeguards which ensure the independence of the judiciary and which keep judicial work of the courts subject to the overriding control of the judges.'[13] In the event, a system of matrix management emerged, under which judges and civil servants worked out between them who should be responsible for what. The system came under occasional sharp pressures, but on the whole worked well enough.

The unified administrative court service has its headquarters in London but is organized on a regional basis. There are six circuits, one of which (the South-Eastern) includes London, each under the control of a circuit administrator who liaises with the presiding judge for his circuit (a High Court judge nominated by the Lord Chief Justice). Each circuit is further divided into a number of areas. The establishment of a single court service, providing administrative services (on the civil side) to both the High Court and the County Courts has brought certain advantages that might otherwise have not been achievable unless the two levels of court were merged. In particular the single service has facilitated the development of court centres out of London where both High Court and county courts may sit and, if the High Court does not sit, where registry facilities for both levels of court can be made available. The Lord Chancellor's Department's court building program has embraced the needs of both levels of court, to the advantages of both and to the users of both.

Over the years, a consistent complaint made by those who have urged the merger of the two levels of civil trial court has been that services of the High Court (which is based at the Royal Courts of Justice in London) are not adequately available in the regions. The planning of the required sittings of the High Court and the county courts is in the hands of the unified court service. By consistently monitoring the position, the court service has been able to minimize the effects of the London bias of the High Court. However, as indicated above, the question of the extent to which greater efforts should be made to carry to the major provincial cities the services of the specialist jurisdictions of the High Court remains controversial.

In England, the High Court judges hold a special constitutional position. This fact makes the development of a single trial court on the civil side difficult but not impossible. From what has been said above it can be seen that the structure of the English civil courts seems unnecessarily complicated, and all the more so when the courts with jurisdiction in family law matters are taken into account. Doubtless this fragmentation causes some practical problems, and it may be that it leads to inefficiencies in the deployment of judge-power and in other ways makes the administration of justice through the civil courts more expensive than it might be. If this is so, it might be expected that, in pursuit of the 'integration without amalgamation' policy, further changes in the relationship between the two levels of court will come forward, and, perhaps, further consideration will be given to the idea that they should be consolidated in a unified civil court.[14]

## The Criminal Courts – Crown Court and the Magistrates' Courts: Closer Alignment

In an earlier section of this paper, I explained that, in England a two-tier trial court system exists on the criminal side. The Crown Court is the superior court; it sits at the Old Bailey in London (where it is known as the Central Criminal Court) and at almost one hundred other cities and towns throughout England. Beneath the Crown Court is a network of inferior courts, the magistrates' courts.

The Crown Court is an unusual superior court. It was created by the Courts Act in 1971 and absorbed jurisdictions (almost exclusively criminal) previously exercised by a variety of courts, both superior and inferior (including courts of assize and courts of quarter sessions). Unlike the other superior courts (including the High Court), the Crown Court does not 'consist of' judges. In fact, the Crown Court has no judges at all. What it has is 'jurisdiction' which, so the relevant legislation says, 'shall be exercisable by' certain judges in certain circumstances. Generally, the jurisdiction of this court may be exercisable by any judge of the High Court and any circuit judge. Such judges, when exercising the jurisdiction of the Crown Court, 'shall be judges of the Crown Court.'[15] The Crown Court borrows judges from the Queen's Bench Division of the High Court and uses judges appointed to the rank of circuit judge. The most serious indictable cases are dealt with by High Court judges temporarily assigned to the Crown Court. The bulk of the work arising in the court is dealt with by circuit judges (some of whom may be specially authorized to take High Court judge cases). The circuit judges in combination form no court of their own; in this sense they are homeless. The Crown Court also makes extensive use of part-time professional judges known as recorders. At present there are 75 Queen's Bench Division judges, 605 circuit judges, and 1,310 recorders in post.

Throughout England there are several hundred magistrates' courts, each with local and limited jurisdiction.[16] The territorial jurisdiction of these courts is based on petty session areas.[17]

The principal distinction between the two levels of court is that, whereas in the Crown Court criminal cases are tried by a professional judge sitting with a jury of twelve, in the magistrates' courts, depending on the circumstances, cases are tried either by a professional judge sitting alone (now known as a district judge), or by a bench of lay justices of peace, discharging the functions of judge and jury. Virtually all criminal cases are started in magistrates' courts and, if not tried there, are committed for disposal in the Crown Court. Historically speaking, the jurisdiction of magistrates to sit as 'examining justices,' preserving evidence and deciding whether or not cases involving indictable offences should be committed to the superior court for disposal (by trial if necessary), was very important. It was a jurisdiction that was best exercised by a tribunal at arm's length from the superior criminal court. In the 1960s and later on the examining magistrate jurisdiction was streamlined.

In recent years, English law has got into a curious muddle over the role of the courts at the pre-trial stages of criminal cases, particularly cases involving the prosecution of indictable offences. Obvious issues that may require judicial attention include the granting of legal aid, the granting of bail, and the disclosure of evidence. Questions have arisen as to the purpose of the examining magistrate function and how it should be structured and organized. The result has been that jurisdiction has been overlaid with a case transfer system for certain cases involving certain kinds of offences under which the role of the magistrates' court is severely restricted, if not cut out altogether. These changes in the pre-trial role of magistrates' courts have done as much as anything else to raise the court unification question.

During 1999 to 2001, the jurisdiction and procedures of the English criminal trial courts were subjected to a detailed inquiry, known as the Criminal Courts Review, undertaken by Sir Robin Auld, an experienced and highly-regarded Lord Justice of Appeal. On occasion, it has been said that this inquiry was the criminal counterpart of the Access to Justice Inquiry conducted by Lord Woolf in relation to civil justice. However, the Woolf inquiry built on the work of the Civil Justice Review Body and drew on that work in a manner that has not been fully recognized. Sir Robin Auld had no such advantage. Further, he suffered from the disability that terms of reference for his inquiry were ludicrously wide (and he also had to contend with an unpardonable amount of unhelpful and distracting political speculation). The terms of reference for Sir Robin's review were as follows:

> A review into the practices and procedures of, and the rules of evidence applied by, the criminal courts at every level, with a view to ensuring that they deliver justice fairly, by streamlining all their processes, increasing their efficiency and strengthening the effectiveness of their relationships with others across the whole of the criminal justice system, and having regard to the interests of all parties including victims and witnesses, thereby promoting public confidence in the rule of law.

In the Auld inquiry the issue of unification of the two levels of court figured prominently. However, the issue of overriding importance was the question of whether the right to jury trial should be curtailed. In England, in cases falling within the exclusive jurisdiction of the magistrates' courts, defendants are denied jury trial. In cases falling within the exclusive jurisdiction of the Crown Court, the defendant pleading not guilty cannot avoid jury trial; that is to say, he cannot waive his right to jury trial in favour of a trial by judge alone (a so-called bench trial). Where a defendant is prosecuted for an offence falling within the concurrent jurisdiction (the 'either way' offences), the position is that the defendant himself may elect whether he is tried in the Crown Court (with a jury) or in a magistrates' court (without a jury). Some of the offences falling within the either way category (notably theft) may be committed in circumstances varying from the very serious to the very minor. Consequently, in England defendants can have a right to jury trial in circumstances that would surprise a foreign observer. Inevitably, in the interests of resource optimization (if not for mere reasons of economy) successive governments have flirted with the idea of limiting jury trial. Invariably (notably in 1974), they have lost their nerve. The Blair government had a run at the issue before the general election in 2001 and stirred up a hornet's nest before dumping the problem on the Criminal Courts Review. The government never managed successfully to rebut the charge that their objective was simply to reduce expenditure on the criminal justice system by forcing cases out of the Crown Court and into the cheaper magistrates' courts' regime without holding out the promise of any compensating benefits elsewhere in the system.

Of course, the issue of trial court unification and the right to jury trial are quite separate. The limiting of the right to jury trial is not dependent on unification. There is no difficulty in contemplating and designing a single trial court in which both jury trials and bench trials are held. If it is necessary to justify the continuation of the two-tiered trial court system on the criminal side, the case for it has to be made on other grounds.

Another issue that figured prominently in the Auld inquiry was whether the arrangements for the administration of the two levels of criminal trial court were satisfactory. After the introduction of the Beeching reforms in 1971, the Lord Chancellor's Department became responsible for the administration of the courts above the level of the magistrates' courts, including the Crown Court. The administration of the magistrates' courts was shared by central government (through the Home Office) and by local magistrates' courts' committees (MCCs) and local authorities. During February to July 1989, the magistrates' courts were subjected to a scrutiny. In the report following, recommendations were made directed at ensuring that the mechanisms, at national and local level, for determining resource levels and resource management and control were best suited to the efficient, economic, and effective discharge of the responsibilities of the magistrates' courts.[18] The scrutiny concluded that the administration of the magistrates' courts should be a central government responsibility and, not surprisingly, suggested that this would best be achieved by a 'next steps agency,' reporting to ministers but operationally independent. It was said that such an arrangement offered the best way of meeting the criteria identified for new management and resourcing arrangements.

This scrutiny report was an opening shot in a very bitter fight between the government of the day and parties involved in the work of the magistrates' courts, including, in particular, members of the lay magistracy (the justices of the peace) and their professional advisors (the justices' clerks). The government conceded that the arrangements for the management of magistrates' courts should continue to be locally based and that local MCCs would survive, but asserted that there was a need to modernize the management structure so as to improve performance and accountability. Inevitably this meant strengthening the role of central government. The government's proposals were set out in a White Paper issued in February 1992.[19]

In this White Paper the government announced that, because of the nature of the changes it intended to make, it would be appropriate to transfer from the Home Office to the Lord Chancellor's Department responsibilities for the finance, organization, and management of the magistrates' courts. The purpose of this change was 'to ensure a more coherent approach to court management within government.' The legislation necessary to effect these reforms was included in the Police and Magistrates' Courts Act 1994.[20] Subsequently, the arrangements for the participation of central government in the administration of magistrates' courts was reorganized and was eventually absorbed within the Courts Service under the Lord Chancellor. Thus, the executive government agency responsible for the administration of the Crown Court became responsible for discharging the central government administration responsibilities for the magistrates' courts. However, the powers of the Court Services Agency over the administration of the Crown Courts were not as great as those exercised over the magistrates' courts (where a certain amount of responsibility lies locally with magistrate's courts committees). For the first time, one administrative agency had both levels of criminal trial court in its sights. And for the first time, the agency responsible for the administration of the Crown Court, in dealing with its own caseloads, could no longer pretend that delays in the processing by the magistrates' courts of cases destined for that court (delays which had previously worked to their advantage) were not their concern.

An examination of the way in which Sir Robin Auld interpreted his terms of reference and carried out his inquiry show how the two issues outlined above (viz., trial court unification and court administration) come together. His lordship interpreted his terms of reference as including, but not as necessarily being limited to, a number of matters which, although they may be stated as discrete issues for purposes of discussion, inevitably overlap. They include, amongst others: the structure and organization of, and distribution of work between, the courts; their composition, including the use of juries and of lay and stipendiary magistrates; and case management, procedure, and evidence (including the use of information technology). In relation to the first of these, Sir Robin sought responses to the following questions: (a) should the present dual structure continue or should there be a single criminal court system covering all levels of offences in which judges and magistrates would all be judges of the court at their different levels, supported by a common administration and, eventually, housed in the same court buildings; (b) if the present dual structure is to continue, should it have a common administration; and (c) in any event, what, in the short and long term, will be a sufficient and efficient provision and distribution of criminal court buildings and their administrative supports?

During his review Sir Robin revealed that, in the course of his consultations with interested parties, it was suggested to him that a unified criminal court would have some advantages. It would result in a more efficient system, it would reduce delays, and it would allow for shared expertise and good practice. It was said by some that present arrangements under which administrative responsibilities for the courts are shared has led to much duplication of effort with consequent inefficiencies. A unified court would allow for cases to enter the system at the appropriate level instead of all being brought in at the magistrates' court level and committed or transferred to the Crown Court as appropriate. A number of respondents argued for the creation of a single criminal court supported by a unified and nationally funded administration, but within a structure which ensures a significant element of local control and accountability at both the summary and indictable offences level. Among those respondents who did not argue for unification there was considerable support for unifying and simplifying the management of the Crown Court and the magistrates' courts.

The *Report of the Review of the Criminal Courts of England and Wales* (October 2001), as Sir Robin Auld's report was entitled, was presented to ministers on 5 September 2001.[21] The report ran to almost 700 pages and made 328 recommendations. When it was published, the government announced that there would be a consultation period, during which comments on the recommendations would be invited, and that a White Paper indicating the government's intentions would follow (see further below). There was much speculation as to which of Sir Robin's recommendations would find favour with the government and which not. For present purposes, fortunately, it is only necessary to explain a few of the recommendations and to indicate the government's response to them.

On the matter of the structure of the criminal trial court and their administration, in summary the report recommended the establishment of a unified Criminal Court to be known as, simply, the Criminal Court. It was proposed that, within that court, there should be three levels of jurisdiction consisting of: the Crown Division to exercise jurisdiction over all indictable-only matters and such either-way cases as are allocated to it; the District Division to exercise jurisdiction over such either-way matters as are allocated to it; and the Magistrates' Division to exercise jurisdiction over all summary-only matters and such either-way cases as are allocated to it. The Crown and Magistrates' Divisions should be constituted as are the Crown Court and magistrates' courts respectively at the present day, and the District Division should consist of a judge, in the main a district judge and at least two experienced magistrates (or if a defendant with the consent of the court so opts, of a judge alone). The District Division's jurisdiction over either-way offences should be limited to those within a likely maximum sentence in the circumstances of the case viewed at its worst (as distinct from the legal maximum for a case or cases of that category) of, say, two years custody, a maximum financial penalty to be determined and/or a maximum of community, or combination of custody and community, sentences to be determined in the light of future reforms of the sentencing framework. The District Division, sitting as a youth court, should also try grave cases against young defendants presently dealt with in the Crown Court.

It might be said that, under these proposals, the 'unified' Criminal Court would be a court unified in name only. In effect, the existing superior Crown Court and network of inferior magistrates' courts would remain, with an additional new court, the District Division, squeezed in between and with the relationships between them smoothed by improved procedural and administrative arrangements. Clearly, if an additional non-jury court (or 'jurisdiction') in the form of the District Division (additional, that is, to the magistrates' courts) was to be established, certain structural problems would have to be addressed. Among the possible options three of them would be to develop the jurisdiction (1) as part of the Crown Court, or (2) as part of the larger magistrates' courts, or (3) as a separate court. Each of these options presented difficulties that the report sought to avoid by adopting a fourth option. Whereas, at the moment, there are two levels of court, under the report's proposals there would be, notionally at least, a single court, but within it three levels of 'division' and each division would look suspiciously like a separate court. It should be noted that no change in the existing stratified orders of judiciary was recommended. Lay magistrates, district judges (formerly stipendiary magistrates), recorders, circuit judges, and High Court judges would retain their ranks and station. Looked at in this way, it appeared that the proposals were consistent with the 'integration without amalgamation' policy. The key recommendation was the creation of the non-jury District Division. If that recommendation had not figured in the report, the case for merging the Crown Court and the magistrates' courts into a single unified Criminal Court would have been significantly weakened. It was the idea that there should be a new non-jury jurisdiction that pointed to and led to the idea that there should be a unified criminal court.

The most controversial feature of the recommended structure was, of course, the recommendation that the District Division should be a non-jury court. There was some doubt as to what might be the effect of the establishment of the District Division on the accused's access to jury trial, but there is no avoiding the fact that the objective behind the recommendation was to reduce the number of jury trials significantly.

During the further consultation period, the recommendation that there should be such a middle tier of jurisdiction designed for this purpose was attacked, notably in a memorandum by Professor Michael Zander.[22] Undenied 'leaks' indicated that the government had abandoned plans to scrap the right to jury trial for many offences as proposed in Sir Robin Auld's report. In April 2002 it became known that the White Paper was likely to contain a number of discrete proposals (some recommended in Sir Robin's report, and some not) which, in their cumulative effects, would reduce significantly the number of Crown Court jury trials (among them is the proposal that the powers of magistrates' courts to jail offenders should be greatly increased). It was estimated that, if implemented, the package of proposals being worked up would have the effect of reducing the number of cases sent to the Crown Court for jury trial by 6,000 a year.

As it became clear that the new non-jury jurisdiction proposed by Sir Robin Auld was almost certainly not going to appear amongst the government's proposals in the expected White Paper, the suspicion arose that the recommendation that there should be a unified Criminal Court would fall with it, because to a large extent the former predicated the latter. However, as is explained further below, Sir Robin's proposals for a new non-jury jurisdiction within a unified criminal court were not based on jurisdictional and procedural considerations exclusively. There remained the possibility that a unified criminal court would be established, not for jurisdictional, but for administrative reasons.

In England, the Court Services Agency, an executive agency coming under the Lord Chancellor's Department, has been responsible for the administration of the Crown Court since the Beeching reforms were introduced in 1972. As we have seen, arrangements for the administration of the magistrates' courts were substantially reformed in 1994, with central government responsibilities being strengthened and shifted to the Lord Chancellor's Department and the role of local Magistrates' Courts Committees (MCCs) being re-defined. In Sir Robin Auld's report, considerable attention was given to the way in which the post-1994 administrative arrangements have worked out in practice and, in particular, to the interface between those arrangements and the administration of the Crown Court.

The report said that the system of administration of the Crown Court is very different from that of magistrates' courts. It is centralized and criticized by some as 'too monolithic and inflexible to meet local needs and the different jurisdictions it has to administer.' The MCCs, despite increasing oversight by the Lord Chancellor's Department, 'are a fragmented and diverse system of local bodies hobbled by difficult financial and managerial mechanisms and with inconsistent practices and procedures.' Further, not only are their great differences between the two systems, 'there is poor co-operation between them.'[23]

The weaknesses in the present dual system of criminal court administration were explained, and proposals for a new management structure were made, in chapter 7 of the Auld report. It was recommended that a single, centrally funded executive agency should be established, as part of the Lord Chancellor's Department, and should be responsible for the administration of all courts, civil, criminal, and family (save for the Appellate Committee of the House of Lords). This new agency would replace the Court Service and Magistrates' Courts Committees. It should be headed by a national board and chief executive. Further, for the purpose the recommended arrangements are not over-centralized, it was recommended that within each circuit the criminal courts should be organized managerially on the basis of the forty-two criminal justice areas, and the implementation of national policy and management at local level for all three jurisdictions should be the responsibility of local managers working in close liaison with local judges and magistrates.[24]

It is perhaps no surprise that Sir Robin found that the arrangements for the administration of the magistrates' courts through the Courts Service Agency and the MCCs, as implemented in 1994, have not worked satisfactorily. As mentioned above, the 1994 reforms were bitterly contested and the central and local structures put in place then represented a grand compromise that was perhaps destined to fail.[25]

In the further consultation period following the publication of the Auld report it became clear that the expected White Paper would contain proposals for significantly reforming the administration of the Crown Court and the magistrates' courts along the lines it had recommended. What was not clear was whether the government would take the view that, as part of that administrative reform, the two levels of court should be merged into a single unified Criminal Court. The then Lord Chancellor, Lord Irvine, was reported as having said that the Auld proposal to combine magistrates' courts and Crown Court into a unified criminal court administered by his own department made 'a vast amount of sense.'[26] This would suggest that the policy of 'integration without amalgamation' was about to be abandoned on the criminal side in England, not for jurisdictional or procedural reasons, but for administrative reasons.

The promised White Paper was published on 17 July 2002.[27] The government rejected Sir Robin Auld's recommendation that there should be a unified criminal trial court consisting of three levels of jurisdiction, with one of them being a District Division in which cases would be tried without juries. The White Paper expressed the view that the benefits identified as flowing from a restructuring of the trial courts into a single court 'can be realised through a closer alignment of the magistrates' courts and the Crown Court, without a complete reordering of the court system.' The rejection of the recommendation that there should be a new non-jury jurisdiction came as no surprise. However, the White Paper did accept that in cases allocated to the Crown Court defendants should have the right to apply to the court for trial by a judge sitting alone. And it was also accepted that in serious and complex fraud cases the prosecution should have the right to apply to the court for the trial to be conducted without a jury.

Generally, the government accepted the Auld recommendations for improving the administration of the two levels of criminal trial court. However, the White Paper did not propose that, for purely administrative reasons, the two levels of trial court should be merged into a single court.

The Auld's inquiry covered a wide range of criminal justice issues, apart from the particular issue of trial court unification. The great majority of its recommendations were accepted, either entirely or in principle or in part, or accepted as worthy of further consideration. During 2003, two major pieces of legislation were enacted for the purpose of implementing major reforms in the English criminal justice system, including those changes recommended by Auld and accepted by the government in the White Paper. The legislation necessary to implement those recommendations, and reforms having a quite separate provenance, is found in two major statutes enacted during 2003.[28] This legislation also paved the way for the closer alignment of the two levels of criminal trial court referred to in the White Paper. This closer alignment, achieved not only by jurisdictional tinkering and the development of uniform rules of criminal procedure, but also by changes to arrangements for court administration, can be seen as based on a criminal side policy of 'integration without amalgamation.' The legislation enacted in 2003 was not immediately brought into force and it is unlikely that all of the provisions will be in force before the middle of this decade.

## Unified Courts and Judicial Orders

Pressure to scrap two-tiered systems builds up when each tier ceases to play the role for which it was designed. If a court system gets to the stage where there is no meaningful distinction between the jurisdictions at the two levels, people are bound to ask: why do we persist with two tiers? The lower court judges are likely to feel affronted by the fact that they discharge the same duties and responsibilities as the higher court judges, but without the same pay and status. The problem is aggravated when, over a period of time, the machinery for appointing judges fails to work properly. If the stratification of orders of judges is to be justified, it has to be ensured that the judges appointed to the higher level are, by some significant and justifiable measure, 'better' (for the sake of a better word) than those appointed to the lower level.

In England, despite the significant overlaps between the jurisdictions of the two levels of trial courts on the civil side, it remains the case that the judicial work falling on the High Court judges is significantly heavier than that discharged by the circuit judges and the district judges. Further, the bulk of the High Court judges are expected to ride circuit for half the year. On the criminal side, although there is again a significant overlap between the two levels of court, the caseload dealt with by the High Court judges and the circuit judges sitting in the Crown Court is heavier than that dealt with by the lay magistrates and district judges in the magistrates' courts.

It is also generally accepted that the calibre of the lawyers appointed to the High Court bench is higher than that of the circuit judges.[29] Of course, from time to time one hears criticism. However, all lawyers appointed to the bench, whether to the High Court level or the circuit judge level, will have spent a number of years sitting as part-time judges dealing mainly with criminal work (i.e., as recorders), and during that period they will have undergone compulsory training. A lawyer who performs poorly as a recorder is unlikely to be offered a full-time appointment. Further, a lawyer who discovers through sitting as a recorder that he does not like judicial work will not accept such an appointment if offered it. Promotions from a circuit judge position to a High Court judge position are still quite rare, though more common than they used to be. Further, it is a professional rule that a barrister appointed as a full-time judge cannot subsequently resign his office and go back to the bar.

In effect, the High Court judges are the 'officer' class of the judiciary and the circuit judges and district judges are the 'other ranks' and this division is tolerated. The lay justices of the peace are 'volunteers' (or, possibly, 'reservists'). The High Court judges are appointed from the upper echelons of the practising bar.[30] They tend to go on to the bench at a significantly later age than the circuit judges. This has one valuable side effect (in addition to minimizing the risk of 'burn out'); it keeps the top flight barristers working at the bar until well into their fifties and this means that the courts have the benefit of their work for longer than they would if they were tempted to take judicial appointments at an earlier age.

Invariably, barristers appointed to the High Court bench take a significant cut in salary. If a barrister accepts an appointment to the High Court bench he will probably do so at an age that enables him to get the full pension entitlement at retirement.[31]

Of course, not all barristers offered appointments to the High Court bench accept. However, it is still the case that the Lord Chancellor gets few refusals, but enough to cause concern about the level of judicial salaries. Barristers who have done well, and who are generally regarded as being of High Court bench calibre, often experience a fair amount of peer pressure to accept, not least from the younger barristers in their chambers who look forward to inheriting some lucrative work when their colleague moves on and up.

I have explained all this at some length because I think it helps to explain why the English have tolerated for so long the divisions between the various orders of judge. If, over the years, a considerable number of inappropriate appointments had been made to the High Court bench, then it is likely that the idea of merging the High Court and the county courts would have developed quite a head of steam. It is significant that in the current debate about the prospect of merging the Crown Court and the magistrates' courts into a single unified criminal court there has been no suggestion that the several judicial orders should be merged. Indeed, many members of the lay judicial order (the justices of the peace) have been against the unified court proposal because they fear the loss of identity of 'their' courts, (i.e., the magistrates' courts).

Of course, it is possible to have a multi-tiered judiciary without having a multi-tiered court system. At the end of the day, whether there is one court or several, the problem of matching caseloads with judicial talent and experience remains. One way of doing that is to have the separate levels of judge corralled in separate levels of court. The other way is to say that courts and judges are quite different and to arrange things so that judges of different orders can sit in the same court, as in the English Crown Court, and possibly, in the unified criminal court proposed by Sir Robin Auld.

All that I have said about judicial orders must be seen in the light of the fact that the arrangements for the recruitment of judges in England are about to change. It does not take a lot of foresight to see that, in England, a judge recruitment and retention crisis is looming. The base for recruitment will have to be broadened. If enacted, the Constitutional Reform Bill (introduced in Parliament in 2004), will bring into being a Judicial Appointments Commission.[32] There is much brave talk about it being important that, under any new arrangements, the present quality of judges be maintained. However, it is doubtful whether the traditional standards for direct recruitment to what I have called the officer class of the judiciary can be maintained. The solution would seem to be to reduce significantly the size of that judicial class. If that happens, the issues of judicial organization and court structure that I have attempted to discuss will be seen in a very different light.

## What Is a Court?

In closing, I would like to draw attention to an old concern of mine, one to which I have alluded on other occasions.[33] It is my belief that we no longer have any idea of what we mean by 'a court'; so how do we know what we mean when we talk of merging courts or creating new courts? At least, there is a cleavage between what judges and lawyers might mean by 'a court' and what court administrators might mean. Judges and lawyers will inevitably give a constitutional and legal definition; administrators will give a definition derived from organization and management thinking.

I am particularly reminded of this whenever I hear lawyers calling for the establishment of yet another new court. In England the latest examples are campaigns for a housing court and for an environmental court. If one attempts to get to the bottom of these crusades one often finds that nothing that is being proposed could not be accommodated within existing court structures (and one often suspects that special interests that ought not to prevail unchallenged are being promoted). In England, at least since the 1870s, the fragmentation of the court system has been resisted. But there has always been a willingness to develop within the basic court system new structures, both horizontal and vertical, to meet changing circumstances and demands. Long ago, Roscoe Pound (the father of American judicial administration) said the ideal arrangement was 'specialist judges, not specialist courts,' a view that has been taken to heart in England.[34]

However, in modern times an additional consideration relevant to court design that Roscoe Pound could not have envisaged has emerged. That is, the administration of the courts. In earlier parts of this paper I explained the ways in which the English executive-based system for the administration of the various courts has emerged and developed. I noted that, initially, matters of jurisdictional and procedural design were treated as forming part of the environment within which the administrative system operates, and were regarded as falling within the exclusive control of the judges (for example, case management). However, in modern times those matters have come to be seen by administrators as issues important to the ability of the administrative system to discharge its tasks (which may involve effective interaction within non-judicial administrative systems) and, indeed, as crucial to the survival of the system, and therefore have become matters that the administrators and their political masters wish to control and manipulate. In this paper I have not regarded it as necessary to enter into the debate as to how court administration functions may be divided into 'judicial' and 'non-judicial.' However, I should not end without saying that this is a matter relevant to the court unification issue, and may prove to be the key to the outcome of the current debate in England as to whether there should be two levels of criminal trial court or a single unified court.

Ever since 1971, when the court administration reforms recommended by the Beeching Commission were brought into effect, with the inevitable result that workings of the courts were drawn ever more tightly into the executive branch of government, English judges and lawyers have been very suspicious whenever changes to court structures and to the jurisdictions and procedures of courts have been mooted by the executive branch. Their suspicion has been that the sole objective has been, not efficiency or effectiveness, but economy. The result has been that good ideas as well as bad have been resisted. On 12 June 2003, the prime minister dismissed the Lord Chancellor, Lord Irvine, and the government announced its intention to abolish the office of Lord Chancellor. In their constitutional ignorance the government failed to realize that the functions of the office could not be transferred to a secretary of state with the stroke of a pen. Lord Falconer was hastily appointed Lord Chancellor and, apparently, given instructions to wind up and dissolve that great office. It is an ill wind that blows no good. In the ensuing uproar the government was forced to concede that the judges should have a far greater role to play in the administration of their courts than heretofore. Under a bargain struck by Lord Falconer and the Lord Chief Justice (Lord Woolf), many of the functions formerly carried out by the Lord Chancellor will become the responsibility of the Lord Chief Justice, and in a variety of ways the hands of the judges will strengthened. The working out of the bargain (or 'Concordat' as it is called) will require new legislation and the amendment of some existing legislation.[35] It may be that, as a result of all this, we are witnessing in England the beginning of an era wherein the prospects for modernization of the court structure, on both the civil and criminal sides, are better than heretofore.

Jurisdictions around the common law world have much to learn from one another about judicial organization. However, whenever I travel to North America or Australia I am always struck by the enormous differences between the 'geography of justice' conditions that prevail there when compared with England. England is a small, densely populated jurisdiction with good communications. There are many sizeable provincial cities where court resources are deployed. It is not unusual there to come across lawyers who practise in half a dozen different court centres. By contrast, the typical North American and Australia jurisdiction is large, and apart from one metropolis and perhaps a small number of other cities, sparsely populated. Frequently, the impacts of these differences are underestimated and the prospects of 'legal transplants' from England to those jurisdictions having the same effects as they do in England are impaired. That is particularly true in relation to the matters I have tried to discuss in this paper. The two-tier trial court structures that are sustained in this country fit with the demographic conditions that exist within it. They may not fit satisfactorily in jurisdictions with markedly different conditions.

NOTES

1  The formal accusatory pleading in the Crown Court is the indictment; consequently offences falling in categories (1) and (3) because, respectively, they may or must be tried on indictment, are known generically as 'indictable offences.'
2  Recently, with the strengthening of the legal framework of the European Union, and the incorporation of the European Convention on Human Rights into English law, and the standardization that these developments has brought, English legal pride has taken a few knocks.

3 *Supreme Court Act,* 1981, section 1. By the *Constitutional Reform Act* of 2005, the Supreme Court becomes the 'Senior Court,' to distinguish it from the proposed Supreme Court of the United Kingdom, which will replace the House of Lords in its judicial capacity. The 2005 act makes some minor changes to the constitution of the Supreme Court.

4 Ibid., section 2.

5 Ibid., 1981, section 4.

6 *Report of the Royal Commission on Assizes and Quarter Sessions,* Beeching Commission), Cmnd 4153 (London: HMSO, 1969), para. 205.

7 See Review Body of Civil Justice, *Civil Justice Review, Consultation Paper No. 6, General Issues* (London: HMSO, 1987), para. 87 et seq.

8 Ibid., *Report of the Review Body on Civil Justice,* Cm 394 (London: HMSO, 1988), para. 104.

9 Ibid., para. 82.

10 Ibid., paras 105–15.

11 Right Honourable Lord Woolf, *Access to Justice: Interim Report* (London: Department for Constitutional Affairs, 1955), ch. 12.

12 See *Courts and Legal Services Act,* 1990 Pt. I.

13 Beeching Commission, para. 170.

14 Well after this paper was written, the Department of Constitutional Affairs (formerly the Lord Chancellor's Department) embarked on an investigation of the scope for unifying the several courts with civil and family jurisdictions. As a result of this exercise, in October 2005 it was announced that the government had 'decided to adopt as a long-term objective' the creation of 'single Civil and Family Courts with unified jurisdictions.' Quite what this means is not clear. In the meantime, procedural and jurisdictional changes, consistent with the 'integration without amalgamation' policy, and designed to smooth out some practical rough edges in the relationship between the High Court and the county courts that have emerged, are expected.

15 *Supreme Court Act,* section 8.

16 The jurisdiction of these courts is not exclusively criminal as they have an important family law jurisdiction; soon to be redrawn as 'local justice areas.'

17 *Justices of the Peace Act* 1997, sections 1 and 2.

18 *Magistrates' Courts: Report of a Scrutiny* (London: HMSO 1989).

19 *A New Framework for Local Justice,* Cm 1829 (London: HMSO, 1992).

20 Further changes were made by the *Access to Justice Act* 1999, Pt. V.

21 The report can be found on the website www.criminal-courts-review.org.uk.

22 See 'Lord Justice Auld's Review of the Criminal Courts: A Response' (November 2001). This memorandum can be accessed and downloaded from the London School of Economics website: www.lse.ac.uk/Depts/law.

23 Auld Report, ch. 3, para. 65.

24 Much as the circuit administrators and presiding judges, Chancery supervising and family liaison judges presently do at circuit level.

25 Justice is not alone here; in the United Kingdom, similar criticisms may be made of central and local administrative arrangements in health, education, and local government.

26 Interview by the legal editor of the *Daily Telegraph*, published April 14, 2002.

27 See Secretary of State for the Home Department, the Lord Chancellor, and the Attorney General, *Justice for All*, Cm 5563 (London: HMSO, 2002).

28 See *Courts Act* 2003 (c. 39), and *Criminal Justice Act* 2003 (c. 44).

29 It should be remembered that the High Court provides the recruiting ground for appointments to the Court of Appeal.

30 There is one High Court judge who was a solicitor, but he had advocacy rights in the higher courts.

31 They have to retire at 72, which means they will have to take an appointment no later than age 57 if they envisage themselves soldiering on to the mandatory retirement age.

32 See Kate Malleson, 'The New Judicial Appointments Commission in England and Wales: New Wine in New Bottles?' in Kate Malleson and Peter Russell eds., *Appointing Judges in An Age of Judicial Power: Critical Perspectives from Around the World* (Toronto: University of Toronto Press, 2006).

33 See Ian Scott, 'Caseflow Management in the Trial Court,' in A.A.S. Zuckerman and Ross Cranston eds., *Reform of Civil Procedure: Essays on 'Access to Justice'* (New York: Oxford University Press, 1995) 28 ff.

34 Roscoe Pound *Organization of Courts* (Boston: Little, Brown and Company, 1940), 273–94.

35 See The Lord Chancellor's Judiciary-Related Functions: Proposals (The 'Concordat'), in House Lords Select Committee on the Constitutional Reform Bill, Volume 1: Report Appendix 6 (HL Paper 125–I, 2 July 2004).

# Conclusion: The Road Ahead

PETER H. RUSSELL

If there is one thing on which all the contributors to this volume agree, it is surely the extraordinary diversity of court structures in this country. Readers too must be struck by the variety of ways in which Canada's provinces and territories have organized their courts. This diversity has developed despite the fact that all of these jurisdictions are subject to the same Constitution. It would seem hard to contend that Canada's Constitution dictates any particular structure for its primary courts.

And yet a difficulty of a constitutional nature does seem to have emerged. The judges of the Superior Courts of the provinces which in the original constitutional architecture were to be responsible for trying the most serious criminal and civil cases have come to share that responsibility with the judges of the 'inferior' Provincial Courts. As Ian Scott explains in his discussion of the English trial courts, there is an inevitable tendency for the pyramid of cases to get out of line with the hierarchy of courts. When more and more of the cases deemed to be important are allocated to lower courts in the hierarchy, adjustments should be made. What makes these adjustments more difficult to make in Canada than in England or in California or any other U.S. state is that Canada's Constitution assigns the power to appoint the provinces' highest trial court judges, the judges of the Superior Courts, to the federal government, and the power to appoint the provinces' other judges and organize the provincial court systems to the provincial governments.

This difficulty, which has its root in section 96 of the Constitution, could be overcome if there were some of that lovely but scarce commodity that David Hancock yearns for, cooperative federalism. But alas, as the accounts given by Friedland and Baar attest, there has been precious little cooperative federalism at the political level in this field. Even though its actions have a vital bearing on Provincial Courts, the federal government has never displayed any interest in or capacity for being a thoughtful and informed policy-making partner with the provinces in this area. It is not only through its responsibilities for staffing the senior provincial judiciaries that the federal government's influence on the Provincial Courts is felt but also through the adjudicative burden its legislation – above all the Criminal Code – imposes on the Provincial Courts. The enormous expansion of the role of provincially appointed judges in trying criminal cases, so clearly documented by Webster and Doob, was the result not of legislative decisions by the provinces but of the federal Parliament's amendments to the Criminal Code. In looking at the passages in *Hansard* through the first two-thirds of the last century when most of these amendments were made, one searches in vain for any indication by the federal law-makers of their thoughts on the impact the changes they were making would have on the lower courts of the provinces. This absence of mind is especially remarkable when we read Friedland's account of just how ill-equipped the provinces' Magistrates Courts were to take on this huge enlargement of their criminal justice responsibilities.

The chapters of this book point to two ways in which a good dose of cooperative federalism would make the road ahead easier. One would be to take up Patrick Healy's suggestion of referring the question of whether the federal Parliament under section 91(27) of the Constitution[1] can confer full criminal trial jurisdiction on the judges of the Provincial Court. A provincial government could make such a reference to its provincial Court of Appeal, as New Brunswick did in 1983. But it would expedite matters if the federal government addressed the reference case directly to the Supreme Court of Canada. The reference should be made even if the federal government is not willing to commit itself to allocating full criminal trial responsibilities to Provincial Court judges. If a majority of the Court follows Healy and removes the constitutional bar to full criminal trial jurisdiction that it erected in *McEvoy*, it would clear the air and require the federal government to give a policy reason for refusing a province that wanted to fill the gaps in the criminal trial jurisdiction of its Provincial Court judges. St-Louis's chapter indicates that Quebec is the province that would be most likely to make such a request. Consideration should also be given to enlarging the reference to include a question asking for reconsideration of previous decisions that reserved a few elements of family law for the exclusive jurisdiction of Superior Court. It is possible that this could result in removal of section 96 barriers to full family court jurisdiction at the Provincial Court level.

It is also possible of course that the Supreme Court will not adopt Healy's position and will identify a constitutional residue of criminal trial responsibility that must remain exclusively with Superior Court judges, and that if asked about family law will continue to insist on a residue of exclusive Superior Court jurisdiction in that field. If so, then the only path to further unification of trial court jurisdiction will be to elevate Provincial Court judges to the Superior Court. Some provinces may prefer to unify at the Superior Court level, particularly those who have already moved part-way along that path in the family law area. It is in proceeding with trial court unification at the Superior Court level that another and most difficult form of cooperative federalism would be needed: intergovernmental cooperation in appointing the judges.

The federal-provincial cooperation called for in the appointment of section 96 Superior Court judges is to have representatives of the provinces and territories included on advisory *nominating* committees. This is the approach recommended many years ago by many academics, by the Canadian Bar Association,[2] and in this volume by Alberta's then attorney general, David Hancock. A first step in this direction was taken in 1988 when the federal minister of justice, Ramon Hnatyshyn, introduced a system of committees to assess persons who had indicated their interest in being appointed to section 96 courts.[3] A representative of the provincial or territorial minister of justice is included on each five-person committee. But these committees are *screening* committees not nominating committees. The committees receive from the federal commissioner of judicial affairs lists of persons who are interested in being appointed and advise the government on those on the list who are not qualified for appointment, who are qualified and (more recently) who are highly qualified. The committees submit to the federal minister long lists of persons deemed to be qualified or highly qualified from which the federal government makes it selection, sometimes appointing persons rated as merely qualified over those rated as highly qualified. What is needed to convert this system into a true merit system is to adopt the practice of the committees and councils that advise the provincial and territorial governments on judicial appointments and have the federal advisory committees submit a short list of the most outstanding candidates available for a given position. Under such a system, the federal government, while retaining its constitutional power to reject any given recommendation, could commit itself, as provincial governments have done, to appoint to the Superior Courts only persons that well-balanced, independent advisory committees have found to merit appointment.

Such a reform of the federal judicial appointing system should be made regardless of the contribution it might make to trial court unification. Ian Scott in his chapter reports that the calibre of the lawyers appointed to the High Court bench in England (the English superior court) remains higher than those appointed to positions lower down in the judicial hierarchy. The same could not be said of the situation in Canada. Political favouritism continues to have an undue influence on federal appointments to provincial Superior Courts, while the provinces have established merit systems of appointment.[4] I had personal experience of the provinces' higher standards, when after several years of chairing Ontario's Judicial Appointments Advisory Committee, I found that some candidates who did not make our short list for appointment to the Provincial Court were appointed to the province's Superior Court. The 'inferior court' status of Provincial Courts that may in the past have been a disincentive for outstanding lawyers to serve on these courts nowadays does not have that effect. The narrowing of salary differentials between federally and provincially appointed judges has certainly contributed to making Provincial Court appointments more attractive. As Martin Friedland observes, first-rate lawyers in criminal law or family law may well prefer an appointment to the Provincial Court where they will be able to focus on administering justice in their areas of expertise. It is high time that the federal government took steps to overcome the ironic and unacceptable fact that in making appointments to the highest provincial courts it is not as assiduous in endeavouring to appoint the best-qualified lawyers available as most provinces are in making appointments to their so-called lower courts.

A more practical obstacle to trial court unification at the Superior Court level is the federal government's reluctance to assume the remuneration burden for the Provincial Court judges elevated to Superior Court status. This does not appear to have been an issue in the piecemeal unification of the Family Court at the section 96 level. But assuming responsibility for remunerating the much larger number of Provincial Court judges who would become Superior Court judges if there were a major trial court unification is another matter. Section 100 of the *Constitution Act, 1867* stipulates that the salaries, pensions, and allowances of section 96 judges be fixed and provided by the Parliament of Canada. But this constitutional provision does not preclude a federal-provincial agreement under which a province that agrees to unification of its trial courts would also agree to share the remuneration costs of the unified court. I would suggest that it would be reasonable for the province to continue to contribute the money it was paying the elevated judges and to be responsible for 50 per cent of the remuneration of all new appointments to the provinces's superior trial court. Such an arrangement would be a logical quid pro quo of the provinces having a significant role in the selection and appointment of these judges. It would ensure that provinces are not using unification simply as a device for off-loading costs to Ottawa. Also, it would reflect the federal-provincial status of these judges and ensure that provinces bear their share of the costs involved when their legislatures expand positions in the courts. Sharing the responsibility of staffing and paying the trial court judiciary might even – and here I may be dreaming – foster a more intelligent and responsible assessment of the personnel needs of Canada's trial courts.

Recently there have been signs that significant reform of the federal judicial appointing system might occur. In the fall of 2005, Justice Minister Irving Cotler introduced a nine-person advisory committee into the process of filling vacancies on the Supreme Court of Canada.[5] The committee's function was to narrow down a list of government nominees to a short list of three, from which the prime minister must choose the appointee or give a public reason for going outside the list. The committee had completed its work when the federal election was called in November 2005. Prime Minister Martin agreed to wait until the election before proceeding with an appointment. After the election the new Conservative prime minister made public his choice of Justice Marshall Rothstein of the Federal Court but before finalizing the appointment Justice Rothstein was asked to be interviewed by an ad hoc parliamentary panel in a nationally televised session. The committee's role in searching for outstanding candidates was too limited, provincial representation too slight (one representative of the three provinces from which the appointee must come) and the whole process too secretive and lacking in transparency.[6] The televised interview of the judge finally chosen was simply banal.[7] Nevertheless, despite its shortcomings, this tinkering with the system of appointing Supreme Court judges was a small step towards a judicial appointing system in which there are some checks and balance on the political agenda of the federal government.

More significant is the work of a subcommittee of the House of Commons Justice Committee that held hearings in 2005 on improving the process for appointment to 'the federal judiciary' – that is, to the courts below the Supreme Court, the Provincial and Territorial Superior Courts, as well as the purely federal courts. The subcommittee's interim report, filed in November 2005 just before Parliament was dissolved for the election, reports agreement on 'the need to limit the recommendations for judicial postings to a short list of three to five candidates.'[8] So far, Vic Toews, minister of justice in the new Conservative government, shows no sign of the zeal he displayed in opposition for reforming the system of appointing judges to the provincial Superior Courts. Without such a reform, provincial governments would be unwise to agree to any expansion of the federal government's power to make appointments to provincial judiciaries.

Even if unification of the trial courts comes about in one or more areas at the Superior Court or Provincial Court level, it is evident that gradations of responsibility will remain and provincial judiciaries will not become one single cadre of judges. All of the chapters above that discuss models of unified trial courts make this point. Baar tells us that the 'subordinate judicial officials' which are a feature of the trial court unification in California described by Kelso are to found in all the unified trial court systems in the United States. Justices of the peace are an important element of Borrows's and Seniuk's House of Justice proposal, and, as Sanders shows, they are in Canada's only working model of a totally unified trial court, the Nunavut Court of Justice. Thus a one-tier trial court system does entail a one-tier judiciary.

The subordinate judicial officers, be they prothonotaries, part-time lawyer-judges, or justices of the peace, in a one-tier trial court are presumably subject to the supervision of one or more of the court's full-fledged judges. That certainly appears to be the case in California's unified court. The Ontario Superior Court judges, however, suggest that a hierarchy managed by an administrative judge might be more difficult for the subordinate judicial officers to accept than a hierarchy created by legislation. Legislation should, as it does now, identify the adjudicative functions that must be performed by professionally qualified judges whose independence and security of tenure are constitutionally protected. Such legislation defines what subordinate judicial officers cannot do, but is no substitute for some kind of human supervision of the services that such subordinate judicial officers are to perform in the justice system. Independence of the judicial branch surely requires that such supervision come from members of the judicial rather than the executive branch of government.

In considering the role of subordinate judicial officers in a one-tier court, it is important to bear in mind the purposes these officers serve in the justice system. Many of the functions they perform are adjudicative in nature requiring a knowledge of the relevant law and independent judgment. In hearing bail applications and police requests for search warrant, justices of peaces are making decisions about citizens' fundamental rights and the security of society. Having highly-paid professional judges available to make the masses of decisions of this kind at all hours and in remote places would be a very extravagant use of judicial resources. Also, it is doubtful that the kind of lawyer we want to try serious civil and criminal cases will take positions that involve a great deal of work that, important as it is to the individual and society, can become very routine to the adjudicator. It is for reasons of this kind that New Brunswick, the one province which, to quote Baar, 'has neither sitting nor signing justices of the peace,' might come to use JPs as subordinate judicial officers in a unified criminal court.

Sanders's account of the Nunavut Court of Justice and Borrows's and Seniuk's House of Justice concept make us aware of another rationale for integrating justices of the peace into the work of a single tier court. The JPs in Nunavut provide a valuable, many would say an essential, link with the far-flung communities served by the territory's Court of Justice. In the Borrows/Seniuk House of Justice, peacemaker JPs perform a similar role. In both these cases, the subordinate judicial officers are lay people, not lawyers. Their inclusion in the court process brings a democratizing influence to a court system that has become dominated by professional lawyers. But not every jurisdiction is enamoured of the idea of lay JPs. Through Tyson's chapter we learn that fear of JPs who live in the local community being too close to the local police has prompted Nova Scotia to move away from lay JPs and create a smaller number of JP centres staffed by legally trained justices of the peace.

Tyson's discussion of the difficulty that Nova Scotia has experienced in finding an appropriate procedure for the handling of civil suits involving small amounts of money points to another kind of hierarchy issue – the possibility of maintaining a hierarchy of procedure. In his chapter Ian Scott discusses the 'procedural compaction' that has taken

place in the English justice system. In Canada, as in England and elsewhere in the common law world, it has been difficult to resist pressure
from lawyers to make simplified summary justice procedure for cases
deemed to be less important and less complex from being made more
and more formal. In an egalitarian age it becomes difficult to maintain
a defensible distinction between serious and trivial cases and cases that
deserve the full panoply of formal procedure as opposed to those that
can be dealt with summarily. Trying to structure a court system on the
basis of such a distinction would seem to be a dubious proposition.
Among Canadian jurisdictions, Quebec has been most innovative in
developing a lawyer-less procedure for small civil suits through its
*Access to Justice Act* as St-Louis mentions. The key to making this simplified procedure work is to have very dedicated and skilled judges,
not part-time lawyer/judges or court clerks, administer this summary
form of justice.

Specialization, like hierarchy, is an inescapable feature of trial court
judiciaries. This is true whether the courts on which judges serve are
organized in one tier or two. Baar comments on how much Canada's
two-tier system is drifting into specialized roles with Superior Courts
increasingly dominated by civil cases and Provincial Courts by criminal cases. On the other hand, one of the advertised features of a single
tier trial court which, like California's unified court, covers several
areas of law, is that it provides room for judicial specialization. One of
the advantages of the Court of Quebec as a structure for unification is
that it encompasses a range of juristic disciplines covering criminal,
family, civil, and administrative law. The specialization that many
jurists oppose is a structure that institutionalizes specialization and
locks trial judges into specializing for their entire career in one area of
law. Indeed, that is one of the fears that Ontario's Superior Court
judges have about a unified criminal trial court. It is also one of the
criticisms of the approach to family law unification under which
appointments of family law specialists to the Superior Court are
strictly to its family law division. Trial courts should not be staffed by
judges who are forever branded as generalists or specialists in one single field. Judges like all professionals, should be free through their
career to move to new fields and change the focus of their work. California's unified trial court certainly facilitates that kind of flexibility
and career development. But, as Baar points out, the interchangeability
of American trial judges is not confined to unified court systems. It is
also evident in two-tiered state court systems. And Scott's chapter

shows how the integrated administration of England's two-tiered system facilitates more flexibility in the deployment of judicial resources than is possible in Canada's two-tiered provincial systems.

There is one judicial function – hearing appeals from lower courts – that we have come to expect in Canada (and elsewhere in the common law world) to be institutionally organized on a specialist and hierarchical basis. As discussed in the introduction, all of Canada's provinces have established courts of appeal as their highest courts.[9] These courts specialize in the sense that they only hear appeals,[10] but they are non-specialist in that they hear appeals in all fields of law, except the few reserved exclusively to the Federal Court. And, of course, as the courts that hear appeals from the Provincial Courts and the trial divisions of provincial Superior Courts, they are at the top of the provincial judicial hierarchy. The only court above them is the Supreme Court of Canada, to which all their decisions are appealable, except those that deal with criminal sentences. These courts of appeal grew out of the provincial Superior Courts and have Superior Court status. Assigning the appellate work of Superior Courts to institutions that are separate from the trial division of the Superior Court was in part a response to concerns of a more liberal, rights-oriented society that judges who hear appeals should not be from the same court as the judges whose decisions they are reviewing. Provincial Courts of Appeal also met the need for a coherent and juristically skilled body to develop the law of the province. But, as the report of the Ontario Superior Court Judges makes clear, the Courts of Appeal do not perform all the appellate work in their jurisdictions. The Ontario Superior Court judges' chapter details the appellate work of their court in criminal, civil and administrative law matters – some of it based on statutes, some on the inherent prerogative writ jurisdiction of Superior Courts. They assert that in Ontario their court performs the function of an intermediate court of appeal.

For the Ontario Superior Court judges, their appellate work is an argument for retaining a trial court hierarchy. The alternative, they suggest, would be loading all of the appellate work now done by the Superior Court onto an already over-loaded Court of Appeal. But there is another alternative: simply recognizing the appellate role of the Superior Court and organizing it on a permanent basis as an intermediate court of appeal. Proposals for intermediate courts of appeal have been brought forward in the larger Canadian provinces since the late 1960s.[11] Many of the larger U.S. state jurisdictions have established intermediate courts of appeal. Because they can be organized on a regional basis, they can make appeals of the more routine kind more accessible than a court of appeal based in the provincial capital. In Ontario it would be possible to staff such an intermediate appeal with judges now serving on the Superior Court. If the Provincial Court were able to hear all criminal cases, this would surely free up Superior Court judges for such appellate work. The Superior Court already has a specialized appellate division, the Divisional Court, that reviews decisions of administrative tribunals and hears appeals in civil suits involving small amounts of money. If, however, there is great concern about judges hearing appeals from judges of their own courts, an intermediate court of appeal could be organized as a separate court with judges appointed to it on a permanent basis.

Though there is not yet a consensus on trial court unification at either the political or juridical level in any province, let alone in Canada as a whole, there is very nearly a consensus on unifying the management and administration of trial courts in each jurisdiction. Tyson, the experienced court administrator, emphasizes the advantages to be gained from having a common management of trial court resources, physical and human. In Alberta, though Hancock's proposed unification of the trial courts has not been carried out, the province is moving ahead with coordinated administration of the Provincial Court and the Court of Queen's Bench in the family law area to provide effective delivery of both courts' processes in all parts of the province. Administrative unification of Ontario's two trial courts on a regional basis is a reform that Ontario's Superior Court judges recommend for consideration. Through Kelso's chapter we learn that administrative unification was the first step to trial court unification in California. And Scott's chapter shows how administrative integration facilitates the effective management of judicial resources in England's two-tier trial court system.

Integrating the administration of trial courts is a worthwhile step to take whether or not a province is moving towards a partial or full unification of its trial courts. But such a strengthening of court administration raises an important constitutional question: who should be in charge of court administration? Professional court administrators with the requisite skills and knowledge should, undoubtedly, do the actual day-to-day court administration. But there are aspects of court administration that involves matters which have a direct bearing on adjudication and must remain under judicial control. In 1985 the Supreme Court of Canada identified three such matters that the constitutional principle of judicial independence requires not be controlled by the executive branch of government.[12] These are the assignment of cases, the sittings of courts, and court lists. It is of vital importance to the principle of judicial independence that the executive branch of government, which is a party to many of the cases the courts hear, not control the cases judges hear and the order in which they hear them.[13] Judges are also in the best position to assess the needs of courts and how they are being served by the court administrators. For these reasons it is essential that court administration be directed by an independent body in which judges play a major role. St-Louis tells us that achieving such administrative independence remains a challenge for the Court of Quebec, and Friedland reminds us of the proposal he made in his report to the Canadian Judicial Council that the courts would function more efficiently and with greater independence if their administration was handled by an independent court services agency. It would seem obvious that such an efficient and independent management of the trial courts of a province can best be achieved if the provincially and federally appointed judiciaries are jointly involved in its direction.

As to what may lie beyond administrative integration, one thing that this book makes clear is that no single approach to trial court restructuring will be adopted at the same time in all parts of the country. The map of the road ahead for the development of Canada's trial courts does not point to a single destination. Quebec appears poised to be the first province to have its Provincial Court (the Court of Quebec) take on a full criminal trial jurisdiction – providing the *McEvoy* constitutional roadblock is cleared away and federal cooperation is forthcoming in making the necessary amendments to the Criminal Code. Borrows's and Seniuk's House of Justice concept provides Saskatchewan with a strong plan of action that would be facilitated if constitutional restrictions on Provincial Court trial jurisdiction were removed. New Brunswick, too, might renew its interest in criminal court unification were *McEvoy* to fall. If the federal government could reform its judicial appointment process, it should be possible to complete family law unification at the Superior Court level in those provinces that have moved part-way along that path. Similarly, if the federal government were willing to involve territorial governments in the selection of Superior Court judges, the Northwest Territories and Yukon might well emulate Nunavut and establish a single territorial trial court.

No matter how fast or how far the trial courts of the provinces are unified, Canadians will continue to be served by two groups of judges:

the federally appointed judges of the Superior Courts and the provincially appointed judges of the Provincial Courts. Even in a province such as Quebec, where trial court unification at the Provincial Court level may be pushed as far as is constitutionally possible, federally appointed Superior Court judges will retain an important role. However much provinces may wish to expand the jurisdiction of the provincially appointed judiciary, they are unlikely to want to make it exclusive, or to be able, in criminal matters, to persuade the federal government to make it exclusive. According to information provided to organizers of the 2002 Saskatoon Conference, at that time the 897 section 96 judges appointed to provincial and territorial trial courts almost equaled in number the 955 provincially and territorially appointed judges.[14] These figures mark a significant shift in growth rates. Twenty years earlier the provincially appointed judiciary out numbered the entire cadre of section 96 judges (i.e., those appointed to courts of appeal as well as trial courts) by 1,013 to 657. In large measure this change can be attributed to two factors: the large number of Superior Court judges who have retired from full-time service but have become part-time 'supernumary' judges; and the amount of judicial work devolved to subordinate judicial officers. The fact remains that nearly a thousand federally paid Superior Court judges are available for trial service in the provinces and territories. Many have a great deal of experience in handling long, complex trials. We can see from the Ontario Superior Court judges' report that while the criminal cases they try constitute a very small fraction of the overall criminal caseload, they are cases that take a great deal of time. It would clearly be unwise for Parliament to exclude this large pool of experienced trial judges from hearing criminal cases. But it seems equally unwise to erect or maintain institutional or constitutional barriers that prevent the most functionally effective use of a province's or territory's judicial resources.

Thus, in whatever diverse ways the question posed in the title of this volume is answered, the Superior Court judiciary appointed through section 96 will continue to be an integral part of the administration of justice in Canada's provinces and territories.The hope is that the full potential of section 96 in helping to knit this country together through its judicial institutions can be realized and that it will not be the basis of dividing trial judiciaries in ways that are seriously dysfunctional and frustrate rather than facilitate the effective administration of justice. Meeting this challenge will require exceptional leadership on the part of both judges and politicians.

In his closing remarks at the Saskatoon Conference, Professor John Whyte, one of Canada's leading legal academics who has held senior government posts in the administration of justice, made the point that court reform must be 'judicogenerative' – meaning, it must be judge-led. In a society that values the independence of its judges and respects their experience, court reform cannot be forced upon a judiciary. But in a society that values accountable and responsible government, no section of the judiciary should exercise a silent veto over court reform. Past experience, as recorded in this book, makes it abundantly cleared that moving forward with structural reform of the trial courts will only happen when political leaders become strongly committed to reform. That has happened several times at the provincial level. It has never happened at the federal level. This book will have served a valuable purpose if it promotes the kind of public dialogue that will mobilize the judicial and political leadership needed to overcome the barriers to taking the next best step in the organization of Canada's trial courts.

NOTES

1 Section 91(27) gives the federal Parliament exclusive jurisdiction with respect to 'The Criminal Law, except the Constitution of Courts of Criminal Jurisdiction, but including the Procedure in Criminal Matters.'
2 Canadian Bar Association Committee on the Appointment of Judges in Canada, *The Appointment of Justice in Canada* (Ottawa: Canadian Bar Foundation, 1985).
3 Minister of Justice and Attorney General of Canada, *A New Judicial Appointments Process* (Ottawa: Ministry of Supply and Services, 1988). There is also a committee for advising on Federal and Tax Court appointments.
4 See Ted Morton, 'Judicial Appointments in Post-Charter Canada: A System in Flux,' in Kate Malleson and Peter H. Russell, eds., *Appointing Judges in an Age of Judicial Power: Critical Perspectives from around the World* (Toronto: University of Toronto Press, 2006).
5 Canada, Department of Justice, *Proposal to Reform the Supreme Court of Canada: An Appointments Process* (Ottawa, September 1, 2005).
6 See Peter H. Russell, 'Selecting Supreme Court Justices: Open Up the System,' *Toronto Star*, 22 September 2005, A21.
7 Campbell Clark, 'Nominee Says He's No Activist, " *Globe and Mail*, 28 February 2006, A1.

8  House of Commons, 'Process for Appointment to the Federal Judiciary: Interim Report of the Standing Committee on Justice, Human Rights, Public Safety and Emergency Preparedness,' Ottawa, November 2005, 1.

9  The courts of appeal of the northern territories are staffed by justices from provincial courts of appeal. For an account of the work of Canadian appeal courts, see Ian Greene, Carl Baar, Peter McCormick, George Szablowski, and Martin Thomas, *Final Appeal: Decision-Making in Canadian Courts of Appeal* (Toronto: James Lorimer, 1998).

10  The main exception is the references case in which provincial governments refer questions directly to their court of appeal for an advisory opinion.

11  For a discussion of these proposals, see Peter H. Russell, *The Judiciary in Canada* (Toronto: McGraw-Hill, 1987), 300–2.

12  See *R. v. Valente*, [1985] 2 S.C.R. 673.

13  On the importance, worldwide, of protecting judicial independence in the administration of the courts, see Peter H. Russell, 'Towards a General Theory of Judicial Independence,' in Peter H. Russell and David M. O'Brien, eds., *Judicial Independence in the Age of Democracy: Critical Perspectives from around the World* (Charlottesville and London: University Press of Virginia, 2001), 19–20.

14  See Peter H. Russell, 'Evolution of Canada's Trial Court System – From Confederation to Today,' Proceedings of Trial Courts of the Future Conference, Saskatoon, 2002.

# Contributors

**Carl Baar** is Professor Emeritus of Political Science at Brock University, and an adjunct professor of political science at York University. For almost forty years, he has focused his academic and professional work on judicial administration, broadly understood; it has taken him throughout North America as well as to Europe, Asia, Africa, and Australia. As a principal in Justice Development International, Ltd., he has taught court administrators in Jamaica, and judges and judicial educators in Ethiopia, India, and Pakistan. His most recently completed Canadian work was with the team developing models of court administration for the Canadian Judicial Council.

**John Borrows** is Professor and Law Foundation Chair of Aboriginal Law and Justice at the University of Victoria Law School. He has held teaching positions at the University of Toronto, the University of British Columbia, and the Osgoode Hall Law School and at the Arizona State University College of Law. He has taught and published widely in the fields of constitutional law, Aboriginal law, and natural resources and environmental law. He is Anishinabe/Ojibway and a member of the Chippewa of the Nawash First Nation in Ontario.

**Anthony N. Doob** is a professor of criminology at the University of Toronto. He has taught at the University of Toronto since 1968, first in the Department of Psychology, and later at the Centre of Criminology. From 1984 to 1987, he was a member of the Canadian Sentencing Commission. Much of his recent work has been in the area of youth justice. His co-authored book (with Carla Cesaroni), *Responding to Youth Crime in Canada*, was published by the University of Toronto Press in 2004.

He has carried out research on attitudes (of the public and judges) about various aspects of the criminal justice system, sentencing, and in 2002 he joined Cheryl Webster in her ongoing program of research on the operation of the adult courts in Canada.

**Martin Friedland** is a University Professor and Professor of Law Emeritus at the University of Toronto, where he was formerly the dean of law. He is the author or editor of seventeen books, including *Detention before Trial, Double Jeopardy, The Case of Valentine Shortis, A Place Apart: Judicial Independence and Accountability in Canada,* and *The University of Toronto: A History.* He has received a number of honours, including the Molson Prize in the Humanities and Social Sciences and the Royal Society of Canada's Sir John William Dawson Medal, and in 2003 became a Companion of the Order of Canada.

**David Hancock** is a graduate in law from the University of Alberta and was a partner with Matheson and Company in Alberta. He was first elected to the Legislative Assembly of Alberta in 1997. Mr Hancock served as minister of federal and intergovernmental affairs and deputy house leader from 1997 to 1999 when he was appointed government house leader and minister of justice and attorney general. Following the 2004 provincial election he moved from the Justice portfolio to become minister of advanced education.

**Patrick Healy** is a professor of law at McGill University. He specializes in criminal law matters, including substantive criminal law, procedure, evidence, sentencing, comparative criminal law and international criminal law, and has published widely in these fields. Professor Healy is a member of the bar of Quebec and, as counsel, has acted for the prosecution and defence in Quebec and elsewhere. He is counsel to the firm of Shadley, Battista in Montreal and has served as a member of the Comité permanent en droit criminel of the Quebec bar and on the executive committee of the Canadian Bar Association (Criminal-Québec).

**J. Clark Kelso** is a professor of law and the director of the Capital Center for Government Law and Policy at the University of the Pacific McGeorge School of Law in Sacramento, California. His work with the California Judicial Council and Administrative Office of the Courts during the 1990s, including work on trial court unification, led to his being honoured with the 1998 Bernard E. Witkin Amicus Curiae

Award, the highest award bestowed upon someone other than a member of the judiciary for outstanding contributions to California's courts. Professor Kelso has also held several top positions in California's executive branch, including service as California's insurance commissioner, director of the Department of General Services and chair of the California Earthquake Authority. In addition to his work at the university, he currently serves as the state's chief information officer and special adviser to Governor Arnold Schwarzenegger on information technology.

**Peter H. Russell** is a university professor emeritus at the University of Toronto, where he taught political science from 1958 to 1996. He has published widely in the fields of judicial, constitutional, and Aboriginal politics. His books include *The Judiciary in Canada: The Third Branch of Government, Constitutional Odyssey: Can Canadians Become a Sovereign People?* and *Recognizing Aboriginal Title: The Mabo Case and Indigenous Resistance to English-Settler Colonialism,* He has co-edited a number of books on the judiciary, including *Judicial Independence in the Age of Democracy: Critical Perspectives from around the World, Judicial Power and Canadian Democracy,* and *Appointing Judges in an Age of Democracy: Critical Perspectives from around the World.* He was the founding chair of Ontario's Judicial Appointments Advisory Committee. He is a past president of the Canadian Political Science Association and the Canadian Law and Society Association. He is an officer of the Order of Canada, a fellow of the Royal Society of Canada, and the holder of a number of honorary degrees from universities, and from the Law Society of Upper Canada.

**Nora Sanders** at the time of writing was the deputy minister of First Nations and Métis Relations for the Government of Saskatchewan. She is now General Secretary of the United Church of Canada. Originally from Ontario, Ms Sanders practised law in her home town of St Thomas and during that time also served as vice-chair of the Health Services Appeals Board. In 1986 she moved to Yellowknife as a legal counsel with the government of the Northwest Territories. She served in successive positions with the Northwest Territories Department of Justice in the 1980s and 1990s. Her time in the north was interrupted when she returned to Ontario in 1992 to serve as chair of the newly created Board of Inquiry under the Ontario *Police Services Act,* before returning to the NWT the following year as the assistant deputy minister of justice. In 1998 she was appointed deputy minister of justice for Nunavut, responsible for setting up the Department of Justice for the new territory, a position she held until May 2004. At the 2002 annual meeting of the Canadian Bar Association, Ms Sanders received the John Tait Award of Excellence in recognition of her contributions to the legal profession in the public sector.

**I.R. Scott** is an Australian, educated at Geelong College and the University of Melbourne. After taking his PhD at the University of London, he entered academic life and became Barber Professor of Law at the University of Birmingham in 1978. He was dean of the Faculty of Law at the University of Birmingham from 1985 to 1994. Since retiring from the Barber Chair of Law in 2000, Dr Scott has been active in legal research and writing, particularly as member of the main editorial board for Civil Procedure (the 'White Book') and as editor-in-chief of the *Civil Justice Quarterly*. Over the years he has been engaged in many judicial administration research projects and consultancies in England, Australia, and the United States.

**Gerald Seniuk** was appointed a judge of the Provincial Court of Saskatchewan in 1977 and appointed chief judge as of January 1, 2001. Chief Judge Seniuk has been active in judicial organizations, serving provincially and nationally, and has also contributed to judicial education programs provincially, nationally, and internationally in Africa, Eastern Europe, and the Caribbean. He has published articles on a wide range of judicial topics in various Canadian legal periodicals and journals. He developed a program on judicial fact-finding that has been used by judicial educators in Canada and other Commonwealth countries. He has also been involved in furthering judicial independence both in Canada and internationally through his published articles, video productions, and educational programs. Through the office of the federal commissioner for judicial affairs he has acted as a judicial consultant to the Canada–Ukraine Judicial Independence project.

**Huguette St-Louis** was born in Montreal, where she completed all of her studies including her law degree from the University of Montreal, and was called to the bar in 1969. From 1969 to 1973 she practised law in the firm St-Louis and St-Louis and then from 1973 to 1984 at the Legal Community Centre of Montreal as lawyer and office director. She was appointed judge of the Provincial Court in 1984 and then associate chief justice of the Civil Chamber of the Court of Quebec from 1988 to 1996. In August 1996, Judge St-Louis was appointed chief justice for a seven-year term. From 1996 to 2003 she was also president of the Judicial Council of Quebec. As chief justice, she was regularly invited to give speeches on various topics, both in and outside Quebec. In 2004 she was on sabbatical leave and since 2005 she is back on the bench.

**Marian Tyson** graduated from the Dalhousie Law School in 1975. After articling in Halifax she joined Nova Scotia's Department of Justice where she served as solicitor for several departments before becoming director of legal services in 1995. In that capacity she appeared in all levels of court, including the Supreme Court of Canada. In 1997 she became executive director of court services in Nova Scotia. She has served on the board of directors of the Association of Canadian Court Administrators (ACCA), and at the time of the Trial Courts of the Future Conference was the president of that association. Shortly after the Saskatoon Conference, Marian Tyson became deputy minister in Nova Scotia's Department of Community Services. In March 2007 she became Deputy Minister of Justice.

**Cheryl Marie Webster** received her PhD in criminology from the University of Toronto in 2003 and is currently an assistant professor at the Department of Criminology, University of Ottawa. Her initial research on adult courts focused on an examination of the role of the two-tiered criminal trial courts in Canada. Subsequently, her work has included an investigation of case processing more generally in the Provincial and Superior Courts. Most recently, she has been examining the use and value of the preliminary inquiry. Some of her other recently published research has focused on general deterrence as applied to sentencing and policies related to imprisonment.